DOCUMENTS OF THE ROSE PLAYHOUSE, ed. by Carol Chillington Rutter.
Manchester, 1985 (c1984). 246p (Revels plays companion library) index 84-
780. 29.50 ISBN 0-7190-0962-6. CIP
This book enriches scholars' knowledge of the background of Elizabethan drama in
performance. Chronologically arranged, these primary sources offer a working account of the Rose (the first of the "South Bank playhouses), its tenants, and plays,
during the ten years it dominated Bankside. Returning to 117 original documents,
ignoring the romantic and often falsely detailed positioning by Victorian "discover-
ers," Rutter supplies connecting headnotes to make a pleasantly readable presentation
of Philip Hensloe and his playhouse. She employs Hensloe's own accounts, players'
letters, Privy Council warrants, Court of Aldermen appeals, plots, parts, inventories,
commissions, bonds, playing schedules, and contracts. Rutter's well-focused and
informative introduction clarifies Hensloe as an individual and as a historical figure.
She also gives information on London courts and councils and players and playwrights
and provides a guide for reading the documents. Meticulous notes to the documents,
appendixes of statutes regulating wages, prices, and apparel, and an index to the plays
precede the general index for the volume. Presupposing a general knowledge of the
period and of the theater, this book will be most welcomed by theater and socio-
political historians. Public and academic libraries serving upper-division undergradu-
ates and above.—*R.G. Whaley, California Polytechnic State University, San Luis*
Obispo

The Revels Plays
COMPANION LIBRARY

E. A. J. HONIGMANN, J. R. MULRYNE
and R. L. SMALLWOOD
general editors

Documents of the
Rose Playhouse

THE REVELS PLAYS COMPANION LIBRARY

Documents of the
Rose Playhouse

edited by
CAROL CHILLINGTON RUTTER

Manchester University Press

© CAROL CHILLINGTON RUTTER 1984

PUBLISHED BY

MANCHESTER UNIVERSITY PRESS

Oxford Road, Manchester M13 9PL

and 51 Washington Street, Dover

New Hampshire 03820, USA

BRITISH LIBRARY CATALOGUING IN PUBLICATION DATA

Documents of the Rose Playhouse.—(Revels
plays companion library)
1. Rose. *Theatre*—History
I. Rutter, Carol Chillington II. Series
792'.09421'64   PN2590.L67

ISBN 0 7190 0962 6
ISBN 0 7190 0981 2 (pbk.)

LIBRARY OF CONGRESS CATALOGING IN PUBLICATION DATA
Main entry under title:
Documents of the Rose Playhouse.
(Revels plays companion library)
Includes bibliographical references and indexes.
1. Rose Theatre. 2. Theatre—England—History—16th century—Sources. 3.
English drama—Early modern and Elizabethan, 1500-1600—Sources. 4. Great
Britain—History—Elizabeth, 1558-1603—Sources. I. Rutter, Carol Chillington.
II. Series.

PN2596.L7R473 1984   792'.09421'2   84-780

ISBN 0-7190-0962-6
ISBN 0-7190-0981-2 (pbk.)

Printed in Great Britain by
Butler & Tanner Ltd, Frome and London

CONTENTS

Since the late 1950s the series known as the Revels Plays has provided for students of the English Renaissance drama carefully edited texts of the major Elizabethan and Jacobean plays. The series now includes some of the best known drama of the period and has continued to expand, both within its original field and, to a lesser extent, beyond it, to include some important plays from the earlier Tudor and from the Restoration periods. The Revels Plays Companion Library is intended to further this expansion and to allow for new developments.

The aim of the Companion Library is to provide students of the Elizabethan and Jacobean drama with a fuller sense of its background and context. The series includes volumes of a variety of kinds. Small collections of plays, by a single author or concerned with a single theme and edited in accordance with the principles of textual modernisation of the Revels Plays, offer a wider range of drama than the main series can include. Together with editions of masques, pageants, and the non-dramatic work of Elizabethan and Jacobean playwrights, these volumes make it possible, within the overall Revels enterprise, to examine the achievement of the major dramatists from a broader perspective. Other volumes provide a fuller context for the plays of the period by offering new collections of documentary evidence on Elizabethan theatrical conditions and on the performance of plays during that period and later. A third aim of the series is to offer modern critical interpretation, in the form of collections of essays or of monographs, of the dramatic achievement of the English Renaissance.

So wide a range of material necessarily precludes the standard format and uniform general editorial control which is possible in the original series of Revels Plays. To a considerable extent, therefore, treatment and approach is determined by the needs and intentions of individual volume editors. Within this rather ampler area, however, we hope that the Companion Library maintains the standards of scholarship which have for so long characterised the Revels Plays, and that it offers a useful enlargement of the work of the series in preserving, illuminating, and celebrating the drama of Elizabethan and Jacobean England.

E. A. J. HONIGMANN
J. R. MULRYNE
R. L. SMALLWOOD

This book is a 'documentary life': a collection of manuscripts selected and arranged to chronicle the day-to-day operation of one Elizabethan playhouse, the Rose, over the fifteen years of its existence. My objectives in compiling this life have been two-fold. First, to present these lively documents in such a way as to release their original energy again, to recreate the push and shove of the Elizabethan playhouse. Second, to introduce students to the possibilities and methods of documentary research by exposing them to the variety of material that survives for this period and by suggesting some ways of interpreting that material.

The documents collected here range from the casual to the formal, from a plot outline scribbled on the back of a letter to official state papers. Some of the documents are crammed with news. A letter to one of Lord Strange's Men sent via the carriers who would find the Company in Shrewsbury, perhaps, or Chester, or York describes how plague was ravaging London and how another company had been among its victims. Other documents are stubbornly reticent. Still others retail gossip or peddle misinformation. Documents do not necessarily speak the truth.

The authors of these documents are as various as the papers themselves. They include the professionals who owned the playhouse, who wrote for it, and who played in it; the bureaucrats on the Privy Council and in the Court of Aldermen who, with the Lord Mayor, regulated it; members of the audience and foreign visitors who only rarely recorded their observations upon it; detractors who decried it from pulpits or in street-corner pamphlets. Women occasionally speak in these documents. The Queen makes known her pleasure through one of her 'mouthpieces'; a player's wife sends word to her husband on tour that his spinach bed is growing well.

As a collection, these documents give an all-round portrait of London's new playhouse industry. Placed chronologically, they reconstruct the day-to-day activity of that industry by showing how pressures outside the playhouse – plague, puritans, petitions, summonses to Court – strained the staggering pressures that were the only way of life inside the playhouse. Companies at the Rose were used to playing fifteen plays in repertoire while they rehearsed and opened new plays fortnightly. Even accident and disaster deferred to this uncompromising production schedule, for the play was the thing, and it would be played whether the players were currently being celebrated or slammed. Playwrights might default; costumes might be gnawed by rats; Court money might remain unpaid for months; or a triumphant opening, as of *Henry VI*, might earn the players triple shares. It was all in a day's work at the Rose.

The Rose is the only Elizabethan playhouse for which it is possible to compile a calendar, and only by virtue of the survival of one document, Philip Henslowe's account book. Henslowe, who built the playhouse in 1587, presided over its hey-day, then abandoned it with a shrug around 1604, kept a near daily record of his financial transactions at the Rose between 1592 and 1603. In the early 1590's Henslowe's chief concern was to record his receipts, the daily share in the box proceeds that the players paid him, their landlord, as rent. Later, when Henslowe became banker to the Admiral's Men then to Worcester's Men, he began keeping itemised records of those companies' expenditures. Comparable records of comparable arrangements were no doubt kept at other playhouses, but Henslowe's Diary (as his account book has been known for the last century) is the only one to survive. It is the essential document on which this calendar depends. To call it a diary, though, is to flatter what is actually a cluttered hodge-podge that frequently reads back to front and conflates memoranda belonging to several years on a single page. The playhouse accounts are wedged between family affairs, a pawn brokerage, and Henslowe's personal pharmacopia of herbal remedies, 'medyson which hathe beene proved.' This means that only part of the Diary appears here and in a restructured format disciplined by the calendar.

None of the documents presented here is new. Indeed, most of them were known to E. K. Chambers when he prepared Volume IV of *The Elizabethan Stage* (1923). But where Chambers's aim was essentially scholarly and definitive, mine is more provisional, more inquisitive of theatre practice, and ultimately less tidy. I allow what Chambers called 'documents of criticism' to jostle against 'documents of control' and to get mixed up with playhouse papers he put elsewhere or omitted entirely. In all cases I have made fresh transcriptions of the documents, and these differ in many details from printed sources students may consult elsewhere.

The chronological arrangement of the documents is a way of insisting, through format, that no document is ever self-sufficient, for while a Privy Council order restraining public playing carries absolute authority in itself, that authority is compromised once the document is placed next to Henslowe's uninterrupted list of daily receipts, evidence that the Rose, for one, was open for business as usual. Sequential format is also a way of attempting to reclaim the impossible: Elizabethan theatre in the present tense. Such reclamation is of course impossible because theatre lives in the instant. Performances may be recalled but they cannot be recovered. Even playscripts, seemingly less ephemeral, are only that part of the player's craft that can be written down. For these reasons and many more Elizabethan theatre cannot be restored to the present. And yet, documents read in sequence, read in the present tense as they were written, might cozen one as admirably as plays themselves do into believing otherwise through the process of re-enactment.

In a book of records I record my thanks to those who supported me: William Ingram, Robert Smallwood and Reginald Foakes; the librarians of the Public Records Office, the Guildhall Library and the Corporation of London Record Office; the British Academy with a grant from the Research Fund in the Humanities; and my husband, a player, like the men in this book, who very sensibly left me in Warwickshire tending his spinach bed while he took up residence in a Bankside London playhouse not far from where the Rose once stood.

It has more than once occurred to me that compiling the documentary life of a playhouse as a way of getting nearer the plays performed there is a bit like Bottom and Company approaching *Pyramus and Thisbe* by calling for the almanac. 'Find out moonshine' is a shout for documentary evidence if ever there was one. Perhaps to insist on facts is to ruin the theatre's magic: it is to name the man behind the lion's mask, to give his address and list his dependants. I cannot argue the point. I only know I feel a special excitement whenever the players arrive on the Elizabethan stage and begin the practical work of making a play happen: when the tragedians of the City, still in travelling gear, con the words and gestures of *The Mousetrap*; when Quince and Snug, apron-men of Athens and actors in more comedies than they know, beat their brains for the solutions to their play's technical problems; when the 'four men and a boy' of *Sir Thomas More* come from behind the arras, stopping their play because one of the troupe has run back to the beard-maker's for a missing chin of hair and has over-stayed his cue. At moments like these the Elizabethan playwright documents his own profession. His players expose the facts behind their fiction, showing us the men at work behind the roles. This, I believe, is what documents do, only one step further removed from the act of stage production. If this volume can stand in relationship to the plays of the Rose as Bottom's almanac stands to *Pyramus and Thisbe*, I am satisfied.

C.C.R.

Introduction

≈◦≈

When Philip Henslowe acquired the lease on the messuage known as the Little Rose and in 1587 began drawing up plans for a playhouse to be built on the property, professional players had been installed in London playhouses for over a decade. The Theater (1576) and the Curtain (1577) stood north of the City in a suburb that was beyond the reach of the Lord Mayor's carping authority but that was likewise remote from the City's centre: fifteen years later the neighbourhood would still be 'in the contrye' as far as Londoners were concerned. A third playhouse, at Newington Butts (1576), seemed no less remote. It was located just a mile down the Kent Road south of London Bridge, but the players evidently found it inaccessible and even the Privy Council agreed that the 'tediousnes of the waie' made the venue unattractive.

Philip Henslowe's innovation was to establish playing on London's South Bank, already notorious for its 'pastymes' and pleasures, its brothels, bowling alleys, bearbaitings. Like Shoreditch and Newington Butts, the Liberty of the Clink was outside the Lord Mayor's direct jurisdiction: it lay on the Bankside between Paris Garden and Southwark, and its 'liberty' or immunity from interference by City authorities derived from the fact that it had once been monastic land, although it was now held by the Bishop of Winchester. Unlike those other suburbs, however, the Clink was linked to the heart of London by the City's arterial highway, the Thames. The same ferries that moved the City's traffic could deliver audiences to landing stairs not five minutes' walk from Henslowe's proposed playhouse. That much Henslowe could have anticipated. What he could not have foreseen was that by putting a playhouse on the Bankside he was setting a precedent that would eventually raise a giant to topple his Little Rose. By 1600 three playhouses would crowd the Bankside. One of them would be the Globe.

Henslowe and the scholars

Philip Henslowe was 'discovered' by the Victorians who, as with Milton's Christ or Sophocles' Oedipus, new fashioned out of what they found in him a creation consistent with their own prepossessions. He was known as early as 1790 to Edmond Malone, but Victorians popularised him: John Payne Collier published the first complete edition of the Diary in 1845 and established the authorised version of Henslowe that still survives today.[1] (Admittedly Collier was an extreme example of the Victorian archetype; his edition of the Diary was discredited when certain forgeries he inserted to enable Henslowe to verify his own version of events were exposed in 1881.) Forty-five years later, F.G. Fleay's *A Chronicle History of the London Stage* established him as 'the only writer who has ever done anything to reduce the detailed evidence of the Diary to workable shape'. That was the opinion of Walter W. Greg who built on Fleay (though sometimes at divergent angles) and produced a scrupulously edited *Henslowe's Diary* in 1904. Four years later it was followed by a companion volume of analysis and interpretation. 'Vol. II' in its turn became the basis of all studies of the Elizabethan playhouse for the next fifty years: Henslowe's account book was so complicated that scholars – most influentially, E.K. Chambers in *The Elizabethan Stage* (1923) – turned to Greg rather than to the original documents. Thus, by a series of begats as sonorous as the Book of Genesis, generations of playhouse historians handed down one Philip Henslowe to the present day. But Collier's original blot on the lineage was prophetic. The Victorians' Henslowe was a changeling.

Fleay stood his creation upon two emotive adjectives, 'illiterate' and 'moneyed'. To his mind, these settled not only the character of Philip Henslowe but the quality of the repertoire and the condition of the companies that played in Henslowe's playhouse. More damagingly, he then went on to make strict distinctions between 'Henslowe's company' and its rival, the Lord Chamberlain's – that is, Shakespeare's – Company. Of 'the assumption that Henslow's [*sic*] was a typical management' Fleay stated flatly:

> This was not so. Henslow was an illiterate moneyed man ... who regarded art as a subject for exploitation, and was alike ignorant of stage management and dramatic literature.... He managed, by a policy well known to the tallymen and money-lenders of the present time, to keep his actors in subservience and his poets in constant need by one simple method, viz., by lending them money and never allowing their debts to be fully paid off. In this conduct he was largely aided by the great competition among the dramatic poets of this period ... [who] were as plentiful as blackberries.... The only rival company to Henslow's was for some six years the Lord Chamberlain's, but the policy of this company was the exact opposite to that of their rivals. Managed by the housekeepers or principal sharers, whose interest was that of the whole company, and not by an independent employer whose object was to fill his own pocket, they sought to produce plays of lasting interest, which would bear revival and be a perennial source of income. They employed few poets, and paid them well ... [while] plays produced for Henslow were continually

rewritten, renamed, and resold to other companies. In fine, the especial value of Henslow's document lies not ... in its showing us what the inner arrangement of Shakespeare's company must also have been, but in setting before us the selfish hand-to-mouth policy on which its principal rivals were guided, and consequently an explanation of their ultimate failure.[2]

Most of this is unfortunate over-interpretation, and Greg, though he admired Fleay's pioneering work on the Diary and saw his own study as building upon Fleay, nevertheless had him in mind when he commented upon 'the serene confidence with which assertions have been made, which one would have thought the most casual perusal of documentary evidence must have at once disproved'.[3] He disposed of Fleay's account in a brisk footnote:

> Of Henslowe's knowledge or ignorance of stagecraft we have absolutely no means of judging; ... it is quite uncertain whether the playwrights who appear in the Diary were often in Henslowe's debt or not. As to the pay given by the Chamberlain's men we are in complete ignorance for we know practically nothing of the internal working of that company. ... Lastly, to suppose that Henslowe's connection with the Admiral's Men led to financial ruin would be grotesquely absurd, for after the accession of James I it was one of the three companies taken under royal patronage and there is nothing to lead us to suspect that it was not in a flourishing condition.[4]

Greg should have added more. Fleay was wrong to suppose that playwrights were 'plentiful as blackberries' and that competition was great among them when the Diary shows the Admiral's Men pursuing every play and playwright that came their way, frequently having to commission three projects to insure delivery of the one play they needed every fortnight. Fleay was likewise wrong to contrast the internal organisation of the Admiral's Men and the Chamberlain's Men; both of them were sharer companies, run by players who had invested money in the company (and whose object was to fill their own pockets). Henslowe, a landlord only, had no management responsibilities. The Chamberlain's Men altered things, but only for financial reasons thrust upon them, when they moved to the Globe in 1599: the sharers put up the money for the playhouse and so became their own landlord or 'housekeepers' as Fleay called them. Either company would have been baffled by Fleay's notions of 'art' or of 'plays of lasting interest' – though one of the signs of a play's 'lasting interest' was that it was 'continually rewritten' since rewrites were only made on old plays that were being revived or prepared for a performance at Court. And as far as 'a perennial source of income' was concerned, the Admiral's Men, in The Jew of Malta, owned a play that attracted audiences for over thirty years. Fleay's most spectacular error was to assert that Henslowe kept 'his actors' perpetually in debt. The players were never 'his', and as the Diary shows, when final reckonings were made, the players paid all their debts. Equally, playwrights Fleay described as working 'for Henslowe' in fact worked for the players, and it was the company's demands, not Henslowe's, they had to meet. Henslowe recorded the details of their transactions in the Diary's loan accounts, but, as Greg made clear, those 'accounts are company accounts'. Henslowe 'never himself bought a play from any author, either directly or indirectly'.[5]

Greg was right. He had the evidence of the Diary to support him. But having 'dismissed at sight' the 'mere rhetorical embroidery' of Fleay's invention, Greg proceeded to capitulate by declaring Fleay's 'comparison to be in the main a true one'. He 'quite agree[d] with Fleay that Henslowe's methods were not those best adapted to the free development of the dramatic energies of the company', and with this he joined those who would not believe that Shakespeare's company could be run on such business-like lines to exploit art: 'What it is important to bear in mind is that the financial arrangements which we find obtaining in the groups of companies under Henslowe's control were the exception rather than the rule.'[6]

Greg's capitulation, particularly his phrase 'Henslowe's methods' (what 'methods'?; 'one would have thought the most casual perusal of documentary evidence ...') made it possible for his followers to skip over his scholarship even as they used its authority to repeat, ever more vociferously, his aberrant conclusions. Each generation took one step further from the documents; each generation grew more confident. Chambers, in The Elizabethan Stage, based his discussion of the Admiral's Men, the playhouses, and the economics of playing directly upon Greg. Greg's 'improvident gang' – the players – became Chambers's 'threadbare companions ... spongers ... frequenters of pawnshops'. His 'stage hacks', Chambers's 'poor devils'; his 'illiterate moneyed man', Chambers's 'capitalist'.[7] Chambers read far enough into Greg to know that Henslowe 'was not in any strict sense the "director" or even the "manager" of the company. Dr Greg more aptly describes him as their "banker"'. But Chambers then declared it 'probable enough' that 'in practice the banker had a considerable say in influencing the policy of the company'.[8] Such sleights were no longer necessary by 1963 when Glynne Wickham's Early English Stages, Volume II, Part I appeared. The documents were so remote that Wickham could state with self-confidence, 'The story of Henslowe's dealings with authors, especially the system of putting them so deeply into his debt as to be obliged to write for his company and no other is too well known to require restating'.[9] Andrew Gurr, in The Shakespearean Stage, wrote with equal certitude: Henslowe 'kept in close touch with several hack-writers. He frequently employed them to patch on additions or alterations to plays he had bought for his companies or to old plays which needed freshening up.'[10] And elsewhere: 'Playwrights were often directly employed by Henslowe, and their products were a regular and major drain on company finances.'[11]

Attempts have been made to tell Henslowe's story straight. T.W. Baldwin, in *The Organization and Personnel of the Shakespearean Company* (1927), did not accept that Henslowe's arrangements with the companies of the Rose were exceptional; instead, he emphasised the similarities in the conduct of the playhouses.[12] R.A. Foakes, the most recent editor of the Diary (1961) and the editor too of the facsimile *Henslowe Papers* (1978) traced in his introduction some of the 'doubtful assumptions and dubious interpretations' that 'Greg took over from Fleay and passed on', and he urged 'further close scrutiny of the evidence' which Henslowe's Diary contains. It and 'other surviving documents need to be fully reinterpreted'.[13] Clearly, Philip Henslowe has suffered at the hands of the scholars. It is undoubtedly time to make a fresh start.

Philip Henslowe, citizen and dyer

London's first playhouse was built by a player. A businessman built its fourth. The distinction, which so impressed the Victorians, is interesting but not qualitative in the ways they imagined, for while it is true that the pedigree Philip Henslowe carried into the public playhouse via commercial London was mixed, so too was the breeding that had, in the 1580s, produced the current generation of professional players: men who might claim descent from Proteus but whose certain lineage connected them to haberdashers' shops and various trade guilds. James Burbage began life as a joiner; John Heminges was a grocer, James Tunstall a saddler, Martin Slater an ironmonger.

Philip Henslowe was a dyer. He served out his apprenticeship to one Woodward, then, when Woodward died, married his master's widow and her wealth sometime in the mid-1580s.[14] His professional life thereafter was occupied with schemes for multiplying that wealth. He dealt in starch and bought goat skins for leather dressing. He investigated the yields of a farm in Gloucestershire. He ran a pawn brokerage in the devastating plague years 1592–3 that may have served his neighbours as an acceptable charity since few of them could have expected to live to redeem their pledges and since Henslowe could have made small profit from their pitiful, contaminated pawns, their 'Reamnant of Brod cloth', 'hood of the old fashen' or 'hoope Ringe of gowld with this poesy hope helpeth hevenes'.

Henslowe was more than a businessman. In the Liberty of the Clink, where he lived, he collected rents on nearly thirty properties, among them taverns, tenements, at least one ordinary (or public eating house), and a brothel. He collected, too, a tidy array of credits to his respectability: Groom of the Chamber to Queen Elizabeth from early in the 1590s; Gentleman Sewer to James I from 1603 (these were minor appointments but ones that required his residence at Court for part of the year); assessor of the tax subsidies collected in the Clink in 1593, 1594 and 1598 (the only years in this decade for which documentation survives); named first among the assessors and given the honorific 'esquier' in the next extant list, 1609; elected vestryman, churchwarden and collector of the poor relief for St Saviour's parish from 1608; selected governor of the free grammar school established by the parish in 1612.[15] Loaded with honours and additions, Henslowe nevertheless continued to style himself 'citizen and dyer' even as he remained phlegmatic about success's outward trappings: the Gentleman Sewer attempted – though unsuccessfully – to sell his office for £200 in 1607; the grammar school governor offered his colleagues his own parcel of land, at a price, for the building. This sort of shrewdness seems always to have been matched with a certain blundering ineptitude: he made a fortune out of the Rose but once was arrested for another man's debts, having stupidly bound himself a guarantor; he doodled on the front of his Diary the rueful apophthegm, 'when I lent I wasse A frend & when I asked I wasse vnkind' and, more resolutely, 'A man withe owte mercye of mersey shall myse & he shall haue mersey *that* mersey full ys'. But he also practised over and over, mindlessly, his own signature – and sometimes other men's.

When Henslowe died in 1616 he was rich enough to endow 'fortie poore men ... eache a mourning gowne to attend my bodye to buryall' and to pay for a tolling of the great bell in St Saviour's. The Rose had long since collapsed. In its place Henslowe held shares in two other playhouses, one of which doubled as a bear-baiting pit. His estate, though never valued, was considerable enough to embroil his survivors in litigation lasting several years.

Such biographical details, spare though they are, give shape to several Philip Henslowes: the courtier, the capitalist, the leather-apron-man, the city squire. Undoubtedly, though, the Philip Henslowe who urges attention today is the man who built the Rose and recorded the life of the playhouse in the pages of his Diary. How does one characterise that diarist? How does one appraise his role in playhouse affairs in the Rose decade, particularly as his relationship to the players changes from one of relative straightforwardness – landlord of the Rose – to one of increasing complexity – financier, banker, 'angel'? And what does one make of the sorest debate attaching to Henslowe's tenure at the Rose, the relationship between the man, his money, the players and profit?

The only answers to these questions reside in the Diary and documents. Their content (what they choose to include and omit) and sometimes their format (the very way they are laid out on a page) provide materials for observing the changes. Henslowe's initial aloofness (take for example his deed of partnership in the Rose playhouse which never mentions the players and which might as well provide for the construction of a tavern or a tenement as a playhouse but for one minor clause that allows each partner to enter friends 'to vew see and heare any playe ... for nothing') grows to intimacy all the more remarkable since he clearly had no proprietary interest in the players (Gabriel Spencer, killed in a duel, becomes 'one of my players'). Henslowe's tentativeness solidifies into confidence. (He was hesitant about the first loans, allocating them only a single page in the Diary, but later, once familiarity bred easiness, did not withdraw their credit even when the Admiral's Men owed him some £400.) Much later, beyond the Rose decade and so outside the scope of these documents, Henslowe's veteran experience in the theatre perhaps elevated him to quasi-managerial authority.[16]

To judge these changes one would do well to keep in mind the comparison that opened this section. Henslowe's playhouse may have been only his latest in a series of speculative schemes. It may have been built entirely on the solid, ungracious foundation of the profit motive. But in this respect it would have been no innovation. From top to bottom the Elizabethan playhouse was organised for profit, and 'mercenary capitalist' – the term fastidious Victorians fixed on Henslowe to single out the Rose from other playhouses they imagined were run on altruism – in fact describes the entire tribe of tradesmen turned players, from Burbage to Ben Jonson, who abandoned steady trades with fixed wages to gamble a stake on the London stage. Henslowe was merely following, at a prudent distance, the footsteps of James Burbage. Their careers bear comparison.

Burbage was the 'first builder of playhouses'.[17] He was also the first builder of playhouse dynasties. A joiner turned player, a leading member of Leicester's Men by 1572, he found himself in a unique position two years later when his company was granted a royal patent which authorised them to 'vse exercise and occupie the arte and facultye of playenge Comedies Tragedies Enterludes stage playes ... aswell within oure Citie of London and liberties of the same as also within the liberties and freedomes of anye our Cities, townes, Bouroughes &c whatsoeuer as without the same thoroughte oure Realme of England'.[18] This privilege was unprecedented. It amounted to an open passport, and Burbage saw its implications for the future. Until then, playing had been an occasional, touring profession. No purpose-built playhouses yet stood. Companies that wanted to perform in London were required to petition the Lord Mayor for a performance licence that named a venue and probably restricted the performance dates. The patent issued to Leicester's Men had the effect of subverting this procedure for that single company, for it gave them leave to perform anywhere they wished at any time (except Sunday). And if anywhere, any time, why not every day, in a permanent playhouse of their own?

Burbage went into action. He leased ground in Shoreditch. He borrowed money, some of it wheedled out of a brother-in-law with 'swete and contynuall' assurances that the enterprise would 'grow to ther contynual great profitt and commodytie'.[19] (It did, for Burbage; the brother-in-law never saw his money again.) He set builders to work, and when the Theater was finished sometime in the summer of 1576, he installed his own company there, charging Leicester's Men rent at the rate of each day's entire gallery receipts. (Landlords after Burbage took only half the galleries.)

Burbage consolidated his dynasty by raising a brace of sons in the profession, the younger, Richard, eventually outstripping his father in fame by having Shakespeare's roles to play. For twenty years until his death in 1597 Burbage held absolute sway over his Theater. He resisted all attempts – some legitimate – by outsiders to alienate shares in his playhouse. He held his creditors at bay with a series of fiendishly complicated lawsuits that none of the principals survived to see settled. He defied contempt of court citations. He taught his sons the wit, and set in motion the stratagem, to preserve their empire: when their landlord refused to renew their ground lease, thinking no doubt to gain a playhouse once the land on which it stood reverted to his own use, the boys dismantled the Theater, transported it across London and the Thames, and reassembled it on land their company took care to own, renaming it in the process the Globe. Perhaps the most notorious scene ever played in Burbage's playhouse was enacted off-stage, by the old man himself. Flanked by his cubs, one armed with oaths, the other with a broomstick, he beat from his door the creditors who would have deposed him.[20] Burbage may have been foolhardy; the Queen did not take kindly to having her bailiffs beaten. But he was not foolish. His pugnacity was solidly rooted in the 'contynual great profitt' his commodity bore him, for as Philip Henslowe would discover when he began keeping track of his own playhouse accounts, from an initial investment of some £500 and an additional £100 every five years or so in maintenance, a landlord's return from his playhouse in a moderately successful year might be £250. That was a weekly income of some £5. By statute, the wage of a skilled tradesman – a joiner, say, or a dyer – was fixed at £5 *per annum*. In some years, Henslowe's playhouse would earn him over £400.

Broken outlines – all that remain of Burbage's tenure at the Theater – are probably sufficient to suggest his style. Much more is known of Philip Henslowe, more that has served to condemn him. His detractors have ten years of the Diary's crammed sequence to watch him entering his receipts, reckoning his accounts, and noting his debts, and to suspect his motives, his capitalism, his money contaminating 'art' and compromising 'artists' – terms the players would have found as ludicrous as Ben Jonson's presuming to call his collected plays 'Works'. But surely, if it is right to offer James Burbage, the profiteer and dynast, as Henslowe's legitimate touchstone, then Henslowe, the entrepreneur and dyer, was an anomaly only in the survival of his records, not in what those records contain, and his transactions at the Rose fit into a grand scheme of playhouse money-making of which James Burbage was the original architect.

It remains to analyse those transactions. Every reader of the documents must make the analysis for himself. He must, of course, see that his interpretation of the Diary will depend on his assessment of Philip Henslowe: what he makes of him will determine what he makes of it. In this respect, the only *a priori* fact a reader needs to know to avoid disaster is the one Walter Greg stated so long ago: 'as far as the evidence of the Diary is concerned, the accounts are company accounts'. Henslowe was landlord of the Rose but never manager of any of the companies that performed there. He did not employ any player or playwright. He did not make policy decisions, either in terms of personnel, repertoire, or style of production. He did not commission any play. If his motives for lending the players money are questioned, one plausible answer is that the landlord became the banker to remain the landlord. The loans – on which he never seems to have charged interest, perhaps indicating that the investment was not directly capitalistic – stabilised the company, and by 1592 Henslowe knew that the stability of his tenants was more important to the Rose than even the stability of its bricks and mortar.

City, Court and Privy Council

Henslowe's papers document the domestic life of his playhouse. Its political life is framed in the official documents that regulated it. These official documents, issued by Her Majesty's Government – the Privy Council – and the Corporation of the City of London – the Lord Mayor and Court of Aldermen – defy simple readings as obstinately as the Diary itself. They present a welter of orders cancelled or contradicted, of demands fobbed off or coldly answered, of swift reversals into acts of solidarity. They show how infrequently the Corporation and the Privy Council saw eye to eye on the playhouses. Co-ordination was rare in their actions, consistency – either internally or successively from one incumbency to the next – even rarer. The Privy Council was composed of factions that periodically split over this as over other issues. A patiently deliberated *modus vivendi* might collapse when a Councillor died and was replaced by a man of different persuasions, or a shift in international politics might change, overnight, the lords' tolerance of some act of stage representation. In the City, the Lord Mayor's attempts to close the playhouses were not always supported by the guilds who, through the Aldermen, elected him, and though hostility to the playhouses was a consistent feature of the office, successive incumbents might pursue the issue with more or less zeal. The Council and the Corporation had a common objective in regulating the playhouses once they became a permanent feature of London life after 1576, but they did not co-operate in achieving

it. Indeed, their policies seem to have worked most habitually by stalemate, cross-purpose and sabotage, for while the Corporation was unequivocal in wanting plays and playhouses suppressed, the Privy Council
pursued courses altogether more ambiguous, tolerating the playhouses
yet tolerating, too, the Corporation's tireless attack on them even as they
made the Corporation responsible for regulation but deprived it of power
of enforcement. The documents show that politically the playhouses
occupied a shifting no-man's-land of bureaucratic expediency that
stretched between Westminster and Guildhall.

The Corporation had excellent reasons for wanting the playhouses
closed. It couched them in moral and ethical language – such was the
frame of Elizabethan cultural reference – but their basis was political, an
extension of the power struggle the City waged with the Court. By ancient
privilege the City of London – the square mile whose boundaries were
still marked by walls the Romans partly built, by eight gates and by the
Tower – was autonomous and reserved freedoms not even the Privy
Council had normal authority to abridge.[21] It was governed by twenty six
Aldermen, elected from the trade guilds (nearly always from the Twelve
Great Companies), and a Lord Mayor, elected annually from among the
Aldermen. Constitutionally, the City's government was solidly conservative. It was also watchfully jealous of its liberty. This was a delicate
matter, however, for everyone knew, despite ancient privilege, that the
City's freedom was respected only so long as the Mayor and Aldermen
maintained order in their jurisdiction. A civil brawl bred of an airy word,
an assault or affray, inevitably termed a 'riot', gave the Privy Council
sufficient excuse to intervene, to dissolve the Court of Aldermen if necessary. As the lords of the Council were not loath to challenge the City's
liberty whenever the excuse of an occasion presented itself, the Aldermen's
vigilance was justified. Any potential breach of peace was bound to shake
their nerves, and their hostility to plays and players was grounded in civic
anxiety rather than in religious or moral scruple. The Aldermen considered 'one of the greatest matters' touching 'the governance of this citie'
to be 'the assemblies of multitudes of the Quenes people'.[22] Plays gathered
'multitudes of the Quenes people' into one place; assemblies meant jost-
ling and shoving; one thing could so easily lead to another, as it did one
day in Finsbury Fields, near Burbage's Theater, when a riot broke out
after one 'Challes alias Grostock dyd turne vpon the Too [i.e., toe] vpon
the belly' of an apprentice who was 'sleping vpon the Grasse . . . whervpon
the apprentice start vp and after wordes they fell to playne bloues',
eventually drawing fifty others into the fracas.[23] No Lord Mayor could
afford to place the City's freedom in jeopardy to such fools. A Mayor had
to play Malvolio, but Malvolio as Malvolio saw himself: not a puritanical
kill-joy but a careful steward of his Lady's household, defending her
peace, and his own self-regard, from pugnacious drunkards and clowns.

The Corporation did have power to regulate players and performances inside the City through their licensing authority, but it was eroded, first by the Privy Council's proposal, early in 1574, that they, through an appointee, take over responsibility for licensing playing places in the City.[24] Naturally enough the Aldermen saw this as an encroachment and rejected the offer. A letter of 2 March 1574 communicated their anxieties over setting a 'precident farre extending to the hart of our liberties'.[25] Next, and perhaps as a direct response to this rebuff, the Privy Council issued the royal patent to Leicester's Men which gave that company authority to behave as if the Lord Mayor, the Aldermen, the Corporation of London and all its guilds, did not exist. The players had been handed the keys to the City, but they prudently declined to use them, for when Burbage built his playhouse on the strength of the patent's immunity, he nevertheless put it in Shoreditch, a suburb that technically lay outside the Corporation's administration. Technically, the Theater fell under the jurisdiction of the Justices of Middlesex, county magistrates and their officers who were closer to Shakespeare's Shallow and Dogberry than to Jonson's Adam Overdo. Having no liberties to defend, very many fewer political axes to grind, and different statutes to uphold, they were more lenient. In any case, the Corporation should not have been responsible for any of the playhouses as, one by one, they were erected outside the City limits. In practice however this was not so. By another of those quirks that so complicated relations between Westminster and Guildhall, the Privy Council made it clear that they expected the Lord Mayor to maintain order not only in the City but in the suburbs and liberties – such as the Clink where the Rose stood – as well. No executive power went with this expectation. The Corporation's muscle stretched no further than the City's gates. Yet any time a disturbance at a playhouse provoked the notice of the Privy Council, the Court of Aldermen were first to hear the lords' displeasure. No doubt the Aldermen felt intimidated; in the absence of a police force psychological pressure was foremost among the Council's repertoire of persuasion, particularly with those susceptible to suggested threats rather than to overt displays of force.

Deprived of effectual power yet needing always to be seen to be doing something, the Lord Mayor retaliated by sending nagging letters, with nagging regularity, to the lords of the Council. The complaints settled into a litany; Sir Nicholas Woodrofe's can be taken as standard. In April 1580 Woodrofe wrote to the Lord Chancellor that, having heard 'on Sundaie last ... some great disorder was committed at the Theatre' he sent 'for the vnder shireue of Middlesex', since only through the sheriff or magistrates could he intervene in county affairs, and even then only under some pretext, i.e., 'because those playes doe make assembles of Cittizens and their families of whome I haue charge'. In the meantime he learned that the Lord Chancellor 'with other of hir Majesties most honorable

Counsell haue entered into examination of that matter' and so, deferring to the Council's higher authority, abandoned his own investigation. Yet he could not forbear taking this occasion to do his 'dutie' to 'informe your Lordship':

> that the players of playes which are vsed at the Theatre and other places and tumbleres and such like are a very superfluous sort of men and of suche facultie as the lawes haue disalowed, and their exersise of those playes is a great hinderaunce of the seruice of God who hath with his mighty hand so lately admonished vs of oure earnest repentance/it is also great corruption of youthe with unchast and wicked matters, occasion of muche incontinence, practises of many ffrayes querrells and other disorders and inconueniences bisid that the assemble of terme and parliament being at hand, against which time the most honorable Lordes haue given vs earnest charge to haue care to avoide vncleanenesse and pestering of the Citty, the said playes are matter of great daunger....[26]

By the time Henslowe built the Rose, the Privy Council had received several versions of this letter. First among the complaints was always the 'very great and dangerous inconuenience' of 'the assemblie of ... great multitudes of the basist sort of people'.[27] Subordinate objections might present themselves from any quarter. In 1582 the Lord Mayor complained that although the players observed the law and 'beginne not their playes till after euening prayer, yet all the time of the afternone before they take in hearers and fill the place with such as be therby absent from seruing God at Chirch'. Ordering them to refrain from admitting audiences until after service would be no remedy, for that 'wold driue the action of their plaies into very inconuenient time of night specially for seruantes and children to be absent from their parentes and masters'.[28] The domestic conservatism of that letter elicited no reformations; neither did the lurid sensationalism of the following year's appeal when the Lord Mayor claimed that 'many enfected with sores runing on them' mingled in the crowds at the playhouse. He added to the conventional assortment of outrages supposedly committed at playhouses – the 'affraies actes and bargaines of incontinencie and thefte stolen contractes and spoiling of honest mens children' – a novel grievance, that the 'vse of archerie and maintenance of good artes are decaied by the assemblers to vnlawfull spectacles'.[29] The Merchant Taylors' Company were worried about another kind of decay when they abolished plays in their Common Hall:

> at our comon playes and suche lyke exercises whiche be comonly exposed to be seene for money, everye lewd persone thinketh himself (for his penny) worthye of the chiefe and most comodious place without respecte of any other either for age or estimacion in the comon weale, whiche bringeth the youthe to

such an impudente famyliaritie with theire betters that often tymes greite contempte of maisters, parents, and magistrates foloweth thereof.[30]

One hardly knows whether it was the levelling influence of the playhouse or of capitalism that most upset the Merchant Taylors, but one senses slightly submerged beneath the arguments a baffled moral outrage provoked to even greater fury for being unable to comprehend how the players had managed to succeed:

> would to god these comon plaies were exiled for altogether, as semenaries of impiety, & theire theaters pulled downe, as no better then houses of baudrie. It is an euident token of a wicked time when plaiers wexe so riche that they can build suche houses.[31]

Over and over the Aldermen point out feebly that they 'do lack power to redresse' the disorders they are describing. 'We cannot remedie it.' They ask the lords 'to geue your allowance of our proceding in such reformaction within our liberties' or to empower the Justices of the Peace, who have authority in the suburbs and 'verye good zeale', but who 'alledge want of Commission' that only the Privy Council can confer. Even when the Aldermen seemed in possession of iron-clad evidence that their complaints and cautions should have been regarded, the sweetness of the moment might be snatched from them. On 14 January 1583, with the restraint of a man who feels himself finally on top, the Lord Mayor wrote to Lord Burghley, Elizabeth's most senior Privy Councillor, of 'a greate mysshappe at Parrise Garden where by ruine of all the scaffold at once yesterdaye a great number of people' – spectators at a bearbaiting – 'are some presently slayne, and some maymed and greviouslie hurte'. That the slaughter happened on Sunday 'giveth great occasion to acknowledge the hand of god for such abuse on the Sabbat daie, and moveth me in conscience to beseche your *Lordship* to geue order for redresse of suche contempt of god*es* seruice'.[32] Burghley replied with devastating cool. He would 'treate with my *Lords* of the Counsell' to find 'some other daie within the weke meeter for bearbaitings and such like worldly pastimes'. But about the incident at Paris Garden he offered only this phlegmatic remark: 'I thinke your learning derely bought by the losse of so many bodies.'[33] The lords had the easy self-confidence of class on their side in these exchanges. It was sufficient to make all Guildhall pause in its tracks for Ambrose Dudley, Earl of Warwick, to write on behalf of one of his entertainers, 'My Lord Maior I cannot thinke my self frendely delt with to haue my seruante put to such publicke disgrace....'[34] If they played it discreetly, the players held an unbeatable trump card in their noble patrons; their nominal servitude gave them access to impressive powers of redress.

For their part, the Privy Council had reasons for wanting the playhouses open. 'Honest recreacion sake' was one. Another was that the playhouses kept in work men of 'pore estates having noe other meanes to sustayne them their wyves and children but their exercise of playing and were only brought up from their youthe in the practise and profession'.[35] It is not just the syntax that makes this statement sound unconvincing, but conviction was probably immaterial, for the Privy Council was not required to justify its decisions to anyone but the Queen. The Council's authority, in E.K. Chambers's dry phrase, was 'ill-defined but imperative', and the playhouses represented an extension of noble prerogative that it was their business to support. Originally players had been servants in the households of the nobility; recreation, 'playing', was the privilege of the elite, and though by Henslowe's day the players had long been independent of such households, residually patronage survived.[36] The players 'belonged' to men like the Earl of Leicester, or George Carey, the Lord Chamberlain, or Charles Howard, the Lord Admiral: men who sat on the Privy Council. The players took their names and wore their liveries. Ultimately, their purpose was to serve the highest patron of 'honest recreacion', the Queen, with 'solace' and 'conuenient matters' at Christmas and Shrovetide. To be in constant 'redinesse' for the royal summons, and 'to the ende they might thereby attaine to the perfectyon and dexteritie in that profession the rather to content her majestie', the players required 'frequent exercise'.[37] They took that 'exercise' in public performances, on public stages. There was nothing more to be said.

But if the Privy Council had reasons for wanting the playhouses open, they likewise had several for agreeing with the Lord Mayor to close them, thereby keeping alive for the Corporation hopes of an ultimate suppression. Chief among those reasons was the plague. The Council did not usually hold the players responsible for the deadly visitations, as the Aldermen frequently did when linking the 'profanity' of the playhouse to what they saw as terrible but just retribution for 'offendinges of God'. The Council was more practical. Plague spread by contamination, so plays had to be restrained as a way of discouraging public assemblies and the communication of infection. A typical Council inhibition began, 'For th'avoiding of the sickness likelie to happen through the heate of the weather and assemblies of the people of London to playes, her Highnes' plesure is ...'. Plague was first cited in a restraint in 1564; in the years before the Rose opened it turned up with depressing regularity: November 1574, August 1577, November 1578, April 1580, July 1581 (the restraint may have stretched into November), spring 1582, May 1583 (perhaps extending into November), and May 1586. Before 1576 a restraint simply meant that the players packed their costumes into skips and left London for a season in the provinces. After 1576 it meant that a purpose-built playhouse stood empty, and a landlord rentless, in their absence. James Burbage may have travelled with his company when inhibitions closed his

Theater; he was still a player and though a touring share was meagre, it was still an income. Philip Henslowe earned nothing while the players were away. He could only lock his playhouse doors and go home, pockets empty, to sit out the term. There was no way of predicting such disasters, but by 1580 anyone could have seen that plague was endemic and that London was likelier to receive an annual visitation than to be spared it; the only question was how long the sickness would persist. Henslowe was not the sort of fool who would have built a playhouse without using Burbage's ten-year-old enterprise and the register of plague bills to calculate how many months a year on average his playhouse would be dark and profitless. His own Diary would later document inhibitions of six months from June to December 1592, ten months from February to December 1593, two months in the summer of 1595, and three months each, July to October, in 1596 and 1597. The next closure would be from June until October 1599, by which time general acknowledgment would date the plague season from Midsummer to Michaelmas, 24 June–29 September, annually. The playhouses were also closed for over a year between the spring of 1603 and 1604.

Not as regularly, the Privy Council ordered the playhouses closed in observation of Lent. In March 1579 they wrote

> To the Lord Maiour of London to take order within the Cittie and in all other places within his jurisdiccion that there be no plaiers suffered to plaie during this tyme of lent, untill it be after Ester weke ... and that this order may be observed hereafter yerelie in the Lent tyme.[38]

It was not, however, 'observed hereafter yerelie'. Henslowe's records in the 1590s show closures of a few days before and after Easter in some years, of several weeks in others, and of none at all in a few.

Finally, any 'disorder' might close the playhouses, not that the 'riot' or 'affray' need have anything directly to do with the players: the incident in Finsbury Fields when Grostock toe-danced on the belly of the sleeping apprentice was a case in point. Still, the ensuing fracas had occurred in the *vicinity* of the playhouse, and that was sufficient to indict the playhouse for having given 'occasion' to the rioters.

Sometimes, of course, the players brought deserved wrath down on their own heads through indiscretion. The Privy Council would not tolerate on stage any action, dialogue or matter that might be construed to be seditious, irreligious, libelous or scurrilous. The categories were deliberately undefined, like a shapeless portmanteau that could be collapsed or expanded as occasion demanded; when, for example, a shift in international politics transformed a harmlessly chauvinistic joke about Dutchmen into a seditious glance at Elizabeth's foreign policy. In practice, the sanctions meant that no living person could be represented on the stage; that religious ceremonies could not be enacted; that satire, particularly any that pointed at the government, was proscribed; and that political matters in general were to be treated with discretion, under cover perhaps of another reign, another generation, another court and country. Lewdness, scandal and bawdry, though likewise prohibited, must have been defined liberally, judging by some of what passed in Marlowe, Shakespeare and Jonson.

The Privy Council's 'ill-defined imperative' shadowed the playhouses constantly, but in fact the Council regulated the playhouses from a distance. While they might personally intervene upon petition or information, when complaint was made to them for indulgence or admonition, or when violation, sometimes amounting to nothing more than rumour, was brought to their attention; and while they might lodge the ostensible onus of regulation with the Lord Mayor, they appointed their own deputy, the Master of the Revels, to oversee the playhouses on a day-to-day basis, giving him authority superior to the Corporation's to regulate those playhouses in ways consistent with the Council's interests.

The first Masters were appointed *ad hoc*, their duties being the seasonal ones of supervising the Christmas and Shrovetide festivities at Court, but the office grew with each monarch's appetite for entertainment so that by 1572 the Master of the Revels was appointed permanently and was responsible for a budget that year of £1,558 17s 5½d, including payments to tailors, property-makers, armourers, embroiderers, haberdashers, mercers, silkwomen, wiredrawers, and someone who supplied a device to simulate thunder and lightning. The Revels Office was enlarged again a few years after the Theater was built: Edmund Tilney was appointed Master in 1577 – his tenure covers the entire Rose period – and in 1581 he was granted a patent in the form of a new commission for managing the office. The first half of the patent pertains to his purely Court functions and authorised him to retain at 'competent Wages' whatever 'propertie makers and conninge artificers and laborers' he required; to purchase whatever 'kindes of stuffe, ware or marchandise' were necessary; to guarantee from forfeiture outside contracts that might have to be suspended when workmen were pressed to the Revels' service; to imprison any who refused the commission and to grant immunity from arrest for the duration of the work to any the Revels employed. Formalising these articles into a patent gave the Master more power and meant that the preparations for the Queen's entertainment – by no means a frivolous occupation – could proceed more efficiently. But the second half of the patent widened the scope of the Master's duties by making him responsible for the professional players who were performing around London daily. This part of the document must be quoted in full:

> We haue and doe by these presents auctorise and commaunde our said Servant Edmunde Tilney maister of our said Revells by himselfe or his sufficient deputie or deputies to warne commaunde and appointe in all places within this our

Realme of England aswell within francheses and liberties as without all and euery plaier or plaiers with their playmakers either belonginge to any noble man or otherwise bearinge the name or names or vsinge the facultie of play-makers or plaiers of Comedies Tragedies Enterludes or what other showes soever from tyme to tyme and at all tymes to appeare before him with all suche plaies Tragedies Comedies or showes as they shall haue in readiness or meane to sett forth and them to presente and recite before our said Servant or his sufficient deputie Whom Wee ordeyne appointe and aucthorise by these presentes of all suche showes plaies plaiers and playmakers together with their playing places to order and reforme auctorise and put downe as shalbe thought meete or vnmeete vnto himselfe or his said deputie in that behalfe, And also likewise we haue by these presentes aucthorised and commaunded the said Edmunde Tylney that in case if any of them whatsoever they bee will obstina-telie refuse vpon warninge vnto them given by the said Edmunde or his sufficient deputie, to accomplishe and obey our commaundement in this behalf then it shalbe lawful to the said Edmunde or his sufficient deputie to attache the partie or parties so offendinge and him or them to commytt to warde to remaine without bayle or mayneprise vntill suche tyme as the same Edmunde Tylney or his sufficient deputie shall thinke the tyme of his or theire ymprison-ment to be punishement sufficient for his or their said offences in that be-halfe....[39]

The terms of the patent meant that Tilney became both playhouse censor and licensor: he approved playing venues by issuing what amounted to operators' licences to playhouse owners like Burbage and Henslowe, and, before any play could be staged, he authorised its performance with a licence certifying that it had been read and allowed by himself or his deputy. In fact the playing companies, who were responsible for securing such licences, did not 'appeare before him ... to presente and recite' the script as the patent instructs; they submitted the plays to be read. Neither did the 'playmakers' participate in this procedure, for once a dramatist handed his manuscript over to a company he had no further rights or responsibilities to it. Licences authorised the performance, not the writing, of a play. However, the Privy Council was not always disposed to hon-ouring such niceties of internal playhouse organisation, so when a play caused offence they usually arrested the playwrights along with the play-ers.

The single surviving example of Tilney's censorship appears on the manuscript of *Sir Thomas More* where he proceeds through the play marking objectional lines 'mend *th*is' or 'all alt*er*' and cancelling some scenes entirely before returning to the opening scene to enter further instructions: 'Leaue out *th*e insur*rect*ion wholy & *th*e Cause ther off ... with a reportt afterward*es* ... A shortt reportt & nott otherwise att your own perrilles.'[40] Players probably grumbled at some of Tilney's decisions; *Sir Thomas More* makes no dramatic sense without the insurrection, and to excise it would have deprived the players of their most effectively theatrical scene. But Tilney was a censor, not an editor. The players did not make a practice of defying him – that was too dangerous and far too costly. An indiscretion – like 'forgetting' to secure a licence or thrusting unauthorised material into an already licensed play – would land them in prison without bail while every playhouse, not just their own, was shut and every player went hungry. When the players did offend the censor it was usually by misunderstanding. But at least once they were disastrously misrepresented. The most furious storm ever to shake the playhouse in Henslowe's memory amounted to nothing more than a tempest in a teapot but nevertheless had dire consequences for the players. A needy informant, in fee to a Privy Council spy, brought evidence – in fact, wild accusation – of a seditious play performed at a Bankside playhouse. Players were arrested, playwrights fled London, playhouse owners listened to rumour and were convinced that their doors were being clapped to in reprisal. But when the Privy Council got round to examining the alleged offenders they discovered no offence had been committed. The informant was wrong.[41] On normal days the players undoubtedly knew far better than any spy how fine a line they were treading between sensation – the kind of thing that pulled audiences into the playhouse – and sedition – the step misjudged that brought their necks to the block – for long years of collaboration, of practically daily communication between the playhouses and the Revels Office, would have taken the mystery out of Tilney's licensing policies. Players may occasionally have been surprised by rejection, when, say, some political adjustment altered the equilibrium of acceptability, but they cannot have been unsure very often of their play's chances of being licensed.

Given Tilney's elaborate commission and the regulatory power that went with it, one question would seem to arise. Why did the Privy Council allow the Corporation of London to go on attacking the playhouses? The answer probably lies at the heart of Queen Elizabeth's philosophy of government by compromise. It was not her style to allow any faction, no matter how golden-haired, an absolute triumph, for any day the weather-cock above Whitehall might swing round and political friends become enemies. A gesture like the granting of the patent to Leicester's Men in 1574 was intended to settle nothing. It merely established a new *status quo*: the Lord Mayor was slapped on the wrist but not manacled; the players were handed a permit that was no guarantee. In sum, the day-to-day survival of the playhouse would hang on the discretion of the Privy Council, but the debate with the City over its ultimate future would never be brought to a final vote in Elizabeth's reign.

Players and playwrights

Over the ten years Henslowe kept his Diary six playing companies occupied the Rose, some for only a matter of days, others for several seasons or years. They were, in order of tenure, Lord Strange's Men, Sussex's Men, Sussex's Men and the Queen's Men together, the Admiral's Men, Pembroke's Men, and Worcester's Men. At least one of these companies died of plague; another probably starved to death on tour in the provinces; a third, recomposed of survivors of two defunct companies, tried like a phoenix to rise out of the ashes but sank again; a fourth outgrew the Rose and moved to grander premises. Most of what is known of the daily life of the Elizabethan player comes from Henslowe's papers where several sorts of documents provide several sorts of information. In the Diary, the receipts accounts, entered as a calendar, set out various companies' playing schedules, repertoires, and earning power. They show two occasions on which a pair of companies played in some kind of partnership and numerous instances when companies played in adversity: when plague or politics closed the playhouses and forced them to tour; when they lost fellow players by death, defection, or retirement. Elsewhere in the Diary the loan accounts itemise the companies' production expenses. They show the players commissioning plays, buying costumes, ordering properties, pensioning off retirees, feeing lawyers, rewarding playwrights for a sensational hit, dividing profits, preparing for trips up to Court – officially their *raison d'être* – or into the country – their *bête noire*. Henslowe's personal accounts with individuals in the companies tell even more about the private responsibilities of the public player, while other memoranda – letters, authorisation slips, bonds, a player's part, a stage plot – place the actor in the tavern and the tiring house, in the wings and on stage.

E.K. Chambers compiled biographies of all the Elizabethan playing companies for *The Elizabethan Stage*. These chapters, being in the main factual rather than interpretative, still carry authority although allowance for his prejudice against Henslowe must be made wherever Chambers uses the Diary subjectively. In respect of the playing companies which appear in the Rose documents, the first difficulty that must be overcome before anything can be discovered about them is the nominal one of identifying them. 'Who is who' must be preliminary to 'what is what', only in this case the 'who' is frequently found behind an alias. Three eventualities might present themselves in the life of a playing company: it might remain intact but change its name several times in as many years; it might disband, reamalgamate with wholly new personnel, yet retain the original company name; or it might split, leaving one player behind in possession of the name while the others went elsewhere to become a new company with a new name. The explanation for such chopping and changing is simple. The players took their names from their patrons and followed their patron's fortunes. When he was honoured with a new title, the title was conferred upon them as well. When he died, his heir might adopt them – so necessitating no change in title – or, bereft of a patron, they might have to seek a new protector with a different title. Lord Strange's Men provide examples of how the system worked. 'Lord Strange' was one of the titles belonging to the Stanley family, who held the Earldom of Derby. It was usually relinquished by the son and heir upon his accession to the Earldom and was given in turn to *his* son and heir. The Stanley family had entertained players since the reign of Henry VIII, but not continuously and not always successively. That is, father and son – the Earl and the Lord Strange – might both patronise a company. If this were the case, when the old Earl died, the heir, Lord Strange, assumed the title. His company became 'Derby's Men' while his father's company, who had been Derby's Men, no longer had a patron and must either have found another, and therefore taken a new title, or disbanded. In 1592 when Lord Strange's Men moved into the Rose, Ferdinando Stanley held the title. He succeeded as fifth Earl of Derby in September 1593, and his company, which had been playing at the Rose, should have become Derby's Men. By then, however, the company was probably defunct, victims of the long plague restraint that closed the playhouses for ten months in 1593. As Strange's Men the company left London in the spring of 1593 to tour, but they did not return as Derby's Men in December when playing resumed at the Rose. Some time over the summer, then, they had probably disbanded. The fifth Earl died in April 1594. If any of his former players did survive the long restraint and the company's disintegration, they might have passed to his heir and perhaps maintained themselves in the provinces, for in the winter of 1599–1600 a company of Derby's Men appeared at Court.

The history of the Admiral's Men is slightly simpler. Their patron, Charles Howard, was appointed Lord Admiral in 1585. His original company probably disbanded in the winter of 1588 when some of the players sold their stock and left for the continent. The remainder attached themselves to other companies, but one of them, Edward Alleyn, who joined Lord Strange's Men, continued to style himself 'seruant to the lord Admiral', thus perpetuating the title until such time as Lord Strange's Men in their turn disbanded. Alleyn then organised a new Admiral's Company which moved into the Rose in May 1594. They continued there until July 1600 when they moved to the new Fortune playhouse. In the meantime, Howard was created Earl of Nottingham in October 1597. The Company's new status should have been reflected in the accounts Henslowe was keeping for them, but perhaps because Howard continued to serve as Lord Admiral, or perhaps simply because Henslowe was never the most scrupulous of record keepers, the Company did not become Nottingham's Men in the Diary until 1599. When Queen Elizabeth died in March 1603 Nottingham's Men were one of the three most prestigious companies that were taken under royal patronage. They became the Prince's Men.

Two more examples can be stated even more briefly. Three separate companies of Pembroke's Men seem to have existed, though whether any of the personnel served continuously is impossible to know. The first amalgamation was the company that Henslowe referred to in a letter of 28 September 1593 as having been worn out by the plodding, profitless summer-long tour in which they were unable to 'saue ther carges with trauell' and so had 'to pane [i.e. pawn] ther parell'. The second company was at the centre of a (misinformed) clash with the Privy Council in the spring of 1597. As a result it collapsed, and its debris was salvaged by the Admiral's Men who first accepted Pembroke's Men as partners in a collaborative company playing at the Rose then simply absorbed them into their own company. The third group of Pembroke's Men played two performances at the Rose in October 1600 then disappeared. Finally, account must be made of a company that did not appear at the Rose but whose fortunes constantly impinged upon it: the Lord Chamberlain's Men, Shakespeare's company. Henry Carey, Lord Hunsdon, was appointed Lord Chamberlain in 1585. An original company he patronised was defunct by 1590, but a new troupe composed of residue Strange's Men who split from Edward Alleyn in 1593 appeared in 1594 as the Chamberlain's Men. This new Chamberlain's Company played continuously for the next twenty-five years, but when Hunsdon died in 1596, the office of Lord Chamberlain passed out of the Carey family to Lord Cobham while the players passed to Carey's son George, the new Lord Hunsdon. Thus, the company became known as 'Hunsdon's Men'. Almost immediately, however, Cobham died; George Carey was appointed to the post his father once held; and the company were the Chamberlain's Men once again from March 1597. Like the Admiral's Men, this company was taken under royal patronage at the accession of James I. They became the King's Men in 1603.

All of the companies whose working habits can be observed in Henslowe's Diary were sharer companies. At their core was a group of perhaps six or eight – the Admiral's Men in 1600 had eleven – sharers who invested money, a share, in the company and who collaborated in running it. They shared the weightiest acting responsibilities, although weight and volume were usually at odds, for the youngest member of the company might have half a dozen roles to play in any given production while the sharer usually took only one or two. They likewise shared all the management decisions. Their accounts with Henslowe show that every member of the company could authorise payment for a playscript or a costume, although in practice responsibility for playbooks seems to have devolved to one sharer for a time while another sharer looked after costuming. Finally, they shared the profits – or losses. Their playhouse income came from two sources, the pit, where spectators stood for a penny, and the galleries, where they paid more to sit. Pit money belonged to the players and probably went for running costs. Half the gallery money was turned over to Henslowe, their landlord, for rent: these are the sums he entered as his daily receipts in the Diary. The other half of the gallery money, unless production costs laid further claims upon it, was the day's profit and was divided equally among the sharers.

Fleshing out the company was a group of perhaps four hired men, adult players whose ability and experience probably equalled the sharers'. Richard Allen, for example, as a hired man in the Admiral's Men, played the same line and weight of roles as the company's sharers did. The difference was that Allen had not staked any money in the company. Presumably therefore he did not enter any of the policy decisions, and at the end of the week he collected a fixed wage while the sharers split profits that might be swollen by throngs crowding into a new play or shrunk by inclement weather or affected by a hundred variables.

The company's investment in the future rested with their boy apprentices who, like every other Elizabethan apprentice, functioned half as servants, half as students. Their jobs on stage consisted of women's roles for the best of the boys, or spear carriers, messengers, supernumeraries for the rest. Off stage, they fetched and carried for their masters, the sharers who had domestic responsibility for supporting them and professional responsibility for training them in the quality. Putting apprentices, hirelings and sharers together, the companies that played at the Rose probably numbered some sixteen players. That was sixteen players for *Dr Faustus*, which names forty-five parts, *The Jew of Malta*, thirty-five parts, and *Henry VI* which, if it is Shakespeare's *Henry VI, Part 1* calls for over fifty.

Sharer companies at the Rose were also repertory companies, maintaining an average of twenty plays and playing them in rotation, a different play each day and a space of a week or ten days between repetitions. This schedule was typical, as the following table shows by summarising the playing seasons at the Rose. The resident company's name and the season's dates are given first. Then follows the number of *possible* performance dates, Sundays having been subtracted across the calendar because such was the law, although the players undoubtedly broke it. Next is given the actual number of performances the company managed in that time, followed by the number of plays in the repertoire, the number of new plays opened, and the weeks in which they were opened. The records for October 1597 are fragmentary, and thereafter Henslowe stopped recording daily receipts. However, repayments attached to the Admiral's Men's subsequent loan accounts show that they performed nearly continuously at the Rose until July 1600 when they transferred to their new

Table 1. The playing seasons at the Rose up to November 1597 when Henslowe's receipts accounts lapse and detailed documentation fails.

Company	Season	Possible performances	Actual performances	Plays	New plays	Weeks in which new plays opened
1. Strange's Men	19 Feb. 1592–22 Jun. 1592	123	105	23	5	2, 8, 10, 14, 16
2. Strange's Men	29 Dec. 1592–1 Feb. 1593	35	29	12	2	2, 5
3. Sussex's Men	27 Dec. 1593–6 Feb. 1594	42	30	12	1	5
4. Sussex's & Queen's Men	1 Apr. 1594–8 Apr. 1594	8	8	5	0	
5. Admiral's Men	14 May 1594–16 May 1594	3	3	3	0	
6. Admiral's Men	17 Jun. 1594–26 Jun. 1595	328	273	36	20	2, 4, 5, 7, 9, 11, 14, 15, 19, 21, 22, 25, 26, 35, 36, 38, 42, 44, 46, 48
7. Admiral's Men	25 Aug. 1595–27 Feb. 1596	187	151	30	10	1, 2, 4, 6, 8, 10, 14, 20, 23, 26
8. Admiral's Men	12 Apr. 1596–28 Jul. 1596	107	84	25	7	3, 4, 6, 9, 11, 12, 15
9. Admiral's Men	27 Oct. 1596–12 Feb. 1597	109	75	18	8	6, 7, 8, 10, 11, 12, 14, 16
10. Admiral's Men	3 Mar. 1597–16 Jul. 1597	136	109	21	6	4, 9, 11, 13, 14, 18
11. Admiral's Men	11 Oct. 1597–5 Nov. 1597	26	9	6	1	1

playhouse, the Fortune. Two years later a newly amalgamated company of Worcester's Men moved into the Rose. They remained until March 1603 when an inhibition, which eventually lasted over a year, closed the playhouses. They did not return to the Rose when playing resumed in 1604.

The performance history of the Rose falls into three periods of major productivity. The arrival of Lord Strange's Men in February 1592 perhaps marked a new beginning for Henslowe and his playhouse. He began keeping his Diary. The Rose had been standing for five years, but whoever his tenants were – indeed, if he *had* tenants in those years – Henslowe did not bother to record any interest he may have shown in them. The composition of the sharer members of Lord Strange's Men is fixed by a Privy Council licence which names Edward Alleyn, 'servaunt to the right honorable the Lord Highe Admiral', William Kemp, Thomas Pope, John Heminges, Augustine Philips, and George Brian as 'al one companie'. It seems likely that Shakespeare played with Strange's Men as well, again based on the assumption that the *Henry VI* in their repertoire was his.[42] Strange's Men were undoubtedly London's premier company in 1592, and the Rose must have gained prestige with them as tenants. In their repertoire they had a half dozen of the most popular, and most lucrative, plays ever staged at the Rose: Marlowe's powerful triumvirate, Kyd's *Spanish Tragedy*, Greene's *Friar Bacon*, *Muly Mollocco* (probably *The Battle of Alcazar*), and *Henry VI*. Initially, Strange's Men were forced to leave the Rose only a year after they arrived because an inhibition fell in February 1593. They spent the next eight months touring the provinces and, possibly as a result of acrimony that festered over those difficult months, when the Company returned to London they split, leaving Edward Alleyn to assemble over the next six months a new company of Admiral's Men that opened at Henslowe's playhouse in May 1594. Henslowe's Diary shows the next six years to have been a period of stability (though agitated by periodic tremors), prosperity (though balanced by hardship and setbacks), and expansion for the Admiral's Men. Alleyn was London's premier tragedian; the Company were favourite at Court; the playhouse, unrivalled on the Bankside, was in her glory. But already in 1597 things were starting to sour. Alleyn retired; players defected; the new Swan playhouse brought competition to the neighbourhood. Still, the Admiral's Men rallied, eventually recalling the renegade players and outlasting the Swan. It was the arrival of the Chamberlain's Men and the Globe in 1599 that ended the domination of the Bank by the Rose. The Admiral's Men moved to a suburb north of the City, and for two years Henslowe's playhouse was unoccupied. Then Worcester's Men breathed new life into it. There were no stars among this new company except the aged clown, Will Kemp, but in Thomas Heywood and Thomas Dekker they had playwrights of long experience and considerable popularity. They had a new, yet untried young playwright, one John Webster. And they certainly had grit. In establishing themselves at the Rose they set themselves in competition with that company at the Globe who had put to flight the Admiral's Men.

Continuity between Lord Strange's Men and the Admiral's Men was effected in the person of Edward Alleyn. He, too, was probably the point of continuity in those companies' tenure at the Rose, for only nine months after Strange's Men moved into Henslowe's house, Alleyn married Henslowe's stepdaughter. Perhaps in that marriage a playhouse dynasty such as James Burbage would perpetuate through his sons at the Theater was contracted. Alleyn's was the brightest success story of the Elizabethan playhouse, though indeed he renounced his quality at least twice and ended his life building almshouses: perhaps the ultimate metaphor of rejection for the profanity of the playhouse. Born in 1566 he was a member of Worcester's Men by 1583; within another six years he was already displaying the business acumen that would make him rich by purchasing other players' shares in joint company stock – costumes, playbooks, instruments. In the 1590s he made famous the roles of Orlando in *Orlando Furioso*, Tamburlaine, Dr Faustus, Barabas in *The Jew of Malta*, Muly Mahomet in *The Battle of Alcazar* and Tamar in *Tamar Cham*. He perhaps stamped his personality too forcefully on Lord Strange's Men: to a man, the sharers named in the 1593 licence abandoned him. The Admiral's Men, however, built a reputation upon him strong enough to survive even when he retired in the autumn, probably, of 1597. Alleyn returned to the Company three years later, propelled more directly by his business sense than his loyalty or love of the profession: there was trouble over the construction of the Fortune, a playhouse in which he owned a large interest, and the weight of his reputation was exactly the pressure Henslowe needed to tip the balance in favour of the project's completion. When the Privy Council finally approved the Fortune their chief reason was the Queen's pleasure, expressed as a desire to see Ned Alleyn perform once again. He did, but perhaps only as a tired ghost from a vaulted, echoing but dead past. He may have settled for reproductions of past performances or he may have been shackled by the fame that still had audiences clamouring for another Tamburlaine, another Jew. Whichever, the Admiral's Men's accounts at the Fortune show them staging a long string of revivals of plays Alleyn had made notorious a decade earlier. Like Shakespeare, though, in Sonnet 111 – 'my nature is subdued/To what it works in, like the dyer's hand' – Alleyn seems to have felt soiled by his profession. Reputation offered no immunity to contamination, and by 1606 at the latest Alleyn had once again, this time finally, severed himself from the players to devote all his energies to the College of God's Gift at Dulwich, built on land that he had been sedulously amassing over the years. It was completed in 1614 at a cost of £10,000. The almshouses he was endowing at his death in 1626 were an extension of the charity attached to his college. The sharp redirection his life took to lead him from playhouses to almshouses might be summarised and denoted in one domestic fact: his first father-in-law, Henslowe, was builder of the Rose; his second, John Donne, was Dean of St Paul's.

Less conspicuously, continuity was achieved between the Admiral's Men and Worcester's Men through a group of playwrights who began with the senior company at the Rose, followed them to the Fortune, then returned to the Rose when the new company arrived in 1602. George Chapman, Henry Chettle, Ben Jonson, Thomas Dekker, Robert Day, Henry Porter, Thomas Heywood, William Haughton, Richard Hathaway, Anthony Munday all wrote for the Admiral's Men at the Rose. Many of them began their careers there. Most continued to supply the Admiral's Men at the Fortune. Several young playwrights – Thomas Middleton and John Webster among them – began at the Fortune under the wings of experienced writers. Webster and Middleton's maiden play was a collaboration with Dekker, Drayton, and Munday. Once Worcester's Men opened at the Rose in August 1602, these loyalties altered somewhat. Perhaps the Admiral's Men – now Nottingham's Men even to negligent Henslowe – with their ancient if popular revivals were seen as the conservative company, Worcester's as more experimental, more vital. Whatever the reason, certain dramatists began writing more consistently for the younger company. Heywood, a sharer in the Company, blossomed as a Worcester playwright. Dekker concentrated his energies there and apparently took Webster and Middleton with him. But what is most interesting about these migrations is that they seem not to have been either exclusive or traumatic, so while Dekker wrote his new plays for Worcester's Men and even transferred to them a play he originally intended for Nottingham's Men – *A Medicine for a Curst Wife* – he revised *Tasso* for the older company and wrote *The Honest Whore* for them in 1604. Heywood was chief dramatist for Worcester's Men by the end of 1602, yet he collaborated with Chettle on *The London Florentine* for Nottingham's Men that December. Day, Hathaway, and Wentworth Smith wrote for both companies simultaneously. So did Henry Chettle. Chettle's availability appears remarkable in that he had signed a bond to write exclusively for Nottingham's Men only a few weeks before handing a play over to Worcester's Men, but then, as Henslowe's copious notes of Chettle's niggling debts would show, the man had a rather vague sense of responsibility. Besides, exclusivity bonds were impossible to negotiate or to enforce on a practical basis. They were merely punitive gestures, and the players' bonds that appear among the Rose documents provide a useful comparison.

The working habits of these playwrights are displayed in the pages of Henslowe's loan accounts with the Admiral's Men and Worcester's Men where one discovers that the typical Rose play was a collaboration involving sometimes as many as five playwrights who frequently submitted their scripts piecemeal and who rarely occupied themselves on one play for longer than a month. Rose playwrights were prolific. In 1597 alone, Chettle, Dekker, and Munday were responsible for twenty-six plays. It was characteristic of Dekker, when he accepted final payment for *Hannibal and Hermes*, to take an advance at 'the same time vpon the next boock called perce of winschester' which he and his collaborators finished a fortnight later. Collaborative teams organised their work in various ways. Once Ben Jonson sold a plot of a play to the Admiral's Men and George Chapman wrote the script. This loosest of associations hardly qualifies as collaboration. Genuine syndicates were sometimes organised from the play's inception and contributed equally from plot to 'exeunt omnes'. The writing was a concentrated team effort. Other syndicates worked differently. In some, a playwright plotted the play, sold the idea to the company, then gathered fellow contributors as he needed them; at stages a single playwright might be writing independently while at others two or three different playwrights wrote in close conjunction. Certain plays seem to have been divided unequally among the syndicate. So, too, were the fees. Elsewhere the syndicate was named in the initial payment but thereafter payments made alternately would seem to indicate that the playwrights, having devised their plot together, went their separate ways to write their separate scenes. Playwrights who submitted their portion of the play to the company were paid whether or not the other collaborators produced the rest.

The method of working prompts questions about the quality of the work, for it must frequently have been the case that a playwright was killing off a character another playwright had devised, without seeing his collaborator's work: the piecemeal system of submission operated positively for the individual dramatist – he collected his fee; another man's sloth was his own affair – but negatively for the play if it is to be judged by modern aesthetic demands that place a high priority on coherence, formal unity, the fusion of the multiple dramatic visions into a single design. Imposing such demands upon the plays of Henslowe's Diary was, to begin with, the work of the Victorians who looked at the conditions in which the Rose playwrights wrote, looked particularly at the strong habit of collaboration, concluded that the playwrights had little artistic investment in their plays, and dismissed most of the repertoire as 'hackwork'. They supposed that Henslowe was primarily responsible for creating those conditions of employment.

They were wrong on all counts. Playwrights worked directly for the playing companies, and it was their demands the dramatists had to meet. That meant supplying the Admiral's Men with some twenty new plays every year: Shakespeare's life's work exhausted in two years. It is probably a fallacy to suppose that collaboration was unhealthy or was forced on the playwrights when Henslowe's Diary shows that they could work as quickly and lucratively alone as in partnership. This must mean that collaboration was a chosen, perhaps even a preferred, method of writing. It may have been more efficient in permitting each playwright to do the job he liked best – kings or clowns, plotting or poetry or prose – in the play. Efficiency was undoubtedly a higher priority to the professional playwrights of the public playhouse than any aesthetic demand, for the playing company, their master, was itself a relentlessly efficient machine that devoured a new play a fortnight. New plays became old plays overnight, their expected stage life a matter of a dozen or so performances across a few months. New plays mostly made money. Old plays mostly did not.

And with that observation this Introduction returns to its opening theme: profit. The Elizabethan playhouse was organised to make money. From Henslowe's point of view, or from Alleyn's, from Burbage's, or from Shakespeare's, the most successful play, the play that would run the longest and reach the widest audience, was the most lucrative play. Obliquely, if financial criteria are allowed to displace aesthetic evaluations, it becomes possible to see collaborative playwriting as a more genuinely Elizabethan way of defining a play, where the quality of the play was in the immediacy of playing the play, and where excellence perhaps resided in the scenic unit, the 'now' on stage that was engaging the audience. For a collaborator, the scenic effect is the primary concern. It must be remembered that it is a modern prejudice which aggrandises and misrepresents the role of the Elizabethan playwright by compiling canons and giving them the dramatists' names. Even Shakespeare's plays were not his own, except in so far as he was a sharer in the Chamberlain's Men. His plays belonged to the company. When a company paid the last instalment on a book, the playwright had sold his entire interest in it. The players were king in the Elizabethan playhouse and perhaps the most exciting story the Rose documents tell is theirs: how they adjusted internally and stretched to fill a repertoire that grew in new directions over the years; how they faced changing realities in the practical circumstances of their profession that were reflected in new arrangements with their landlord; how they came to terms with and finally tamed the antagonism that surrounded them in the community. The end of that story was – predictably – a money deal.

Editorial procedures

Reading Henslowe. The Rose documents are produced here in old spelling. To have modernised the spelling would have meant making interpretative decisions that eradicated some of the information the documents contain and that compromised their integrity as primary sources. Old spelling will present few problems to the modern reader even though spelling was not standardised by the end of the sixteenth century and writers from formally-trained Privy Council scribes to literate players and playwrights to unlettered businessmen were all capable of rendering basic English vocabulary in permutations of the alphabet that would look wild in the modern reader's conservative, not to say crabbed, lexicon. Today's reader will need to read more slowly, certainly more patiently, than he is used, but he will not meet many impasses that ingenuity and the *OED* will not be able to break through. Most Elizabethan writers were at least consistent. Their eccentricities, once identified, supply a scribal fingerprint of sorts that turns informant upon the whole document. The single exception is Henslowe. Spelling, as so much else in his life, was an *ad hoc* arrangement for Henslowe. He did not commit himself to a spelling once decided upon; he did not copy the spelling of play titles from one entry to the next even though the titles appeared over and over in his receipts lists; he did not even apply the experiment of one spelling upon the invention of the next. So 'suit', 'sewte', 'sewt', and 'sewtte' all appear; *Muly Mollocco* comes in five versions on the first page of the receipts accounts; and *Tis No Deceit to Deceive the Deceiver* is rendered as 'tis no desayt to deseaue the deseuer'.

Henslowe must be read as he himself wrote – phonetically – and then most of the Diary is straightforward enough: *howse: house; owt: out; grene; green; fostes: Faustus; payer: pair.* Some spellings are more recondite: *goyne: join; bodeyes: bodice; geylous: jealous; meghellmas: Michaelmas; sraftid: Shrovetide.* In some cases the context will show that the phonetic word cannot be correct and that alternatives should be tried: 'eares', 'eayeares' and 'ers' are 'heirs'; 'fuschen', 'fustian'; a 'rich clock', a 'cloak'; 'ales' is 'alias'; 'mean' and 'mane' are usually 'men' or 'man' as in the play title 'made manes mores', *The Madman's Morris*.

Titles are frequently difficult. They were for Henslowe as well. The 'spanes comodye donne oracioe' is *The Spanish Comedy of Don Horatio*; the 'masacar', Marlowe's *Massacre at Paris*; 'tittus & ondronicous', *Titus Andronicus*. But clearly, Henslowe's spellings are important indicators of Elizabethan pronunciation: 'hewen of burdockes' is *Hugh of Bordeaux*; 'godfrey of bullen', *Godfrey of Boulogne*; 'owld castell', *Oldcastle*; 'matchevell', *Machiavelli*. An index of all the play titles of Henslowe's Diary appears at the back of this volume; difficult titles are cross-indexed to alternate renderings. Identifications that cannot be resolved by consulting this index should be referred to the title index in Foakes and Rickert's *Henslowe's Diary*.

Henslowe was consistent in using several abbreviations: 'pd' for 'paid', 'rd' for 'received', 'dd' for 'deliver' or 'delivered', and 'mr' for 'master' as in Master of the Revels. The ampersand, &, could be 'and' or 'an'.

Henslowe almost never used 'ye' for 'the', but he frequently put 'yt' for 'that'. He usually used 'yt' for 'it' and sometimes for 'yet'. Other contributors to the Diary conflated words: 'one thone ptye' for 'on the one part' or 'fulpemente' for 'full payment'. Henslowe did not. His recurring habit was to separate them: *a bowe; a monste; a poyntement; a dicyons* (additions); *be gynynge; des carge* (discharge), *cone tenew*. With Henslowe, familiarity is the only teacher. Sometimes even that fails: when their edition of the Diary went to press Foakes and Rickert were still bewildered by 'dornackes' and 'colysenes'.[43]

In all of the documents, words, spellings, or sections of the writing that were crossed out or cancelled by the author have been indicated with square brackets. (Henslowe's entries in particular show several important cancellations.) Standard Elizabethan abbreviations, such as 'Matie' and 'wch' have been expanded: 'Ma*jes*tie' and 'w*hi*ch'.

Dates. The Elizabethan civil calendar dated the new year from 1 January. The older ecclesiastical calendar began the new year on Lady Day – the Feast of the Annunciation – 25 March. Civil documents could be dated by either convention; Henslowe used both, never systematically. Thus, a potential area of confusion arises in the period 1 January–25 March each year when scribes observing the ecclesiastical system retained the old year date for months modern readers of the Rose documents would date in the new year. Such discrepancies are acknowledged in the headnotes to the documents by recourse to split dates which juxtapose the ecclesiastical date as it is found on the document with the civil equivalent. An example is Henslowe's first receipts account with Lord Strange's Men which he dates '1591 beginge the 19 of febreary'. The headnote gives the date as '19 February 1591/2'. Split dates are sufficiently clumsy to jog the reader's attention to this problem while avoiding the confusion, invited by silent modernisations, of an evident contradiction between the date on the document and the date in the headnote. They likewise alert the reader to what he should be looking for if he consults the original manuscript. Dates must always be scrutinised carefully, particularly Henslowe's dates, for Henslowe did not observe either the civil or the ecclesiastical system consistently, even in a single year. Entries in the receipts accounts for January might be dated according to the new civil calendar year. A few pages later, however, entries belonging to that same January might be dated in the old year. Occasionally Henslowe dated receipts by the old year far into April or May. Thus, where an isolated entry dated January, February, or March occurs in the Diary, the year date is open to question. Context or disposition may determine the matter. That is, the entry may refer to transactions clearly dated elsewhere or may fall among other entries that suggest which reading is correct. Otherwise, tentativeness is the best one can do.

Two other dating conventions are relevant to these documents. The regnal year was dated from the anniversary of the Queen's accession, 17 November 1558. Thus, '33 Elizabeth I' ran from 17 November 1588 to 16 November 1589. Again, therefore, a discrepancy between this and the civil or ecclesiastical calendar exists. Regnal years were used exclusively on some documents such as lay subsidy rolls and royal proclamations, and they appeared together with civil dates on most other legal documents. Finally, quarter days throughout the year were conventionally designated for payments of all kinds. The quarter days were 25 March (Lady Day), 24 June (the Feast of John the Baptist), 29 September (Michaelmas), and 25 December (Christmas). Michaelmas was the beginning of the fiscal year.

Monetary conversion. Before 1972 when decimalisation reorganised the English monetary system, the '£ s d' (liber, shilling, denarius) system had been standard from pre-Elizabethan times. The pound was worth twenty shillings and the shilling worth twelve pence. Henslowe normally entered his receipts in roman numerals and frequently wrote them as composites, that is, 'xxv s' for '25 shillings', equivalent to £1 5s, or 'xxiv d' for 14 pence, equivalent to 1s 2d. In the accounts *ob = obolus = a* halfpenny; *ob. q. = obolus + quarter =* three farthings. A mark was worth 13s. 4d.

Notes

(For abbreviations used in these notes, see pp. 218-19.)

1 John Payne Collier, *The Diary of Philip Henslowe, from 1591 to 1609* (London: Shakespeare Society, 1845). G.F. Warner listed the Collier forgeries in his *Catalogue of Manuscripts and Muniments of Alleyn's College of God's Gift* (1881). Excerpts from the Diary were scattered through Edmond Malone's ten-volume *Shakespeare* (1790). Others appeared throughout James Boswell's 'Variorum' *Shakespeare*, 21 vols. (1821).
2 F.G. Fleay, *A Chronicle History of the London Stage* (1890), 117.
3 Walter W. Greg, *Henslowe's Diary*, Vol. *II* (London: A.H. Bullen, 1908), 111.
4 Greg, *Vol. II*, 112.
5 Greg, *Vol. II*, 111.
6 Greg, *Vol. II*, 113.
7 E.K. Chambers, *The Elizabethan Stage I* (Oxford: Clarendon Press, 1923), 351, 363. Chambers did not, however, accept all Greg's conclusions, as is stated in his review of the *Diary* in *Modern Language Review* 4 (1909), 407-13.
8 Chambers, *ES I*, 363.
9 Glynne Wickham, *Early English Stages II, Part I* (London: Routledge, 1963), 129.

10 Andrew Gurr, *The Shakespearean Stage 1574-1642* (Cambridge University Press, 1970), 16.

11 Gurr, *Shakespearean Stage*, 51.

12 T.W. Baldwin, *The Organization and Personnel of the Shakespearean Company* (Princeton University Press, 1927), 321-31. The book is too schematic and the picture of the Admiral's Men too neat, but at least Baldwin did not consider Greg's interpretation of the Diary final. He was more generous toward Henslowe than Greg had been.

13 R.A. Foakes and R.T. Rickert, *Henslowe's Diary* (Cambridge University Press, 1961), xxv. Foakes's introduction is still the best place to begin with the Diary, but steps toward reinterpretation have been taken by Neil Carson in two articles, 'Literary Management in the Lord Admiral's Company, 1596-1603' and 'Production Finance at the Rose Theatre, 1596-98', both of which appeared in *Theatre Research International* new series, 1977 and 1979. Bernard Beckerman contributed an important essay entitled 'Philip Henslowe' to *The Theatrical Manager in England and America*, edited by Joseph W. Donohue (1971). And Cambridge University Press have commissioned from Neil Carson and C.C. Rutter a replacement for Greg's *Vol. II*.

14 Henslowe's dates are a matter of conjecture in the absence of baptismal or deposition records, one of which would have suggested a date of birth, the other of which would have stated his age. Surviving documents locate him first in 1585 in the Liberty of the Clink when he took the lease on the Rose property. (Walter Greg's belief that Henslowe lived there from 1577 was a mistake based on a misreading of a letter in the *Henslowe Papers* which actually belongs to 1597.) Ironically, most factual information on Henslowe's life is contained in litigation surrounding his will after his death in 1616. Edward Alleyn deposed that Henslowe had married the widow Agnes Woodward 'about seaven and Thirtie yeares sithence'. That dates the marriage around 1580. Henslowe was a 'servant' to Agnes when they married, which probably means that his apprenticeship to Woodward had not yet expired when Woodward died. Henslowe, then, may have been under twenty-four years of age in 1580 since according to apprenticeship law he must have reached at least twenty-four by the time his articles expired. Thus, when he acquired the Rose property in 1585 he may have been about thirty. Henslowe's will survives in the Public Records Office (PCC 6 Cope, now PRO Prob. 11/127). The litigation surrounding the will likewise survives (PRO C.24/431/23 and ST.CH.168/18) and has been thoroughly analysed: W. Rendle transcribed part of the Chancery suit in 'Philip Henslowe' in *The Genealogist*, new series 4 (1887), 149-59. C.J. Sisson discussed the Star Chamber depositions in 'Henslowe's Will Again', in *Review of English Studies*, 5 (1929), 308-11. John Brierley reviewed the entire case in 'Edward Alleyn and Henslowe's Will' in *Shakespeare Quarterly*, 9 (1958), 321-30. None of them had discovered the existence of the actual will itself, which was first transcribed by Carol Anne Chillington in an unpublished dissertation, *Philip Henslowe and His Diary* (Ann Arbor: University of Michigan, 1979), 268-9.

15 Lay Subsidies: PRO E.179/186/349; E.179/186/362; E.179/186/370; E.179/186/375a; E.179/186/377; E.179/290/40-47. Henslowe was among the wealthiest men in the Clink, rated at £10 worth of earthly possessions. Francis Langley,

his playhouse rival and owner of the Swan in Paris Garden, seems to have been substantially wealthier, being rated at £20 in 1594 and 1598. But then Paris Garden as a district was more affluent than the Clink: twenty-seven households there were assessed £42 8s in taxes in 1593 while that same year sixty households in the Clink paid £48 2s 8d.

Certificates of Residence: PRO E.115/199/130; E.115/206/137; E.115/207/15; E.115/207/17; E.115/208/58; E.115/211/137; E.115/213/31; E.115/214/28; E.115/219/79; E.115/219/82. These Certificates were issued in connection with the assessment of the lay subsidies to any person who might be in danger of facing an assessment in two jurisdictions. They verified to the assessors in one jurisdiction that the tax had been collected in the other. Henslowe's Certificates were all issued from the Court and repeated the same information, that 'Phillip Henslowe one of the groomes of her ma*jestie* chamber beeing rese*d*aunt and abyding at the Courte at the tyme of taxac*i*on and most parte of the yeare before is assessed and rated before vs at iij£ in fees and therefore ought to be dischardged of the same in all other places wheare he shalbe taxed'.

Poor Relief: *Henslowe Papers*, MSS. I, Art. 70.

Grammar School: PRO Patent Rolls C66/1926. Henslowe's vestry duties should not be depreciated, for as Frank Freeman Foster points out in *The Politics of Stability* (London: Royal Historical Society, 1977), vestrymen normally served for life and churchwardens were the chief administrative officers in the parish (p. 31). The parish was both a secular unit of political influence and local government and also an ecclesiastical institution, so that the vestrymen's jurisdiction 'reached into what could be called police power, public works, sanitation, tax collecting, and old age insurance'. Their business was dispatched 'not like modern bureaucrats representing a collective authority but as prominent parishioners acting individually and frequently relying on their own judgment' (p. 41).

16 Bernard Beckerman, 'Philip Henslowe', *The Theatrical Manager in England and America*, edited by Joseph W. Donohue, pp. 19–62. I entirely support Beckerman's reconstruction of Henslowe's relationship with the players in the Rose decade but retain misgivings about his interpretation of the direction Henslowe's career would take at the Hope playhouse after 1612 (and so beyond the scope of the present volume). Readers should be aware, however, that the documents upon which Beckerman must base his comments are difficult in the extreme and admit no superficial explanations. The so-called 'Articles of oppression' can stand for an example. In 1615 a group of players at the Hope formulated their alleged grievances against Henslowe into these 'Articles'. They accused him of financial double-dealing, of withholding their stock and playbooks, binding hired men in his own name instead of in the company's name, of entering players' private debts against the company's accounts, of selling their stock to 'strangers', of reneging on his promise to pay them for 'lying still' one day each fortnight while he used his playhouse for bear baiting, and, most heinously, of systematically reducing the players to ruin: 'with in 3 yeares hee hath broken and dissmembred five Companies'. 'The reason', so they said, 'of his often breakinge with vs hee gave in these word*es* should these fellowes Come out of my debt, I should have noe rule with them' (*Henslowe Papers*, M.S. I, Art. 108). The 'Articles' indicate the scope of interference that might have been

possible from an enterprising and experienced playhouse landlord: Henslowe is accused of meddling in nearly every aspect of company finance and production. But whether in fact he *did* interfere in the ways alleged is open to serious doubt. One way of evaluating the players' claims is to observe what they accepted in settlement of them, for having itemised £567 damages against Henslowe they eventually adjusted their claims, agreed that they *owed* him £400 and gratefully accepted an abatement of £200.

17 'The Sharer Papers', printed by J.O. Halliwell-Phillipps, *Outlines of the Life of Shakespeare* (London, 1884), 366.

18 *ES II*, 87.

19 The Burbage–Brayne litigation is printed in a full text by C.W. Wallace, *The First London Theatre, Materials for a History* (*Nebraska University Studies*, xiii.1, 1913). Chambers summarizes the suit in *ES II*, 387–93.

20 Burbage *v*. Brayne in Wallace, *First London Theatre* and in *ES II*, 392.

21 For a comprehensive guide to the administration and government of London and the suburbs in the reign of Queen Elizabeth I see Frank Freeman Foster, *The Politics of Stability* (London: Royal Historical Society, 1977).

22 *Cotton* MS. Roll xvi, f. 41. Printed: *ES IV*, 271.

23 *Lansd.* MS. 41, f. 31. Printed: *MSC i*, 163; *ES IV*, 297.

24 The Privy Council letter does not survive, but its contents can be reconstructed from the Aldermen's reply of 2 March 1574. (See following note.)

25 *Cotton* MS. Roll xvi, f. 41. Printed: *ES IV*, 271-2.

26 *Remembrancia i*, 9. Printed: *MSC i*, 46; *ES IV*, 279.

27 *Remembrancia i*, 538. Printed: *MSC i*, 63; *ES IV*, 294.

28 *Remembrancia i*, 319. Printed: *MSC i*, 54; *ES IV*, 288.

29 *Remembrancia i*, 520. Printed: *MSC i*, 64; *ES IV*, 294.

30 C.M. Clode, *Early History of the Guild of Merchant Taylors* (1888), 235; Guildhall Library Microfilm 326 (30) vol. 3. Printed: *ES II*, 75.

31 *ES IV*, 269.

32 *Remembrancia i*, 456 (misdated 18 January). Printed: *MSC i*, 58; *ES IV*, 292.

33 *Remembrancia i*, 458. Printed: *MSC i*, 60; *ES IV*, 292.

34 *Remembrancia i*, 383. Printed: *MSC i*, 56; *ES IV*, 289.

35 *Remembrancia i*, 317. Printed: *MSC i*, 52; *ES IV*, 287. And Privy Council Minute 3 December 1581, printed by Dasent *APC xiii*, 269; *ES IV*, 284.

36 Patronage survived as an effective administrative tool for enforcing one of Elizabethan society's highest social priorities: mastery. In a society where order was maintained by the authority and awe of master over servant, and where that domestic relationship stood as the paradigm of all relationships from the apprentice at his master's table to the Privy Councillor in his Queen's audience chamber, masterless men could not be tolerated. Stiff penalties were set out in *An Acte for the punishement of Vagabondes and for Releif of the Poore & Impotent* (14 Eliz. c. 5, printed in *Statutes iv*, 590; amended by 18 Eliz. c. 3, printed in *Statutes iv*, 610; and augmented by 37 Eliz. c. 11, printed in *Statutes iv*, 718) for 'All & every person ... being above thage of fourtene yeres ... taken begging in any parte of this Realme, or taken vagrant wandring and misordering themselves ...'. Article 5 of the act described as vagabonds 'All and everye persone and persones beynge whole and mightye in Body and able to labour, havinge not Land or Maister, nor using any lawfull Marchaundize Crafte or Mysterye ... and can gyve no

reckninge howe he or shee dothe lawfully get his or her Lyvinge; & all Fencers Bearewardes Comon Players in Enterludes & Minstrels, not belonging to any Baron of this Realme or towardes any other honorable Personage of greater Degree . . .'. Conviction on the first offence carried the punishment of whipping and burning 'through the gristle of the right Eare with a hot Yron of the compasse of an Ynche about'. A third conviction meant death as a felon and loss of land and goods. To avoid indictment as vagabonds, to prove that they were not masterless men, the players wore the household livery of the master who legitimised them. As far as the rulers of London were concerned, the outward badge of livery made their job of discriminating felons from freemen significantly more straightforward; the trade guilds, too, identified their brethren by company livery.

37 *Remembrancia i*, 317. Printed: *MSC i*, 52; *ES IV*, 287.
38 Dasent, *APC xi*, 73; *ES IV*, 278.
39 Patent Roll 1606, m.34.46. Printed: *ES IV*, 285.
40 *Harl* MS.7368. Edited by Walter W. Greg, Malone Society (Oxford, 1911).
41 See document nos. 52–4 and the notes attached to them.
42 See document no. 16 and the note attached to it.
43 J.M. Nosworthy, 'Dornackes and Colysenes in Henslowe's Diary', *Notes and Queries*, 213 (1968), 247–8. 'Dornackes' is a corruption of *Dornick*, a kind of fabric; 'colysenes' is Henslowe's spelling of *cullisance*, a corruption of cognizance, a badge.

The Documents

⬦⊙⬦

1. 10 January 1586/7. Deed of Partnership in the Rose Playhouse.

The messuage known as the 'little rose' with two gardens adjoining was
held in trust by the parish of St Mildred's, Bread Street. Philip Henslowe,
'cittizen and Dyer of London', acquired the lease for a period of 21 years
at £7 rent per year in March 1584/5. Within two years he had begun to
erect a playhouse on the property that stood not far from his own house
'on the bank sid right over against the clink', the prison that was one of
Southwark's landmarks. This deed of partnership with John Cholmley,
who is described as 'cittizen and grocer', is something of a mystery, for
although the agreement was not due to expire until April 1595, Cholmley
does not figure anywhere else in the Rose documents. Henslowe scribbled
his name in several places on the front page of the Diary but made no
reference to him otherwise. The following deed sets out certain financial
matters. It includes sufficient detail to permit an estimation of the cost of
the playhouse; it shows that profits were to be divided equally between
the partners and that Cholmley's victualling house was to be a prominent
feature of the premises. But it is silent on what might be taken to be the
most important arrangements. It makes no specific provision for tenants:
it does not indicate which company of players was to occupy the new
house, nor what their share of the proceeds was to be. Perhaps their
arrangement would have been the same as the Burbage syndicate had
evolved at the Theater: receipts in any playhouse came from two sources,
the standing money from the spectators who paid perhaps a penny to
stand in the pit and the gallery money from patrons who chose to sit
above and probably paid twice as much. The standing money had always
been the prerogative of the players, but at first the Burbages claimed all
the gallery money for themselves. Later, they began splitting the galleries
with the players, and this seems to have become the normal provision in
all playhouses. One other detail of the deed is striking. The designations
'dyer' and 'grocer' suggest that the playhouse had established itself as an
attractive investment not just to theatrical dynasties like the Burbages but

to speculating tradesmen whose only similarity to the players was an
equal determination to make money. Once solid citizens began investing
in the young enterprise, detractors must have found it increasingly difficult
to diagnose the playhouse as an unnatural growth on the face of society.
The new playhouse – the first on the South Bank – was open by the
autumn of 1587 (see no. 4). A Sewer Commission Report for Surrey
described it as 'new' in April 1588.

———

This Indenture made the Tenthe daye of Januarye Anno domini 1586 ...
Betwene Phillippe Hinshley cittizen and Dyer of London one thonne
partye and John Cholmley cittizen and grocer of London one thother
partye ... for the greate zeale and good will that is betwene them and
tothentente that they maye better increase theire substance are entrid into
partner shippe ... in the ... posessinge ... of all that parcell of grownde
or garden plotte contayninge in lenghe and bredthe sqare every waye
ffoorescore and fourteene foote of assize little more or lesse As allso ... of
all the beniffytte somes of moneye proffitte and Advauntage of a playe
howse now in framinge and shortly to be ereckted and sett vppe vpone
the same grounde or garden plotte from the Daye of the Date of these
presentes for and duringe and vntill the ende and terme of Eighte yeares
And three monthes from thence nexte ensuinge ... if the saide partyes doe
so long Lyve Whereuppone yt is ... agreed ... That yt shall and maye be
lawfull to and for the saide John cholmeley ... To have ... The moytie or
one halfe of All suche some and somes of moneye gaynes profytt and
comodytye which shall arysse growe be colectted gathered or become due
for the saide parcell of grounde and playe howse when and after yt shalbe
ereckted and sett vpe by reasonne of any playe or playes that shalbe
showen or played there or otherwysse howsoever And ... the saide
Phillippe Hinshley ... To have ... The other moytie ... And further That
he the sayde John cholmley ... shall ... have ... All that small tenemente
or dwellinge howsse scittuate and standinge at the sowthe ende or syde of
the saide parcell of grownde or garden plotte to keepe victualinge in or to
putt to any other vse or vsses whatsoever ... with the whole beniffyte ...
which he ... shall ... make ... by the same howse neare adioyninge vnto
a lane there comonly called mayden Lane now in the tenure of the saide
John Cholmley or his assignes with free ... passage ... as well in by and
throughe the Alleye there called Rosse Alleye leadinge from the Ryver of
thames into the saide parcell of grownde As allso in and by and throughe
the waye leadinge into the saide mayden Lane ... And likewyse That he
the saide Phyllipe ... shall ... at his ... owne proper coste and chargis
with as muche expedicion as may be ereckte fynishe and sett vpp or cause
to be erected finished and sett vpe by John Grygges Carpenter his servantes
or assignes the saide play house with all furniture therevnto belonginge

... All which premisses ... ar scittuate ... on the bancke syde in the
paryshe of St Savoyes in Sovthworke in the County of Surrey In consideracion whereof the saide John Cholmley ... dothe covenant ... with the
saide Phillippe Hinshley ... well and truly to paye ... for a yerlye anuyttie
the some of Eighte hundreth and Sixteene Poundes of lawfull moneye of
Englande in manner and forme followinge that is to saye One the feaste
Daye of the Nativitie of St John Baptiste ... Twentie five Poundes and
Tenne shillinges ... And so further after that from feaste daye to feaste
Daye quarter to quarter and yeare vnto yeare ... vntill all the saide somme
of Eighte hundreth and Sixteen Poundes be so truly contented and payde
... And yf yt shall happen the saide ... quarterly paymentes ... to be
bhinde and vnpayde in parte or in all by the space of Twentye and one
dayes ... after any feaste daye ... then and from thencforthe the saide
copartner shippe ... shalbe voyde ... And that yt shall and maye be
lawfull to and for the saide Phillipe Hinshley ... to renter And the saide
John Cholmley ... vtterly to expell ... And further ... yf yt happen eyther
of the saide partyes ... dye or decease this mortall lyffe before thende of
the saide terme ... yt shall ... be lawfull ... for thexecutors ... to have
... the parte ... of him so deceasinge as copartner with the surviver ...
And further the saide partyes doe ... graunte eyther with the other by
these presentes that yt shall and may be lawfull to and for the saide
Phillype Hinshleye and John Cholmley ... joyntly to appoynte and permitte suche personne and personnes players to vse exersyse & playe in the
saide playe howse at theire wills and pleasures beinge for the profytt and
Comodytie of them bothe And likewaye that the saide Phillype Hinshley
and John Cholmley when any playe or playes shall be played or showen
in the saide playe howse ... shall and wilbe there present them selves or
appoynte theire sufficiente debutyes or assignes with them selves or otherwysse at their Choyse to Coleckte gather and receave all such some and
somes of moneye of every personne & personnes resortinge and Cominge
to the saide playe howse to vew see and heare any playe or enterlude at
any tyme or tymes to be showed and playde duringe the saide terme of
Eighte yeares and three monethes excepte yt please any of the said partyes
to suffer theire frendes to go in for nothinge And that all suche some and
somes ... so colected ... shall ymediately that nighte after accompte made
by them selves theire debutyes or assignes be equally devided ... whereof
the saide Phillipe Hinshleye ... to have the one halfe ... And ... John
Cholmley ... to have the other ... And further the saide Phillipe Hinshleye
... shall ... paye ... All and all manner of quitte rentes and other rente
Chargis due and payable to the Lorde or Lordes of the premisses ... And
likewayes shall ... repaire and amende all the brigges and wharffes
belonginge to the saide parcell of grounde ... at or before the xxixth daye
of September nexte cominge ... And likewayes the saide John Cholmleye
and Phillipe Hinshleye ... doe ... graunte eyther with the other ... That

they ... shall ... after the saide xxixth daye of September nexte Cominge ... repare amende sustayne mantayne and vpholde the saide play howse brigges wharffes and all other the wayes and brygges now leadinge ... into onto and from the saide parcell of grownde ... when and as often as neede shall require ... And further the saide Phillipe Hinshley ... dothe ... graunte to and with the saide John Cholmleye ... That he ... will not permitte or suffer any personne or personnes other then the saide John Cholmley ... to vtter sell or putt to sale in or aboute the saide parcell of grownde ... any breade or drinke other then suche as shalbe solde to and for the vse and behoofe of the saide John Cholmley ... In Witness Whereof the saide partyes to theis presente Indentures Interchaungeably haue sett their Seales the day and yeres firste aboue Written

> Sigillatur et deliberatur in
> presentia mei
> Cut: Jones Scriviener
> Edward Pryce

(On verso) By me John Cholmley grocer

2. 25 January 1587. Letter (extracts).

The writer of this anonymous letter to Sir Francis Walsingham, Secretary to the Privy Council, was probably not a soldier – as he claimed – but a petty spy who specialised in exposing papists. His rhetoric is typical of those moralisers who attacked the public playhouse, and his dire contrast between 'proud players' who 'jett in their silkes' and 'pore people' who 'sterve in the Streetes' is a conventional one that would dog the players until the public playhouses were closed in 1642. The letter shows the degree of hostility a builder of a new playhouse might expect to face from certain sectors of the community. But (even allowing for deliberate ex-aggeration in the service of self-righteous fury) it likewise indicates how popular plays were proving to be. The one constructive comment, that the players should 'paye a weekly pention to the pore', was eventually adopted by the players themselves who saw that local approval could be bought with a contribution to parish relief.

———

I haue often tymes proposed to attempt your honores patience in vewing this disscource followinge: but fearing lest I should be thought two officious I have lett sleape my determynation in hope that tyme woulde take away th'occation ... The thinge is this the daylie abuse of Stage playes is such an offence to the godly, and so great a hinderance to the gospell, as the papistes do exceedingly rejoyce at the bleamyshe thearof, and not without cause: for every day in the weeke the playeres billes are sett vpp in sondry places of the Cittie, some in the name of her *Majesties* menne, some the Earl of Leic*ester*, some the *E*arl of Oxfor*des*, the L*or*d Admyralles & dyvers others so that when the belles tole to the Lecto*res*, the Trumpet*tes* sound to the Stages, whereat the wicked faction of Rome lawgheth for joy, while the godly weepe for sorrowe. Woe is me, the play howses are pestered when the churches are naked, at the one, it is not possible to gett A place, at the other, voyde seates are plentie, the p*ro*faning of the Sabaoth is redressed, but as badde a custome en*ter*tayned, and yet still our long suffering God forbayrith to punishe. Yt is A wofull sight to see two hundred proude players *j*ett in their silkes, wheare five hundred pore people sterve in the Stree*tes*: but yf needes this mischief must be tollorated, whereat (no doubt) the highest frownith: yet for god*es* sake (sir) lett every Stage in London pay a weekly pention to the pore, that *ex hoc malo proveniat aliquod bonum*: but yt weare rather to be wisshed, that players might be used as Appollo did his lawghing, *semel in anno*. The lord of hostes will surely forsake to dwelle amongst the tentes of Israell yf the synnes of the people do still p*ro*voke hym ... nowe mee think*es* I see yo*ur* honor smyle, and saye to yo*ur* self, theise thing*es* are fit*t*er for the Pullpit, then A Souldiers penne: but God (who searchith the hart and reynes) know*eth* that I write not hipocritically: but from the veary sorrowe of my soule.

3. 7 May 1587. Privy Council Minute.

Ostensibly the Council issued this restraint as a precaution against the spread of plague, but the allusion to 'outrages and disorders' suggests a more immediate provocation. The order was signed by, among others, the Earl of Leicester, the Lord Admiral, and the Lord Chamberlain, all of whom retained players. St Bartholomew's Day – 24 August – was the opening date of one of the greatest of the London fairs. Bartholomew Fair was set in Smithfield and ran for ten days, during which time goods were sold wholesale and retail. Booths offering entertainment and food were set up to pleasure the fair-goers, for this fair was not only the most important event on London's trade calendar, it was likewise a time of holiday humour. The Privy Council was acting advisedly in this Minute by dating the lifting of the restraint to coincide with St Bartholomew's Day: the fair was so popular, and was so material to the success of so many tradesmen, that the authorities were reluctant to interfere with it even in summers when the pestilence raged unremittingly.

———

A let*tr*e to the L*or*d maio*ur* of the citie of London: that whereas their l*or*dshipes were giuen to vnderstand that certaine outrages and disorders were of late committed in certaine places and Theaters erected within that Citie of London or the suburbes of the same where enterludes & comedies were vsuallie plaied, and for that the season of the yeare grew hotter and hotter it was to be doubted least by reason of the concorse of people to such places of common assemblies there might some danger of infeccion happen in the Citie Their lordshipes thought it expedient to have the use of the said Interludes inhibited both at the Theaters, and in all other places within his jurisdiccion And therefore required him accordinglie to take presente order for the stayinge of the same, chardging the plaiers and actors to cease and forbeare the use of the said places for the purpose of playinge or shewinge of anie such Enterludes or Comedies vntill after Bartholomew tide next ensuinge.

4. 29 October 1587. Privy Council Minute.

The unnamed playhouse referred to in this minute must have been Henslowe's Rose since the Rose was the only playhouse on the South Bank at this date. His neighbours tolerated Henslowe's newest business venture for a mere six months before complaining to the Privy Council that the statute forbidding performances on Sunday was being abused at the Rose. The lords referred the matter to the Justices of Surrey, in whose jurisdiction the playhouse stood. For good measure, the Council sent a similar letter to the Justices of Middlesex: the Theater and the Curtain came under their surveillance.

A lettre to the Justices of Surry: that whereas thinhabitauntes of Southwark had complained vnto their lordshippes declaring that th'order by their lordshippes sett downe for the restrayning of plaies and enterludes within that countie on the Saboath daies is not obserued, and especiallie within the libertie of the Clincke and in the parish of St. Savours in Southwarke: which disorder is to be ascribed to the negligence of some of the Justices of peace in that countie: They are required to take suche stricte order for the staying of the said disorder, as is allreadie taken by the lord Maiour within the liberties of the cittie, so as the same be not hereafter suffred at the times forbidden in any place of that Countie.

A lettre to the Justices of Middlesex: that forasmuch as order is taken by the lord Maiour within the precinctes of the cittie for the restrayninge of plaies and interludes on the Saboath daie according to such direccion as hath been heretofore giuen by their lordshippes in that behalfe: They are required to see the like obserued and kept within that Countie, aswell in anie places priviledged as otherwise.

5. 16 November 1587. Letter (extracts).

Philip Gawdy, the correspondent, was a student at Clifford's Inn and a remote satellite of the Court. It is not known in which playhouse this accident occurred, but it is quite possible that the Admiral's Men were playing at the Rose. The deaths were interpreted by some as God's 'judgementes' upon a profession that 'hurte' by 'fooling'. The letter provides a rare note on theatre practice: if Gawdy reported the incident accurately, the players were attempting – in the event, disastrously – an impressive stage device that imitated life most dangerously.

————

You shall vnderstande of some accydentall newes heare in this towne thoughe my self no wyttnesse thereof, yet I may be bold to veryfye it for an assured troth. My Lord Admyrall his men and players having a devyse in ther playe to tye one of their fellowes to a poste and so to shoote him to deathe, having borrowed their callyvers one of the players handes swerved his peece being charged with bullett missed the fellowe he aymed at and killed a chyld, and a woman great with chyld forthwith, and hurt an other man in the head very soore. How they will answere it I do not study vnlesse their profession were better, but in chrystyanity I am very sorry for the chaunce but God his judgementes ar not to be searched nor enquired of at mannes handes. And yet I fynde by this an old proverbe veryfyed ther never comes more hurte than commes of fooling.

6. 3 January 1588/9. Deed of Sale.

The men named in this sale of playhouse property had all been Admiral's Men, but Robert Browne had recently left England with part of the Company to set up a touring troupe on the continent. Richard Jones may have been selling his domestic playing stock before joining Brown in Germany, and this deed may be evidence of the London Company's disintegration. By buying up Jones's costumes, 'Instrumentes', 'commodities' and, most importantly, playbooks that would have come into his possession as his personal share in joint company stock and that represented any playing company's surest assets, Alleyn prevented the Company's repertoire from falling into the hands of some rival cry of players. Alleyn also demonstrated shrewd business sense of the kind that eventually transformed him into the richest, instead of merely the most celebrated, of all Elizabethan players. Following these negotiations, Alleyn aligned himself with Lord Strange's Men (but continued to style himself 'seruant to the lord Admiral') and in 1594 emerged as the head of a newly amalgamated Admiral's Company (see no. 30). By then Jones had returned, both to England and to the Company, probably ruing this sale. John Alleyn, Edward's elder brother, had been an innholder before joining the 'quality' and may have returned to that more stable way of life in the years before his death in 1596. The Robert Browne referred to in this deed is probably 'that Browne of the Boares head' playhouse whom Alleyn's wife mentions as having 'dyed very pore' in 1603 (see no. 113). For an itemised inventory of the range of 'commodities' the Admiral's Men accumulated as playing stock, see no. 65.

——

Be it knowen vnto all men by theis presentes. That I Richarde Jones of London yoman for and in consideracon of the Some of Thirtie Seauen poundes and Tenne shillinges of lawfull mony of Englande to me by Edwarde Allen of London gentleman well and trulie paid. Haue bargayned and solde and in playne and open Market within the citie of London haue delyured to the same Edwarde Allen All and singuler suche Share parte and porcion of playinge apparrelles playe Bookes, Instrumentes, and other comodities whatsoeuer belonginge to the same, as I the saide Richarde Jones nowe haue or of right ought to haue Joyntlye with the same Edwarde Allen John Allen Citizen and Inholder of London and Roberte Browne yoman, To haue holde and enjoye All and singuler my said Share of playinge apparell Playe bookes Instrumentes and other commodities whatsoeuer aboue Bargained and solde, to the same Edward Allen his Executors administrators and assignes as his and theire owne goodes freelie peaceablie and quyetelye foreuermore without let clayme or dysturbaunce of me the saide Richarde Jones my executors Administrators or assignes or any of vs or of any other person or persons by our meanes consent or procurement, In witnes whereof I the saide Richarde Jones to this my present writinge haue set my hande and Seale the Thirde daie of Januarye anno domini 1588 And in the one and Thirteethe yeare of the raigne of our souraigne Ladie Elizabethe by the grace of god Queene of England fraunce and Irelande defendor of the ffaithe &c/
By me Richard Jones
Sigillatur et deliberatur in presentia mei Johnnis Haruey apprentice
Thomas Wrightson Scrivener/

7. 6 November 1589. Letter.

Lord Burghley, the Lord Treasurer of England and the most powerful member of the Privy Council, had ordered a restraint of plays (the order itself has not survived), but Sir John Harte, Lord Mayor of London, could report only limited success in enforcing it. Edmund Tilney's normal scope as Master of the Revels was to censor individual plays, but here he seems to have been initiating an inhibition against playing in general. This unusual intervention may have been directed against a controversy that was raging outside the playhouse. For many months an anonymous group of radical puritans had been conducting a pamphlet war against the episcopacy, signing their scurrilous attacks 'Martin Marprelate'. They were answered in kind, at first with the bishops' approval, but *quid pro quo* did not end the matter. The exchanges grew more violent and, by a proclamation dated 13 February 1589, the authorities finally called the controversy sedition. In the Queen's name they ordered the destruction of 'sundry schismatical and seditious bookes, diffamatorie Libels, and other fantasticall writings ... in rayling sorte, and beyond the bounds of all humanitie'. Robert Greene, John Lyly and Thomas Nashe all contributed to the anti-Martinist campaign; all of them wrote for the players as well. It is possible that Tilney's 'mislike' indicates that Martin's enemies had been speaking in 'rayling sorte' from the public stage. The wording of Harte's letter reveals a level of bureaucratic muddle the players must frequently have exploited to their own advantage: Harte could send his summons only vaguely to 'suche players as I coulde here of', the implication being that he did not know how many companies were performing in London or where they were playing. The Cross Keys, in Grace Church Street, was a well-known inn and playing venue. James Burbage performed there in 1579, and by 1594 the Cross Keys served the Chamberlain's Men as winter quarters.

———

My very honourable good Lord. Where by a lettre of your Lordships directed to mr. yonge it appered vnto me, that it was your honours pleasure I sholde geue order for the staie of all playes within the Cittie, in that mr Tilney did vtterly mislike the same. According to which your Lordships good pleasure, I presentlye sente for suche players as I coulde here of, so as there appered yesterday before me the Lord Admeralles and the Lord Straunges players, to whome I speciallie gaue in Charge and required them in her Maiesties name to forbere playinge, vntill further order mighte be geuen for theire allowance in that respecte: Whereupon the Lord Admeralles players very dutifullie obeyed, but the others in very Contemptuous manner departing from me, went to the Crosse keys and played that afternoone, to the greate offence of the better sorte that knewe they were prohibited by order from your Lordship Which as I might not suffer, so I sent for the said Contemptuous persons, who haueing no reason to alleadge for theire Contempt, I coulde do no lesse but this evening Comitt some of them to one of the Compters, and do meane according to your Lordships direction to prohibite all playing, vntill your Lordships pleasure therein be further knowen. And thus resting further to

trouble your Lordships I moste humblie take my leaue. At london the
Sixte of Nouember 1589.
Your Lordships moste humble
John Harte maior
To the righte honorable my very good Lorde, the Lorde highe Tresaurer
of Englande.

8. 12 November 1589. Privy Council Minute.

In line with Harte's letter, the Privy Council issued stiff instructions for
the suppression of blasphemous plays. Although Lord Strange's Men were
evidently the original offenders, all the playing companies were ultimately
affected: they were ordered to surrender their playbooks for reconsidera-
tion by the Master of the Revels and the Archbishop of Canterbury who
between them controlled not only the performing but the printing of
plays. The Revels Office had authority to license performance; the Archbishop, as head of the Ecclesiastical Commission, had authority over the
Stationers' Office and hence over printing. The terms of the order specify
public performance. Presumably private playing was unaffected.

———

At the starrechamber 12 Nouembris 1589.
A lettre to the lord Archbishop of Canterbury. That whereas there hathe
growne some inconvenience by Comon playes and enterludes in and about
the Cyttie of London, in the players take upon them to handle in their
plaies certen matters of divinytie and of State unfitt to be suffred: for
redresse whereof their Lordships have thought good to appointe some
persones of Judgement and understanding to viewe and examine their
playes before they be permitted to present them publickly: his Lordship is
desired that some fytt persone well learned in divinity be appointed by
him to Joyne with the master of the Revells and one other to be nominated
by the Lord Mayour and they Joyntly with some spede to viewe and
consider of suche Comedyes and Tragedyes as are and shalbe publickly
played by the Companies of players in and aboute the Cyttie of London,
and they to geve allowance of suche as they shall thincke meete to be
plaied and to forbydd the rest.

A lettre to the master of the Revelles, requiring him with two others the
one to be appointed by the Lord Archbishop of Canterbury: and the other
by the lord mayour of London to be men of learning and Judgement and
to Call before them the severall Companies of players (whose servauntes
soever they be) and to require them by authorytie hereof to delyver vnto
them their bookes that they maye consider of the matters of their com-

edyes and tragedyes, and therevppon to stryke oute or reforme such partes and matters as they shall fynd vnfytt and undecent to be handled in playes, bothe for divinitie and state, comanding the said Companies of players in her majesties name, that they forbeare to present and playe publickly anie Comedy or Tragedy other then suche as they three shall have seene and allowed which if they shall not observe they shall lett them knowe from their Lordships that they shalbe not onely sevearely punished but made Capable [sic] of the exercise of their profession forever hereafter.

9. 23 August 1589. Prefatory Epistle (extracts).

Thomas Nashe addressed this letter 'To the Gentlemen Students of Both Universities' by way of preface to Robert Greene's *Menaphon*. For Nashe, the endeavours of art were the legitimate occupation of university men, not of newfangled poets such as Thomas Kyd, whom he glanced at as the 'Kidde in Aesop' and scorned for reading Latin with a dictionary. The decay of poetry was the fault of the 'tragedians', the common players who, ignorant yet pretentious, dressed up their plays in brave speech rather than in excellent action. The players' 'ideot art-masters' were their playwrights who abetted them by turning their pens to the 'swelling bumbast of a bragging blanke verse'. This last was probably a sneer at Marlowe, a friend of Nashe's and a university man, but one whom Nashe feared was conspiring in the decadence of poetry by prostitution to the drama. Nashe probably gave a fair indication of the standard repertoire in the public playhouse when he referred to 'English Seneca ... let blood line by line'. But his contempt only serves to show the shape of things to come: the players, not the scholars, were to be the new lords of dramatic poetry, and the next generation of playwrights would be men who learned their craft in playhouses like the Rose.

I am not ignorant how eloquent our gowned age is grown of late; so that euery mechanicall mate abhorres the english he was borne too, and plucks with a solemne periphrasis, his *vt vales* from the inkehorne: which I impute not so much to the perfection of arts, as to the seruile imitation of vain glorious tragedians, who contend not so seriously to excell in action, as to embowell the cloudes in a speech of comparison; thinking themselues more than initiated in poets immortalitie if they but once get *Boreas* by the beard, and the heauenlie Bull by the deaw-lap. But heerein I cannot so fully bequeath them to follie, as their ideot art-masters, that intrude themselues to our eares as the alcumists of eloquence, who (mounted on the stage of arrogance) think to out-braue better pennes with the swelling bumbast of a bragging blanke verse ... It is a comon practise now a daies amongst a sort of shifting companions, that runne through euery art and thriue by none, to leaue the trade of *Nouerint* whereto they were borne, and busie themselues with the indeuors of Art, that could scarcelie latinize their necke verse if they should haue need; yet English *Seneca* read by candle light yeelds many good sentences, as *Blood is a begger*, and so foorth; and if you intreate him faire in a frostie morning, hee will affoord you whole *Hamlets*, I should say handfuls of tragicall speeches. But O griefe: *Tempus edax rerum*, whats that will last alwayes? The Sea exhaled by droppes will in continuance bee drie, and *Seneca* let blood line by line and page by page, at length must needes die to our Stage: which makes his famished followers to imitate the Kidde in *Aesop*, who, enamored with the Foxes newfangles, forsooke all hopes of life to leape into a newe occupation.

10. *c*. February 1592. Rose Repairs Account (extracts).

Between autumn 1587 and February 1592 it is not known which company or companies occupied the playhouse, or indeed whether the playhouse was in continuous use over the five years. The Rose may have fallen derelict, or it may have been such a popular playhouse that the constant push and shove of audiences over the years had worn the structure into disrepair. In any case, early in the New Year 1592 Henslowe undertook major repairs that totalled over £105. He entered his itemised account for building materials, wages, and so on – 110 entries in all; about half are reproduced here – on folios 4 and 5 of his Diary. An inspection of the materials gives some idea of what the playhouse must have looked like and what sort of improvements Henslowe had in mind. It is impossible to know whether he was redesigning the entire playhouse or making interior alterations to accommodate more spectators perhaps. His total expenditure, at roughly one eighth of the probable cost of erecting the playhouse in the first place (see no. 1), suggests major alterations, and it seems clear that certain features of the original design were to be improved: the room over the tirehouse (which ultimately would be used for storing costumes and properties, see no. 65) and the lords' room were to be plastered. ('Sellynge' probably means 'sealing' in this case rather than 'ceiling'.) A 'penthowsse shed at the tyeringe howsse doore' was added on, though Henslowe only saw fit to use 'owld' timber for this project. This shed, too, was probably used for costumes. The disbursement for 'payntinge my stage' is particularly tantalising: nothing more is known about the interior of the Rose than this bare statement, but it is known that the pillars in another playhouse, the Swan, were painted cunningly to look like marble. The 'fryingpan' was evidently Henslowe's local ironmongery. Only a few of the entries are dated, the earliest being 6 February. The dates provide the explanation for Henslowe's present outlay. On 19 February Lord Strange's Men moved into the Rose.

———

Jesus 1592

A note of suche carges as I haue layd owt a bowte my playe howsse in the yeare of our lord 1592 as ffoloweth

Itm pd for a barge	iij *li* x *s*
Itm pd for breacking vp & palynge	xx *s*
Itm pd for wharfyng	viij *s*
Itm pd for tymber & bryngen by watter	vij *li* ix *s*
Itm pd for lyme	ix *s* ij *s*
Itm pd for wages	xix *s*
Itm pd for bryngen of dellberds	ij *s* vj *d*
Itm pd for ij hunderd of lyme	xj *s*
Itm pd for iij quarters of A hunderd of deall bordes	iij *li*
Itm pd for A maste	xij *s*
Itm pd for A some of lathe naylls & hafe	
Itm pd for wages	iiij *li* x *s*
Itm pd for iiij hundred of iij peny naylles	xij *d*
Itm pd for j lode of Rafters	
Itm pd for j lode of quarters	
Itm pd for j thowsen of lathe naylles	
Itm pd vnto the thecher	vij *s*
Itm pd for bryngen of stvfe	vj *d*
Itm pd for j hunderd of lyme	v *s* vj *d*
Itm pd for iij dayes for A workman	iij *s* vj *d*
Itm pd for A [illegible] for iiij days	iij *s* 4 *d*
Itm pd vnto the thecher	xx *s*
Itm pd for sande	iiij *s* vj *d*
Itm j thowsen of lath nayelles	
Itm pd for xxvj fore powlles	x *s* vj *d*
Itm pd vnto my workmen for A weckes wages	vj *li*
...	
Itm pd the vj of febrearye for wages	iiij *li* iij *s* 4 *d*
...	
Itm pd for brycklaynge	ij *s* ij *d*
...	
Itm pd for payntinge my stage	xj *s*
...	
pd in fulle paymente the 7 of march 1591 vnto the Iornmonger in sothwarke at the fryingpan three pownd & xij *s* I saye R	iij *li* xij *s*

pd in fulle paymente the 28 of marche 1591 vnto mr lee tymber man for Rafters & quarters & laths & bordes the soms of	v *li* xiiij *s*
pd vnto my cossen adren for money w*hi*ch I owght him the 28 of marche 1591	vij *li*
pd vnto the paynters the 28 of marche 1591	xxvj *s*
pd vnto my cossen adren the 13 of aprell 1591	xxij *li* x *s*
pd for sellynge the Rome ouer the tyerhowsse	x *s*
pd for wages to the plasterer	iiij *s*
pd for sellinges my lords Rome	xiiij *s*
pd for makeinge the penthowsse shed at the tyeringe howsse doore as foloweth pd for owld tymber	x *s*
pd for bordes & quarters	xviij *s* vj *d*
pd for bordes	xiij *s* vj *d*
pd for naylles & henges & bowlltes	xix *s*
pd the carpenters for wages	ix *s*

11. 19–26 February 1591/2. Rose Playhouse Receipts.

These document the opening week's performances by Lord Strange's Men in the playhouse that was to be their home for the next two years. How the Company became Henslowe's tenants is impossible to know, for the Company's history is both long and cloudy. The Stanley family inheritors to the Earldom of Derby were known as the Lords Strange, a title they relinquished upon accession to the Earldom. They had retained players since the reign of Henry VIII, but not continuously nor entirely successively, for heirs frequently entertained players in their fathers' lifetimes. Lord Strange's Men existed as a distinct company in 1589, when they were named in a contempt citation (see no. 7). In 1590 they were probably playing with the Burbages and the residue of the Admiral's Men (see no. 6) at the Theater. James Burbage proved difficult to deal with. There were quarrels, and in May 1591 John Alleyn, Edward's brother, was witness to a dispute 'in the Attyring housse or place where the players make them ready'; James Burbage argued with some of the Admiral's Men about 'the dyvydent money between him and them', which Burbage had detained, and was derisive about their patron, the Lord Admiral, swearing 'by a great othe, that he cared not for iij of the best lordes of them all'. Alleyn's reverence for his lord being complete, Burbage's pugnacity probably strained their relationship to the breaking point. A company formed itself around Edward Alleyn and undoubtedly began looking for a new home. Henslowe's Rose may not have been immediately available, or it may have required repairs before occupation. It is clear, however, that Lord Strange's Men had been formed and working at a high level for several months before moving into the Rose, for over the Christmas season (December 1591–January 1592) they gave no fewer than four perform-ances at Court. They returned to Court for the Shrovetide revels in February, when they performed twice, and on 20 February they were paid a sumptuous £60 for their efforts. Three other companies also performed, but only one play each; it seems clear that when Strange's Men opened at the Rose they were London's most prestigious company. The £60 Court money would have been sufficient working capital to underwrite several new productions. In their opening week, however, they relied entirely on old plays: Robert Greene's *Friar Bacon* and *Orlando Furioso*; Marlowe's *Jew of Malta*; *The Spanish Comedy*, which, though difficult to imagine, was the companion to the play known either as *Jeronimo* or *The Spanish Tragedy*. *Muly Mollocco* might be George Peele's *The Battle of Alcazar*, but nothing more is known about *Sir John Mandeville* or *Henry of Cornwall* except that they remained in the repertoire to a venerable age; *Cornwall* was popular enough eighteen months later to be one of the plays the Company performed on tour (see no. 25). The Company began playing on 'satterdaye' according to Henslowe's account, and they gave a performance the next day as well, so evidently the statute against Sunday playing was being infringed now as it had been in 1587 (see no. 4). The daily entry of receipts probably represents Henslowe's share in the tak-ings, that is, half the gallery money. The other half, together with the standing money collected from spectators in the pit, would have been divided among the Company sharers, partly as their own profits, partly as capital to reinvest in the Company: to buy costumes and playbooks, to pay hired men and boys, to construct scenery and properties. Henslowe's portion was actually a form of rent; his sole responsibility to the players was to maintain the playhouse as its landlord. But his decision in 1592 to begin keeping daily records of his playhouse transactions may indicate that he was contemplating a more permanent relationship with these tenants than he had achieved with other companies in the past. His willingness to undertake extensive rebuilding might point to the same thinking. It may be a romantic coincidence, or a calculated ratification of a dynastic settlement such as the Burbages already had, that within nine months Edward Alleyn had married Henslowe's stepdaughter. The re-ceipts, which continue in no. 16, document the Company's daily perform-ance schedule: they show the range of repertoire, the rate of production, and the relative popularity of various plays.

———

In the name of god A men 1591
beginge the 19 of febreary my
lord stranges mene A ffoloweth
1591

Rd at fryer bacvne the 19 of febreary … satterdaye …	xvij *s* iij *d*
Rd at mvlomvrco the 20 of febreary	xxix *s*
Rd at orlando the 21 of febreary	xvj *s* vj *d*
Rd at spanes comodye donne oracioe the 23 of febreary	xiij *s* vj *d*
Rd at syr John mandevell the 24 of febreary	xij *s* vj *d*
Rd at harey of cornwell the 25 of febreary 1591	xxxij *s*
Rd at the Jewe of malltuse the 26 of febrearye 1591	l *s*

12. ?21 February 1592. Player's Part (extracts).

Orlando Furioso, with Edward Alleyn in the title role, was among the first plays Lord Strange's Men performed at the Rose. This manuscript may belong to that occasion. A player learned his lines by studying a 'part'. He did not hold a complete copy of the script. Instead, his lines, introduced by cue lines from other characters, were written on slips and pasted together in a long roll. Only the bookholder, whose job it was to act as prompter during rehearsal and performance, needed the full text. This procedure probably owed more to economy than to caution, for relatively few plays were worth pirating by another company either for unauthorised performance or publication. The typical play needed to be learned, rehearsed, and opened in just over a fortnight, with the expectation that it would remain in the repertoire for a matter of months. To transcribe, say, twelve copies of *Friar Bacon* or *The Jew of Malta* would have cost the Company too much both in time and money. Storing twelve manuscripts per production over a season of perhaps thirty plays would have been impractical. This cheaper, speedier method of distributing a manuscript in fragmentary parts must indicate something about the Elizabethan player's attitude to the play as a whole and about the practicalities of rehearsal. He could not, as some modern actors do, begin developing his character by studying the play's other characters and seeing what they reveal about him. He probably did not 'build a character' at all, and the notion of a 'subtext' would have been completely alien, for, although he would have heard the complete play once in a pre-rehearsal read-through, he would not have had more than a gist of what other characters were doing in the play until he arrived at rehearsals. To imagine his situation one would have to see oneself playing Polonius without knowing any of Hamlet's lines or any of the stage action while Polonius is off. Life must have been even more complicated for the player who was doubling several roles and was seeing the play in segments of five or so lines between frantic entrances and exits. Alleyn, though he undoubtedly carried the weight of *Orlando Furioso*, at least had the relative security of knowing where he was for most of the play: he was centre stage. His part in *Orlando* contained 530 lines; some stage directions were included but no indication was made of what was happening on stage between Orlando's entrances. The manuscript from which the following transcription was made is now badly decayed. One of the more legible portions is reproduced. Argalio enters to Orlando who has just discovered his beloved's name carved in 'true loue knot*tes*' with the name of his rival on trees throughout the forest. Orlando laments, then vows revenge and finally runs mad. A portion further along gives these stage directions down the left margin: 'here he harkens'; 'he walketh vp & downe'; 'he singes'; 'he whistles for him'; 'he beat*es* A'. Alleyn corrected several mistakes in the manuscript. The mistakes appear in square brackets; the corrections are placed in angle brackets. One omission was inserted later. It is indicated by soliduses. The version of the play given in this part differs considerably from the extant printed edition of *Orlando Furioso* by Robert Greene, and the performance of 21 February seems to have been the only time *Orlando* was performed at the Rose: the play appears nowhere else in Henslowe's Diary.

———

Argalio————————————my Lord
come hether Argalio, Vilayne behold these lynes
see all these trees, carued with true loue knot*tes*
wherin are figured Medor and Angelica.
what thinkst thou of it——————is a woema*n*
and what then——————some newes
what messenger hath Ate sent abrode
with Idle loo*k*es to listen my lament
sirha who wronged happy nature thus
to spoyle thes trees with this Angelica
yet in hir name Orlando they are blest.
————————folow loue
As follow loue, darest thou disprayse my heaue*n*
[and for] ⟨offer⟩ disgrace, and prejudice hir
name
is not Angelica the quene of Love
deckt with the co*m*pound wreath of Adoms
flowers
she is, then speak thou peasant what he is
that dare attempt, or court my quene of loue
or I will send they soule to Charons charge.

—————————————————& Medors loue
Nought but Angelica, and Medors loue
shall medor then posesse Orlandos loue
danty, and gladsome beames of my delight
why feast your gleames on others lustfull
thought*es*
delicious browes, why smile your heaue*n* for
those
that woundring you proue poor Orlandos foes.
Lend me your playnt*es* you sweet Arcadian
nimphes
that wont to sing your late dep*ar*ted loues.
thou weping floud leave Orpheus: wayle for me
proud Titans neces gather all in one
those fluent spring*es* of your lamenting eyes
and let th*em* streame along my [faithfull] ⟨faint-
full⟩ look*es*.

———————————————of S[   ]ant
Argalio seek me out Medor, seek out *that* same
dogg
that dare inchase him w*i*th Angelica
—————————————————be content

      O feminile ingegno di tutti mali sede
      come ti vuolgi et muti facilmente
      Contrario oggetto proprio de la fede
      O infelice, o miser [   ]credi
      inportune, superbe, ett dispettose
      priue d'amor di fede et di Consiglio
      temerarie, crudeli, inique, ingrate
      per pestilenza eterna al mundo nate

Vilayne Argalio whers medor / medor is medor a knave /
what lyes he here

dragges   and braues me to my face, by heaue*n* Ile tear
him in.   him pecemeale in despight of these.
—————————————————on his neck

enters with Villayns provide me straight a lions skyn*n*e
a mans legg for I thou seest / I am mighty Hercules
see whers my massy clubb vpon my neck
I must to hell to fight w*i*th Cerberus
and find out medor ther, y[ou] ⟨ea⟩ Vilaynes or
Ile dye

13. 25 February 1591/2. Letter.

In the same week as playing began at the Rose, William Webbe, Lord Mayor of London, wrote to John Whitgift, the Archbishop of Canterbury, to enlist his influence with Edmund Tilney and the Revels Office. His was not a private or a personal war against the theatre, for the anti-playhouse campaign seems to have been one of those responsibilities successive Lord Mayors inherited with their chain of office. Usually within weeks of being installed, new mayors sent copies of a *pro forma* appeal to the Privy Council reciting complaints and calling for the abolition of the playhouses. Webbe's letter was drafted from a standard catalogue of grievances that had been, and would be, duplicated by his brethren in office. In addressing the Archbishop instead of the Privy Council, however, Webbe was showing some initiative – or perhaps some cunning born of frustration. By 6 March Whitgift had responded, and Webbe replied with a letter thanking him for 'voutchsafing vs your help for the removing of this great inconvenience'; he did not indicate what that 'healp' entailed but said that 'certain of our Brethren' – meaning the Aldermen – had been appointed to 'confere' with Tilney. Two of Webbe's observations should be specially noted, since, conventional though they were, upon them hung the debate between the Court and the City over the future of the public playhouses: Webbe was willing to concede, albeit disparagingly, that 'wee vnderstand that the Q. Ma*ie*stie is & must bee served at certen times by this sort of people.' 'Sort' expresses his contempt explicitly enough, but Webbe would dare go no further, to expose as a fraud the legal fiction that the players existed to entertain the Queen. Instead he argued that the Queen's pleasure could be served 'by the privat exercise of hir ... own players in convenient place'. His most biting remark has to do with the Revels Office, which, he implied, was sheltering playhouses that formerly 'lay open to all the [City] statutes for the punishing of these & such lyke disorders'.

———

Our most humble dueties to your Grace remembred. Whereas by the daily and disorderlie exercise of a number of players & playeng houses erected with in this Citie, the youth thearof is greatly corrupted & their manners infected with many evill & vngodly qualities by reason of the wanton & prophane divises represented on the stages by the sayed players, the prentizes & servants withdrawen from their woorks, & all sorts in generall from the daylie resort vnto sermons & other Christian exercises to the great hinderance of the trades & traders of this Citie & prophanation of the good and godly religion established amongst vs. To which places allso doe vsually resort great numbers of light & lewd disposed persons as harlotts, cutpurses, cuseners, pilferers, & such lyke, & thear vnder the collor or resort to those places to hear the playes divise divers evill &

vngodly matches, confederacies, & conspiracies, which by means of the opportunitie of the place cannot bee prevented nor discovered, as other wise they might bee: In consideration whearof wee most humbly beeseach your Grace for your godly care for the refourming of so great abuses tending to the offence of almightie god the prophantation & sclaunder of his true religion & the corrupting of our youth, which ar the seed of the Church of god & the common wealth among vs, to voutchsafe vs your good favour & help for the refourming & banishing of so great evill out of this Citie, which our selves of loong time though to small pourpose have so earnestly desired and endeavoured by all means that possibly wee could. And bycause wee vnderstand that the Q. Maiestie is & must bee served at certen times by this sort of people, for which pourpose shee hath graunted hir lettres Patents to Mr Tilney Master of hir Revells, by virtue whearof hee beeing authorized to refourm exercise or suppresse all man-ner of players, playes, & playeng houses whatsoeuer, did first Licence the sayed playeng houses within this Citie for hir Maiesties sayed service, which beefore that time lay open to all the statutes for the punishing of these & such lyke disorders. Wee ar most humbly & earnestly to beeseach your Grace to call vnto you the sayed Master of hir Maiesties revells with whome allso wee have conferred of late to that pourpose, and to treat with him, if by any means it may bee devised that hir Maiestie may bee served with these recreations as hath ben accoustomed (which in our opinions may easily bee don by the privat exercise of hir Maiesties own players in convenient place, & the Citie freed from these continuall disorders, which thearby do growe, & increase dayly among vs. Whearby your Grace shall not only benefit & bynd vnto you the politique state & government of this Citie, which by no one thing is so greatly annoyed & disquieted as by players & playes, & the disorders which follow thearvpon, but allso take away a great offence from the Church of god & hinderance to his ghospell to the great contentment of all good Christ-ians, specially the preachers, & ministers of the word of god about this Citie, who have long time & yet do make their earnest continuall com-plaint vnto vs for the redresse hearof. And thus recommending our most humble dueties and service to your Grace wee commit the same to the grace of the Almightie. ffrom London the 25th of ffebruary. 1591.

Your Graces most humble.

To the right reverend ffather in god my lord the Archbisshop of Cantur-bury his Grace

14. 22 March 1592. Minute from the Guild of Merchant Tailors.

In his campaign against the playhouses, Lord Mayor William Webbe canvassed support from each of the City guilds. His strategy was to approach the problem via Edmund Tilney, by proposing that Tilney severely restrict London's rapidly growing playhouse industry. In essence, this meant requiring Tilney to restrict his own business, for in holding the Mastership of the Revels, Tilney held a monopoly from the Queen such as other subjects held on starch or the importation of sweet wines. Tilney would not have relinquished the power, or the profit, he derived from licensing plays and playhouses without compensation, so the Lord Mayor circulated letters among the trade guilds to test reaction to raising an annuity for Edmund Tilney. Having considered the matter, the Merchant Tailors replied. If they seem less worried about the players than their own purses it may be because the trade guilds had long-standing affiliations with the players: not only were plays performed at Guildhall – the Lord Mayor's Pageant rivalling in civic terms the Christmas revels at Court – but guilds like the drapers and merchant tailors would have been linked to the players professionally since costumes were by far the most important visual aspect of production, and guildsmen could expect to make part of their living dressing players for the stage.

———

A precepte directed frome the Lord Mayor to this companie shewinge to the companie the great enormytie that this Citie susteyneth by the practice and prophane exercise of players and playinge howses in this Citie, and the corrupcion of youth that groweth thereupon invitinge the companie by the consideration of this myscheyfe to yeilde to the paymente of one Anuytie to one Mr. Tylney, mayster of the Revelles of the Queene's house, in whose hands the redresse of this inconveniency doeth rest and that those playes might be abandoned out of this citie vpon consideracion of which precepte albeit the companie think yt a very good service to be performed yet wayinge the damage of the president and enovacion of raysinge of Anuyties upon the Companies of London what further occasions yt may be drawne unto, together with their great chardge otherwyse which this Troublesome tyme hath brought, and is likely to bringe, they thinke this no fitt course to remedie this myscheife, but wish some other waye were taken in hand to expell out of our Citye so generall a contagion of manners and other inconveniency wherein if any endeavors or travile of this companie might further the matter they would be readye to use their service therein. And this to be certified as the companies answere if yt shall apeare by conference with other companies that the precepte requireth necessarilie a returne of the companies certificate, and answere in this behalf.

15. February 1591/2 – June 1592. Rose Licensing Fees.

These records may suggest why the Master of the Revels would remain unimpressed by offers of an annuity. Tilney's office carried with it an annual stipend from the Queen of £66 6s 8d in consideration of his employment at Court to arrange the revels at Christmas and Shrovetide. A more lucrative income came from the playhouses: owners, like Henslowe in these entries, paid him £1 (eventually rising to £2 then £3) per month to license their playhouses for operation; playing companies paid him 7s to license each play for performance. The fact that 'tyllnes man' collected the monthly fee should not obscure the fact that Tilney and Henslowe were well acquainted; indeed, their familiarity may have benefited Henslowe years later when he was building his second playhouse (see no. 98).

_____

Itm pd vnto mr tyllnes man the 26 of febreary 1591	v s
Itm pd vnto mr tyllnes man the 4 of marche 1591	v s
Itm pd vnto mr tyllenes man the 10 of marche 1591	v s
Itm pd vnto mr tyll*nes* man the 17 of marche 1591	v s
Itm pd vnto mr tyllnes man the 24 of marche 1591	v s
Itm pd vnto mr tyllenes man the 28 of marche 1591	v s
Itm pd vnto mr tyllnes man the 7 of aprell 1591	v s
Itm pd vnto mr tyllnes man the 14 of aprell 1591	v s
Itm pd vnto mr tyllnes man the 21 of aprell 1591	v s
Itm pd vnto mr tyllnes man the 28 of aprell 1591	v s
Itm pd vnto mr tyllenes man the 5 of maye 1592	v s
Itm pd vnto mr tyllnes man the 10 of maye 1592	v s
Itm pd vnto mr tyllnes man the 13 of maye 1592	xij s
Itm pd vnto mr tyllnes man the 20 of maye 1592	vj s 8 d
Itm pd vnto mr tyllnes man th 9 of June 1592	vj s 8 d
Itm pd vnto mr tyllnes man the 14 June 1592	vj s 8 d

16. February 1591/2 – June 1592. Rose Playhouse Receipts.

A direct continuation from no. 11, this calendar of receipts completes the first season of playing by Lord Strange's Men at the Rose. In nineteen weeks the Company gave 105 performances of twenty-three plays and paid Henslowe £181 9s 11d as his share in the proceeds. Five new productions, which Henslowe identified as 'ne' in the margin of the Diary, entered the repertoire. 'Harey the vj', perhaps Shakespeare's, was one of the season's most popular plays. It opened on 3 March, earning for Henslowe £3 16s 8d; by the end of the run, fifteen performances later, its receipts had dropped to £1 11s. Even though this play's fortunes were brighter than most, its steady decline gives a fair indication of how most plays held the stage. Even hits – which can be roughly identified from the receipts as Henslowe's £3 plays – rapidly wore thin. The explanation for this probably lies in the audience. A regular audience, one that attended the playhouse frequently, would demand a constantly changing repertoire. Their displeasure might have immediate impact: seven plays this season were performed only once. But they might also have favourites they paid to see again and again. Some crowd-pleasing classics held the stage not just for months but for years. *The Jew of Malta* and *Jeronimo* were already old plays this season but they were enormously popular. And they were still being revived in 1600. The new play *Tambercame*, i.e. *Tamar Cham*, is not to be confused with Marlowe's *Tamburlaine*, first performed in 1587. Part of this playing season fell during Lent, supposedly a time of restraint, but no observation seems to have been made except Good Friday, 24 March. Henslowe wrote 'Ester' in the margin between his entries for 25 and 27 March; he also marked Whitsuntide. To indicate playing weeks he put dashes in the margin. Henslowe's calendars are rarely completely accurate; around 8 May his dates are muddled by a misreading of his own handwriting. He continued to write the year date as '1591' until the end of April although according to the ecclesiastical calendar the new year commenced on Lady Day, 25 March.

————	Rd at clorys & orgasto the 28 of febreary 1591	xviij s
	Rd at mvlamvlluco the 29 of febrearye 1591	xxxiiiij s
	Rd at poope Jone the 1 of marche 1591	xv s
	Rd at matchavell the 2 of marche 1591	xiiij s
ne————	Rd at harey the vj the 3 of marche 1591	iij li xvj s 8 d
	Rd at bendo & Richardo the 4 of marche 1591	xvj s
————	Rd at iiij playes in one the 6 of marche 1591	xxxj s vj d
	Rd at harey the vj the 7 of marche 1591	iij li
	Rd at the lockinglasse the 8 of marche 1591	vij s
	Rd at senobia the 9 of marche 1591	xxij s vj d
	Rd at the Jewe of malta the 10 of marche 1591	lvj s
	Rd at harey the vj the 11 of marche 1591	xxxxvij s vj d
————	Rd at the comodey of doneoracio the 13 march 1591	xxviiij s
	Rd at Jeronymo the 14 of march 1591	iij li xj s
	Rd at harey the 16 of marche 1591	xxxj s vj d
	Rd at mvlo mvllocco the 17 of marche 1591	xxviiij s vj d
	Rd at the Jewe of malta the 18 of marche 1591	xxxix s
————	Rd at Joronymo the 20 of marche 1591	xxxviij s
	Rd at constantine the 21 of marche 1591	xij s
	Rd at Q Jerusallem the 22 of marche 1591	xviij s

	Rd at harey of cornwell the 23 of marche 1591	xiij s vj d
	Rd at fryer bacon the 25 of marche 1591	xv s vj d
Ester		
———	Rd at the lockinglasse the 27 of marche 1591	lv s
	Rd at harey the vj the 28 of marche 1591	iij li viij s
	Rd at mvlimvlucko the 29 of marche 1591	iij li ij s
	Rd at doneoracio the 30 of marche 1591	xxxix s
	Rd at Joronymo the 31 of marche 1591	iij li
	Rd at mandefell the 1 of aprell 1591	xxx s
———	Rd at matchevell the 3 of aprell 1591	xxij s
	Rd at the Jewe of malta the 4 of aprell 1591	xxxxiiij s
	Rd at harey the vj the 5 of aprell 1591	xxxxj s
	Rd at brandymer the 6 of aprell 1591	xxij s
	Rd at Jeronymo the 7 of aprell 1591	xxvj s
	Rd at mvle mvloco the 8 of aprell 1591	xxiiij s
	Rd at the comodey of Jeronymo the 10 of aprell 1591	xxviiij s
ne———	Rd at tittus & vespacia the 11 of aprell 1591	iij li iiij s
	Rd at byndo & Richardo the 12 of aprell 1591	xxiiij s
	Rd at harey the vj the 13 of aprell 1591	xxvj s
	Rd at Joronymo the 14 of aprele 1591	xxxiij s
	Rd at mandevell the 15 of aprell 1591	xxvj s
———	Rd at mvllo mvlluco the 17 of aprelle 1591	xxx s
	Rd at the Jewe of mallta the 18 of aprell 1591	xxxxviij s vj d
	Rd at the lockingglasse the 19 of aprell 1591	xxiiij s
	Rd at tittus & vespacia the 20 of aprell 1591	lvj s
	Rd at harey the vj the 21 of aprell 1591	xxxiij s
	Rd at the comodey Jeronymo the 22 of aprell 1591	xvij s
———	Rd at Jeronymo the 24 of aprell 1592	xxviiij s
	Rd at Jerusalem the 25 of aprell 1592	xxxxvj s
	Rd at fryer bacon the 26 of aprell 1592	xxiiij s
	Rd at mvlo mvloco the 27 of aprell 1592	xxvj s
ne———	Rd at the second parte of tamber came the 28 of aprell	iij li iiij s
	Rd at harey of cornwell the 29 of aprell 1592	xxvj s
———	Rd at mvlo mvlluco the 30 of aprell 1592	lviij s
	Rd at Jeronymo the 2 of maye 1592	xxxiiij s
	Rd at titus & vespacia the 3 of maye 1592	lvij s vj d
	Rd at harey the vj the 4 of maye 1592	lvj s
	Rd at the Jewe of mallta 5 of maye 1592	xxxxj s
	Rd at fryer bacon the 6 of maye 1592	xiiij s
———	Rd at brandimer the 8 of maye 1592	xxiiij s
	Rd at harey the vj the 7 of maye 1592	xxij s

Rd at tittus & vespacia the 8 of maye 1592	xxx s
Rd at Jeronymo the 9 of maye 1592	xxvj s
Rd at the 2 parte of tambercam the 10 maye 1592	xxxvij s
Rd at the Jew of mallta the 11 of maye 1592	xxxiiij s

whittsvn tyde

———Rd at Jeronymo the 13 of maye 1592	iij li 4 s
Rd at harey the 6 the 14 of maye 1592	l s
Rd at tittus & vespacia the 15 of maye 1592	iij li
Rd at mandevell the 16 of maye 1592	xxxx s
Rd at mvllomvloco the 17 of maye 1592	xxxvj s vj d
Rd at harey of cornwell the 18 of maye 1592	xxvj s
———Rd at harey the vj the 19 of maye 1592	xxx s
Rd at the Jewe of mallta the 20 of maye 1592	liiij s
Rd at the comody of Jeronymo the 21 of maye 1592	xxviij s
Rd at Jeronymo the 22 of maye 1592	xxvij s
ne———Rd at the taner of denmarke the 23 of maye 1592	iij li xiij s vj d
Rd at titus & vespacia the 24 of maye 1592	xxx s
———Rd at harey the vj the 25 of maye 1592	xxiiij s
Rd at tambercame the 26 of maye 1592	xxxvj s vj d
Rd at Jeronymo the 27 of maye 1592	xxiij s
Rd at matchevell the 29 of maye 1592	xxvj s
Rd at the Jewe of malta the 30 of maye 1592	xxxiij s
Rd at mvlemvloco the 31 of maye 1592	xxiij s
———Rd at Bendo & Richardo the 5 of June 1592	xxxij s
Rd at tittus & vespacia the 6 of June 1592	xxxxij s
Rd at the lockinglasse the 7 of June 1592	xxix s
Rd at the tambercame the 8 of June 1592	xxxx s
Rd at Jeronymo the 9 of June 1592	xxviij s
ne———Rd at a knacke to knowe a knave 1592	iij li xij s
———Rd at harey the vj the 12 of June 1592	xxxij s
Rd at mvlemvloco the 13 of June 1592	xx s
Rd at the Jewe of malta the 14 of June 1592	xxxviij s
Rd at the knacke to knowe a knave the 15 of June 1592	lij s
Rd at mandevell the 16 of June 1592	xx s
———Rd at Joronymo the 18 of June 1592	xxiiij s
Rd at harey the vj the 19 of June 1592	xxxj s
Rd at the comodey of Jeronymo the 20 of June 1592	xv s
Rd at tambercame the 21 of June 1592	xxxij s
Rd at the knacke to knowe A knave the 22 of June	xxvij s

17. 12 June 1592. Letter (extracts).

William Webbe, Lord Mayor of London, wrote to Lord Burghley of a tumult in Southwark. The connection between the affray and the play-house, tenuous though it was, nevertheless gave Webbe the opportunity to mention that the law against performances on Sundays had been breached in Southwark. Webbe could not make Henslowe's playhouse responsible for the actual riot – indeed, the 'doers and authors of the disorder' may not have been locals; they issued from the Blackfriars, on the opposite side of the river from the Rose – but he could still implicate it for having given 'opportunitie', and not only to 'these' but to 'such lyke disorders'. Webbe clearly wanted the playhouses held accountable for any civic disturbance whatsoever. The final paragraphs of his letter represent a partial backing down from his original stance though. He had to report what he had been told by 'men of reputation' in Southwark, that in fact the apprentices had the right of it on this occasion. They had been provoked by the marshal's men who set upon them 'with their daggers drawn & with Bastianadoes in their hands', even attacking innocent bystanders, 'whearof soom cam that way by chance soom cam but to gase as the manner is'. This mitigating evidence modified Webbe's judgement upon the apprentices; he ended by excusing those who 'otherwise would obey in all duetifull sort'. But he did not allow such mollifying circumstance to complicate his opinion of the playhouse. That condemnation stood.

––––

My humble duetie remembred to your good Lord. Beeing infourmed of a great disorder & tumult lyke to grow yesternight about viij of the clock within the borough of Southwark I went thither with all speed I could taking with mee on of the Sherives whear I found great multitudes of people assembled togither & the principall actors to bee certein apprentices of the ffeltmakers gathered togither out of Barmsey street & the Black fryers with a great number of lose & maisterlesse men apt for such pourposes. Whearupon having made proclamation and dismissed the multitude I apprehended the doers and authors of the disorder & have committed them to prison to bee farther punished as they shall bee found to deserve. And having this morning sent for the Constable of the Borough & the Deputie with divers other of best credit who wear thear present, to examine the cause & manner of the disorder I found that it beegan vpon the serving of a warrant from my Lord Chamberlein by on of the Knight Mareschalls men vpon a ffeltmongers servant who was committed to the Mareschallsea with certein other that wear accused to his Lord by the sayed knight mareschalls men without cause of offence (as them selves do affirme). ffor restraining of whome the sayed apprentices & maisterless

men assembled themselves by occasion & pretence of their meeting at a
play which bysides the breach of the sabboth day giveth opportunitie of
committing these & such lyke disorders. The principall dooers in this
rude tumult I mean to punish to the example of others, whearin allso it
may please your Lordship to give mee your direction, if you shall advise
vpon any thing meet to bee doon for the farther punishment of the sayed
offenders.

18. 23 June 1592. Privy Council Minute (extracts).

These orders to set 'a stronge and substancyall watch' at midsummer
evidently responded to Webbe's letter ten days earlier (see no. 17). But
given the moderating comments with which Webbe ended, the Council's
rhetoric seems over-reactive and its severity puzzling. What had been
reported as a tumult in Southwark was here eliciting a comprehensive
night-watch over the whole city: constables from St Giles-in-the-Fields, in
the north, to Newington Butts, in the south, and from Whitechapel
westward to the Strand were alerted. The Lord Mayor had already been
charged. So had the Justices of Surrey for all of Southwark, the Clink, the
Bankside and Paris Garden. Strangely, though, the clause ordering the
playhouse closures is almost an afterthought to the main business of
setting the watch. The period of restraint, from June until the Feast of St
Michael, 29 September, suggests that the measure was more precautionary
than punitive, for that was the plague season. The apprentice fracas may
have been a convenient expedient for action the Council intended to take
anyway.

———

A lettre to the master of the Rolles Sir Owen Hopton knight John Barnes
and Richard yonge Esquiours ... whereas her majestie is informed that
certaine Apprentyces and other idle people there adherentes that were
authors and partakers of the late mutynous and foule disorder in Southwarke in moste outrageous and tumultuous sorte have a further purpose
and meaninge on midsommer eueninge or midsommer nighte or about
that tyme to renewe theire lewd assemblye ... To prevente in tyme theis
wicked and mischevious purpose we have giuen straighte order to the
maior of London ... to set a stronge and substancyall watch. ... Moreover
for avoydinge of theis unlawfull assemblies in those quarters yt is thoughte
meete you shall take order that there be noe playes used in anye place
neere thereaboutes as the Theator, Curtayne or other usuall places there
where the same are comonly used nor no other sorte of vnlawfull or
forbidden pastymes that drawe togeather the baser sorte of people from
hence forth untill the feast of St. michaell.

19. 13 July 1592. Warrant.

If the Privy Council worried about plague in June, their fears were rapidly justified. From August onwards the sickness intensified; Michaelmas came and went but the restraint was not lifted. Lord Strange's Men, as this warrant from the Canterbury Chamberlain's account shows, were on tour in Kent, and Henslowe's Rose remained shut until the end of the year.

———

Itm payd the xiij day of July to the lord straunge his players when they playd in the courte hall before mr leedes maior & other his brethren xxx^s

20. Undated.

These three documents are traditionally grouped together but possibly more by convention than conviction. Since none bears a date, internal evidence supplies the only evidence for relating them. The documents share key allusions – to the watermen, a bankside playhouse and a restraint – so possibly they cross reference and belong to the same event. On the other hand, it is possible that the repetitions are simply coincidental; the documents could apply to a number of separate incidents. The Watermen's Petition, for example, is the sort of permanently useful appeal Henslowe might have held in reserve to issue – in compassion's name – whenever his playhouse was threatened. Henslowe seems to have organised the petition in the first place (otherwise, his name appears inexplicably, for he was certainly not, among all his other ventures, a waterman) and the signatories were not just the Queen's poor watermen but Henslowe's neighbours, some of whom were his tenants. Moreover, a careful reading of the documents reveals subtle discrepancies that may point to separate events. The petition submitted by Lord Strange's Men refers to 'this longe vacation' (from July to October after which the law courts reconvened for Michaelmas term), to 'travellinge the Countrie' and to 'this our restrainte'. From this it can be gathered that the Company was on tour over a summer while a restraint was in effect. But whether that restraint was general, and extended to all the companies, or particular in applying solely to Strange's Men at the Rose, is rendered obscure by the petition calling it 'our restrainte'. The Watermen's Petition is equally ambiguous. It asks that Henslowe be permitted 'to have playinge in his saide howse during such tyme as others have'. But this might mean 'as others have now' – i.e., because other playhouses were in operation – or 'as others have usually'. This second reading would mean that Henslowe and the watermen were petitioning for a normal resumption of playing when a general restraint was lifted. The third document does not seem to relate to a general inhibition, but to a specific closure of the Rose, for the Company, having clearly been instructed some time earlier to quit the Rose, was evidently permitted to play in the playhouse at Newington Butts, a mile south. This allowance, though, does not square with the Company's assertion, in the first petition, that they had been 'travellinge the Countrie' and incurring 'chardge intollerable'. Of course, it would be helpful to know exactly what the Council meant by 'three days': whether in all or in a week. But if the warrant answers the Company's petition it seems peculiar that the lords would mention complaints the Company had not even raised: the 'tediousnes of the waie' to Newington Butts and '*tha*t of longe tyme plaies haue not there bene vsed on working daies'. It seems peculiar, too, that the warrant should be so clearly directed toward the Rose rather than toward Lord Strange's Men: the Company is permitted to play, but so is 'any other ... in suche sorte as they haue don heretofore'. It is the playhouse's liberty that seems the issue. The playhouse in Newington Butts was used as a transfer venue on at least one other clearly documented occasion that may be pertinent to these vexing documents. In June 1594 the Lord Admiral's Men in association with the Chamberlain's Men appeared there (see no. 31). The involuntary amalgamation was not happy, and within a week the Admiral's Men had arranged to return to the Rose. The Watermen's Petition could belong to that later event. If so, there is a double appropriateness in its being addressed to the Lord Admiral – who ruled the waters but who happened to patronise the company that would be affected. The Privy Council Warrant might then relate to an earlier occasion when Lord Strange's Men had been forced to play at Newington Butts and were equally dissatisfied, and the Company's petition might be an example of the sort of appeal players had in readiness to submit against any inhibition. One other comment is pertinent here: evidently the watermen were not exaggerating. The progressive settlement of the theatre industry, playhouse by playhouse, on the South Bank worked to their great profit so that when Henslowe reversed the trend in 1600 by building his new playhouse north of the City the watermen were vehement in their protests. Out of this emerges the realisation that playhouse audiences in Southwark were not mainly local but came from the more affluent north bank. Hence the need for water transport.

A. Petition from Lord Strange's Men

To the righte honorable *our* verie good Lord*es*, the Lord*es* of her ma*j*esti*es* moste honorable privie Councell Our dueties in all humblenes rembred to y*our* honors. fforasmuche (righte honorable) oure Companie is greate, and thearbie our chardge intollerable, in travellinge the Countrie, and the Contynuaunce thereof, whilbe a meane to bringe vs to division and seperacion, whearebie wee shall not onelie be vndone, but alsoe vnreadie to serve her majestie, when it shall please her highenes to comaund vs, And for that the vse of our plaiehowse on the Banckside, by reason of the passage to and frome the same by water, is a greate releif to the poore watermen theare, And our dismission thence nowe in this longe vacation, is to those poore men a greate hindraunce, and in manner an vndoeinge, as they generallie complaine, Both our, and theire humble peticion and suite thearefore to your good honnores is, That you wilbe pleased of your speciall favor, to recall this our restrainte, And permitt vs the vse of the said Plaiehowse againe And not onelie our selues But alsoe a greate nomber of poore men shalbe especiallie bounden to praie for your Honors

> Yor honors humble suppliantes
> The righte honorable the Lord Straunge
> his servantes and Plaiers

B. Petition from Her Majesty's Watermen

To the right honnorable my Lorde Haywarde Lorde highe Admirall of Englande and one of her majesties moste honnorable previe Counsayle. In most hvmble manner Complayneth and sheweth vnto your good Lordeshipp your poore suppliantes and dayly Orators Phillipp henslo, and others the poore watermen on the bancke side whereas your good Lordshipp hathe derected your warrant vnto hir majesties Justices, for the restraynte of a playe howse belonginge vnto the saide Phillipp henslo one of the groomes of her majesties Chamber So it is if it please your good Lordshipp that wee your saide poore watermen have had muche helpe and reliefe for vs oure poore wives and Children by meanes of the resorte of suche people as come vnto the said playe howse, It maye therefore please your good Lordshipp for godes sake and in the waye of Charetie to respecte vs your poore water men, and to give leave vnto the said Phillipp henslo to have playinge in his saide howse during suche tyme as others have according as it hathe byne accustomed And in your honnors so doinge you shall not onely doe a good and a Charitable dede but also bynde vs all according to oure dewties, with oure poore wives and Children dayly to praye for your honnor in muche happynes longe to lyve.

Isack Towelle

William dorret master of her maiestes barge

Gylbart Rockett marke on of her majesties wattermen

wyllm hodgyes quens man

Edward Robartes marke on of her majesties wattermen

Thomas Jarmonger on of her majesties wattermen

thomes toy

william M Tuchenner on of her majesties mean

Thomas Edmanson marke
Edwarde Adysson on of her majesties wattermen

James Russell

W T

Henry Draper

Jeames Granger

fardinando Black

Christoffer topen marke

Parker Playne

C. Privy Council Warrant

Wheareas not longe since vpon some Consideracions we did restraine the Lorde Strainge his servauntes from playinge at the rose on the banck side, and enioyned them to plaie three daies at newington Butts, Now forasmuch as wee are satisfied that by reason of the tediousnes of the waie and that of longe tyme plaies haue not there bene vsed on working daies, And for that a nomber of poore watermen are therby releeved, You shall permitt and suffer them or any other there to exercise them selues in suche sorte as they haue don heretofore, And that the Rose may be at libertie without any restrainte, solonge as yt shalbe free from infection of sicknes, Any Comaundement from vs hereto fore to the Contrye notwithstandinge: ffrom. To the Justices Bayliffes Constables and others to whome yt shall Apperteyne.

21. December 1592 – February 1593. Rose Playhouse Receipts.

The inhibition ordered in June, though set to be recalled on 28 September, was not lifted until late December. The Rose stood empty for six months, but Lord Strange's Men must have been 'exercising' elsewhere, for they had plays in readiness when they were called to Hampton Court on 27 December, two days before they reopened to the public at the Rose. Their readiness shows their resilience to six months' durance, either trudging from guild hall to guild hall through the provinces or idling in London, plucking the grass that grew in the streets in plague time. They may have been too preoccupied to care, in August, that Thomas Nashe's *Pierce Peniless his Supplication to the Divell* had been entered in the Stationers' Register, and that Nashe, normally contemptuous of the public playhouse, defended plays as 'a rare exercise of vertue' which 'shewe the ill successe of treason, the fall of hastie climbers, the wretched end of vsurpers, the miserie of ciuill dissention, and how just God is euermore in punishing of murther'. More gratifyingly, Nashe defended the players: they were 'not as the players beyond sea a sort of squirting baudie Comedians, that have whores and common Curtizens to playe womens partes, and forbeare no immodest speech or vnchast action that may procure laughter', for on the English stage 'our Sceane is more statelye furnisht than euer it was in the time of Roscius'. But Nashe's unexpected tribute was more than cancelled by unlooked for defamation from another quarter. On 3 September the playwright Robert Greene, Nashe's friend, died 'very poor', even at the moment of death adding one more worthless debt to his blackened credit: he promised £10 to the man who carried his farewell letter home to his wife. When Greene died Lord Strange's Men lost a valuable playwright, for *Friar Bacon and Friar Bungay* was among the Company's most popular plays. Even worse, in his death they encountered an implacable enemy. Penury had embittered Greene, but it had not silenced him, and he left his posthumous invective, *A Groat's-worth of Wit, Bought with a Million of Repentance*, in which he savaged the players for exploiting poets of his calibre. He put into the mouth of one of his characters, a dandified Player, the smug brag that 'men of my profession get by schollars their whole living' and later he warned three fellow university wits (probably George Peele, Nashe and Marlowe) to beware the perfidious players, 'those Puppets that spake from our mouths, those Anticks garnisht in our colours'. 'Trust them not,' he intoned, 'for there is an vpstart Crow, beautified with our feathers, that with his Tygers hart wrapt in a Players hyde supposes he is as well able to bombast out a blank verse as the best of you: and beeing an absolute *Johannes fac totum* is in his owne conceit the only Shakes-scene in a countrey. .... Yet, whiles you may, seeke you better Maisters; for it is pittie men of such rare wits, should be subject to the pleasures of such rude groomes.' Greene was hitting at Shakespeare, who was probably with Lord Strange's Men, by parodying the line 'O tiger's heart, wrapp'd in a woman's hide' from *Henry VI Part III*, with which the Company may have planned to open their previous season. Lord Strange's Men may not have been in London to feel the first full blast of Greene's attack when it was made public; it was entered in the Stationers' Register on 20 September. But evidently shock waves were felt throughout the profession, for in a matter of weeks Henry Chettle issued an apology and a retraction. Chettle, himself a playwright who would eventually be employed by companies at the Rose, admitted in his preface to *Kind-Hart's Dream* (a rueful glance at 'Tygers hart'?) that he had escorted the *Repentance* into print. It had been, he said, Greene's dying wish. But he bitterly regretted the offence it had given, and protested 'with neither of them that take offence was I acquainted, and with one of them I care not if I neuer be: The other, whome at that time I did not so much spare, as since I wish I had, ... my self haue seene his demeanour no less ciuill than he excellent in the qualitie he professes: Besides divers of worship haue reported his vprightness of dealing, which argues his honesty, and his facetious grace in writting, that aprooues his Art.' While Greene shot his dead thunder, and Chettle trembled to pull it back, Lord Strange's houseless players weathered the more dangerous storm. Perhaps on tour, perhaps in town, they held themselves together, maybe even staking a permanent claim in the Rose through their leading actor, for in October Henslowe entered this statement in his Diary: 'Edward alen wasse maryed vnto Jone Woodward the 22 daye of october 1592 In the iiij & thirtie yeare of the Quene ma*jesties* Rayne elizabeth by th*e* grace of god of Ingland france & Iarland defender of the fayth'. The language is peculiarly formal for Henslowe. Perhaps he was impressed with a sense of occasion, the Queen's name shedding some of its power on to a reign he hoped he was establishing in the playhouse. Finally, in December, the Rose reopened. Five weeks later it was shut again. The plague had not been defeated even by the cold weather. In this short season, Lord Strange's Men managed twenty-nine performances of twelve plays. They brought two new plays into the repertoire – 'the gvyes' is probably Marlowe's play on the Duke of Guise, *The Massacre at Paris* – and they earned Henslowe £48 9s. On New Year's Day the Company gave a public performance of *The Jew of Malta* in the afternoon, then appeared at night at Hampton Court. When he wrote the account heading to these receipts Henslowe first gave the year as '1592' then changed it to 1593. He marked new plays 'ne' and put marginal dashes to mark off the playing weeks. Typically, he misdated his calendar, this time at the end of the season. Playing probably ended a couple of days earlier, as an accurate numbering would have indicated, for a Privy Council restraint was issued on 28 January and compliance did not usually take four days to enforce.

In the Name of god Amen 1593
be ginnge the 29 of desemb*er*

	Rd at mvlomulluco the 29 of desemb*er* 1592	iij *li* x s
	Rd at Joronymo the 30 of desemb*er* 1592	iij *li* viij s
	Rd at the cnacke the 31 of desemb*er* 1592	xxx s
	Rd at the Jewe the 1 of Janewary 1592	lvj s
	Rd at the cnack the 3 of Jenewary 1592	xxix s
	Rd at mandevell the 4 of Jenewary 1592	xij s
ne——	Rd at the gelyous comodey the 5 of Jenewary 1592	xxxxiiij s
——	Rd at titvs the 6 of Jenewary 1592	lij s
——	Rd at Jeronymo the 8 of Jenewarye 1593	xxij s
	Rd at mvlo mulocko the 9 of Jeneway 1593	xx s
	Rd at frier bacon the 10 of Jeneway 1593	xxiiij s
	Rd at the comodey of cosmo the 12 of Jeneway	xxxxiiij s
	Rd at mandevell the 13 of Jeneway 1593	ix s

	Rd at the cnacke the 14 of Jenewary 1593	xxiiij *s*
———	Rd at tittus the 15 of Jeneware 1593	xxx *s*
	Rd at harey the 6 of 16 of Jeneware 1593	xxxxvj *s*
	Rd at frer bacon the 17 of Jeneware 1593	xx *s*
	Rd at the Jew the 18 of Jeneway 1593	iij *li*
	Rd at tambercam the 19 of Jenewaye 1593	xxxvj *s*
	Rd at m*v*lomuloc the 20 Jeneway 1593	xx *s*
———	Rd at Jeronymo the 22 of Jeneway 1593	xx *s*
	Rd at cossmo the 23 of Jeneway 1593	xxx *s*
	Rd at the knacke the 24 Jenerye 1593	xxiiij *s*
	Rd at titus the 25 Jenewaye 1593	xxx *s*
ne———	Rd at the tragedey of the gvyes 30	iij *li* xiiij *s*
	Rd at ma*n*devell the 31 *of Jenewarye*	*xij s*
	Rd at frier bacon the 30 of Jenewarye 1593	xij *s*
	Rd at harey the vj the 31 of Jenewarye 1593	xxvj *s*
	Rd at the Jewe of malta the j of febreary 1593	xxxv *s*

22. 28 January 1593. Privy Council Minute.

This restraint, occasioned by the most severe outbreak of plague London had experienced since Chaucer's time, remained in effect for nearly a year. The 'Certificate' alluded to was the plague bill, the official certificate of deaths attributable to plague. The seven-mile *cordon sanitaire* the Council ordered to encircle the city was a normal precaution, its radius usually calculated from the residence of the Queen.

———

A le*tt*re to the l*or*d maior and Aldermen of the Cittie of london. forasmuch as by the Certificate of the last weeke yt appearethe the infection doth increase w*h*ich by the fav*o*ur of God, and w*i*th yo*u*r diligent obseruance of her ma*i*esti*es* Comandement*es* and the meanes and orders prescribed to be put in execution w*i*thin the Cittie of london maie speedelie cease yeat for the better furderance therof we thinke yt fytt that all manner of concourse and publique meetinges of the people at playes, beare-baitinges, bowlinges, and other like assemblyes for sportes be forbidden and there-fore doe hereby requier you and in her ma*i*esti*es* name straightlie charge and com*m*ande you forthw*i*th to inhibite w*i*thin yo*u*r Jurisdiction all plaies baiting of beares, bulls. Bowling and any other like occasions to assemble any nombers of people together (preacheing and devyne service at Churches excepted), wherby no occasions be offred to increase the infection w*i*thin the Cittie, w*h*ich you shall doe bothe by p*ro*clamacion to be published to that ende and by spetiall watche and observacion to be had at the places where the plaies beare-baitinges bowlinges and like pastimes are usually frequented and if you shall upon this publicacion finde any so undutifull and disobedient as they will notwithstanding this prohibition offer to plaie, beate beares or bulles bowle, &c. you shall presentelie cause them to be apprehended and comitted to prison there to remaine untill by their order they shalbe dismissed And to the end the like assemblies within the out liberties adjoyning to the Cittie [be likewise restrained] we have given direction to the Justices of the peace, and other publique officers of the Counties of middelsex and Surrey to hold the like course not onlie within the said liberties but also within the distance of seven myles about the Cittie which we doubte not they will carefullie see to be executed as you for your partes within the Cittie will doe the like, in reguarde of her maiesties comandement the benefitt of the Cittie; and for the respectes alreadie signified unto you.

Two other lettres of the like tenour written to the Justices of the peace within the Counties of Surrey and meddelsex for the prohibition of like assemblies in the out liberties and within seven miles of the Cittie of either countie.

23. 6 May 1593. Performance Licence.

During the first three months that the inhibition was in effect, none of the London playing companies seems to have decided whether to wait out the plague at home – it was, after all, winter and a remission could be hoped for – or to admit defeat, load their hampers and take to the road. Lord Strange's Men perhaps could afford to defer their decision since on 7 March they had been paid £30 for performances they had given before the Queen at Christmas; £30 would tide them over several weeks. By 29 April, another company, Sussex's Men, could wait no longer. The Privy Council issued that company a licence permitting them 'to exercyse theire qualitie ... in any County Cittie towne or corporacion not being within vij^{en} miles of london'. On 8 May Henslowe noted in his Diary a loan of £15 to his nephew Francis, a player, 'to laye downe for his share to the Quenes players when they brocke & went into the contrey to playe'. Evidently players had to stake a share in the touring company, and Francis's debt was witnessed by three other players, all of them Queen's Men, so that company too was heading for the provinces. On 6 May the following warrant was granted to Lord Strange's Men, belatedly, as it turned out, for the Company had already been on the road for several days. Edward Alleyn had already received a letter from home by 2 May when Strange's Men were performing in Chelmsford (see no. 24). Performance licences, or warrants, were vital to companies on tour. They identified the company and authorised their performance should any provincial magistrate demand proof of their legitimacy. Naming the company's prominent members was one attempt by officials to forestall the abuse of such warrants, for licences were frequently duplicated or forged. Companies on tour, like kings in combat, sometimes put more than one version of themselves into the field. It is not clear whether this warrant listed the entire Company or just its leading personnel, for although six players seems about right for a touring company, all the men named were Company sharers. Boy apprentices travelled with their company, at least on one tour when Edward Alleyn's boy, John Pigg, wrote a letter home to Alleyn's wife while the Admiral's Men were on the road. Unfortunately that letter is not dated, but Pigg figures in Henslowe's Diary after 1597. Apprentices were the financial and professional responsibility of their masters, and they may have toured on this basis. Hired men were a different case entirely. Since they were paid on a wage basis, they may have been made redundant in plague-time, left to fend for themselves in London and re-hired when the Company returned. Hired personnel may not have been required on tour since plays were undoubtedly edited into shortened touring versions and may have been selected in the first place to avoid large casts. Of the players named in this performance licence, it is known that Alleyn and the others parted company after this tour. By the summer of 1594 he had become the centre of a new Admiral's Company at the Rose. They, recruiting Shakespeare, had formed the Chamberlain's Men by then, and five years later they would settle at the Globe, a stone's throw from the Rose on the South Bank. Will Kemp, the famous clown and Shakespeare's reputed target in Hamlet's tight-lipped advice to the jester, eventually left the Chamberlain's Men to join Worcester's Men in 1601. This performance licence must have struck the players as gratifying in one supportive detail: in times of plague their profession and its much decried impiety became the target of loud hostility, being supposed by some to be the cause of the divine fury that was being expressed so lethally in the devastating sickness. Who knows how much the players shrugged at this? Or shuddered. Many have left evidence in letters and wills of God-fearing dispositions. How much, then, it must have helped morale to know that their Queen was defending them. She clearly expected to see them again, for the overriding consideration in granting the warrant was that the players should stay in condition, well 'exercized', in order to 'be in the better readiness hereafter for her *majesties* service whensoeuer they shalbe therunto called'.

———

Whereas it was thought meet that during the time of the Infection and continewaunce of the sicknes in the citie of London there shold no plaies or Enterludes be usd, for th'avoiding of th'assemblies and concourse of people in anie usual place apointed nere the said Cittie. And though the bearers hereof Edward Allen *servaunt* to the right honorable the *Lord* highe Admiral, William Kemp, Thomas Pope, John heminges, Augustine Phillipes and Georg Brian being al one companie servauntes to our verie good the Lord the Lord [sic] Strainge ar restrained their exercize of Playing within the said Citie and Liberties thereof; yet it is not therby ment but that they shal and maie in regard of the service by them don & to be don at the Court, exercize their quallitie of playing Comodies, Tragedies & such like in anie other Cities Townes & corporacions where the Infection is not so it be not within seaven miles of London or of the Coort that they maie be in the better readines hereafter for her majesties service when-soeuer they shalbe therunto called. Theis therfore shalbe to wil and require you that they maie without their Lett or contradiccion use their said exercize at their most convenient times and places (the accustomed times of devine praiers excepted).

24. 2 May 1593. Letter.

This is the earliest surviving in a series of letters exchanged by Edward Alleyn, on tour with Lord Strange's Men, and the Henslowe household with whom his wife Joan remained in London while plague ravaged the city. These letters are the evidence to measure the quality of Alleyn's marriage, whether it was a dynastic settlement or a marriage of true minds. Here Alleyn jested with his wife – carting was the common punishment for whores – and the joke would be all the more loving if by 'your felowes' Alleyn meant the wives other players had left behind, especially if they had been left behind only days before. Players' wives must have felt abandoned, particularly if they were left head of the household and responsible for its survival through the plague. Touring was certainly not an easy life, but at least the players did not face the fear and horror of the infection. It may have helped the women's self-esteem to be imagined by their player-husbands as exchanging huswifery for red petticoats and domesticity for a life as fantastic as the fustian players once those players were safely out of London. The jest is savoured in Alleyn's Marlovian vaunt, 'mouse when I com hom Il be revengd on them'. Alleyn referred to Philip Henslowe and Agnes, his wife, as 'father' and 'mother'; 'Bess Dodipoll' was Joan's sister Elizabeth. The interest of this letter lies more in the personality that shines through it than in anything said. The address in this respect is significant. Edward Alleyn was famous enough on the Bankside for letters to reach him bearing that information alone.

———

My good sweett harte & loving mouse I send the a thousand comendations wishing thee as well as well may be & hoping thou art in good helth with my father mother & sister I haue no newes to send thee but that I thank

god we are all well & in helth which I pray god to continew with vs in the contry and with you in london, but mouse I littell thought to hear that which I now hear by you for it is well knowne they say that you wear by my lorde maiors officer mad to rid in a cart you & all your felowes which I ame sory to herar but you may thank your ij suporters your stronge leges I mene that would nott cary you away but lett you fall in to the handes of suche Tarmagants but mouse when I com hom Il be revengd on them till when mouse I bid thee fayerwell I pre thee send me word how thou doste & do my harty comendations to my father mother & sister & to thy own self and so swett hart the lord bless thee.
from Chellmsford the 2 of maye 1593
thyn ever & no bodies els by god of heaven
Edwarde Alleyn
farewell mecho mousin & mouse
& farewell bess dodipoll

[addressed:] To E Alline
         on the bank side

25. 1 August 1593. Letter.

On 5 July Henslowe wrote to Alleyn conveying family greetings but little news. Had he chosen he could have filled his letter with news of a shocking murder whose circumstances were darkly suspicious. Perhaps Henslowe had not heard of the killing. That seems unlikely for a man who kept his ear to the ground in Southwark and his fingers on the Court pulse. Perhaps he omitted to report it, not appreciating what the victim's death would mean to Lord Strange's Men. Or perhaps he did report the death of Christopher Marlowe, and the letter has been lost. In May the circulation of a series of malicious libels against 'straingers' – immigrants – had prompted the Privy Council to order a special inquiry into the matter. Society itself grew feverish in plague time. Scapegoats, anyone who could be blamed for the sickness, were looked for. Graffiti scrawled on the wall of the strangers' church might incite street violence. In this volatile climate the Privy Council took no chances. They ordered the author of the libels to be discovered, seized and, if necessary, tortured. The following day, 12 May, Thomas Kyd was arrested after an officer of the Lord Mayor searched his rooms for links to the libel investigation. Libels had not been found, but other papers that might be taken in evidence in a trial for atheism were confiscated. Under torture Kyd confessed. He said that the papers were not his, that they belonged to Christopher Marlowe. Marlowe was summoned by the Privy Council on 18 May. He entered his appearance on 20 May and was ordered to give daily attendance until his case could be heard. Ten days later Marlowe was dead, stabbed through the eye by one Ingram Frizer in a squabble over the reckoning at the 'house of a certain Eleanor Bull, widow'. On 1 June the coroner's inquest found Frizer guiltless; he had acted in self-defence. Marlowe's death may not have been a personal loss to any one of Lord Strange's Men, but his plays were the backbone of their repertoire, and Alleyn had built his massive reputation on the towering figures of Faustus, Barabas and Tamburlaine. Could he have seen what was coming, Alleyn might have appreciated the irony at hand: within months Lord Strange's Men would disband, perhaps having made the decision while still on tour and ignorant of Marlowe's death. Alleyn with his fame would pull together a new company at the Rose. The remnant Strange's Men, not a colossus among them, would limp together toward an uncertain future. With Marlowe dead, the picture altered. Overnight Alleyn's strongest blood line as an actor dried up. He could still play Faustus or the Jew, but there would be no new mighty lines to thunder. By then, Heminges and the rest might have been reflecting how things were looking up for them. They had accepted into their company a young actor, Richard Burbage, who seemed to promise much, and they had probably moved into his father's playhouse, the Theater. They might have believed the giant who was Marlowe could never be surpassed, yet they might have looked hopefully to their own young playwright, who had not yet hit his stride: Shakespeare. All these events were months ahead; the new partnerships would not be fully documented until 1594. On 1 August 1593, however, Alleyn and Lord Strange's Men were still 'al one companie' and were in Bristol preparing to play *Henry of Cornwall*. They did not expect to return to London until All Hallows (1 November), so Alleyn instructed his wife to send further letters to Shrewsbury, Chester and York. Thomas Pope and Richard Cowley were both players: Pope had been with the Company since the beginning of the tour (see no. 23), and Cowley may have been joining them. John Griggs, the carpenter who had supervised the Rose repairs in 1592, was now busy on alterations to Alleyn's house. The famous man's concern for his spinach and his orange stockings is endearing; his instructions for warding off the plague by casting water before the doors and hanging rue in the windows seem pitiful gestures, superstitious or at best simple-minded, until it is remembered that the disease was a complete mystery. Alleyn was advising cleanliness; in the event it was the most effective deterrent available.

———

Emanell

My good sweett mouse I comend me hartely to you And to my father my mother & my sister bess hoping in god thought the siknes beround about you yett by his mercy itt may escape your house which by the grace of god

it shall therfor vse this corse kepe your house fayr and clean which I
knowe you will and every evening throwe water before your dore and in
your bakcsid and haue in your windowes good store of rwe and herbe of
grace and with all the grace of god which must be obtaynd by prayers and
so doinge no dout but the Lord will mercyfully defend you: now good
mouse I haue no newse to send you but this thatt we haue all our helth for
which the Lord be praysed I reseved your Letter att bristo by richard
couley for the wich I thank you I haue sent you by this berer Thomas
popes kinsman my whit wascote because it is a trobell to me to cary it
reseave it with this Letter And Lay it vp for me till I com if you send any
mor Letters send to me by the cariers of shrowsbery or to west chester or
to york to be keptt till my Lord stranges players com and thus sweett hartt
with my harty comendacions to all our frends I sess from bristo this
wensday after saynt Jams his day being redy to begin the playe of hary of
cornwall mouse do my harty comendacions to mr grigs his wif and all his
houshould and to my sister phillyps.

Your Loving housband E Alleyn

mouse you send me no newes of any things you should send of your
domestycall matters such things as hapens att home as how your distilled
watter proves or this or that or any thing what you will

[written vertically in left-hand margin]

and Jug I pray you lett my orayngtawny stokins of wolen be dyed a very
good blak against I com hom to wear in the winter you sente me nott
word of my garden but next tym you will but remember this in any case
that all that bed which was parsley in the month of september you sowe
itt with spinage for then is the tym: I would do it my self but we shall nott
com hom till allholand tyd and so swett mouse farwell and broke our
Long Jorney with patienc

[addressed]

This be delyvered
to mr hinslo on of the
gromes of hir maisties
chamber dwelling
on the bank sid
right over against
the clink

26. 28 September 1593. Letter.

On 17 July 149 plague deaths per week were recorded in London; on 5
August, the weekly death count was 1103. Henslowe continued to send
Alleyn news about the terror and devastation that surrounded them at
home: 'we haue be flytted with feare of the sycknes but thanckes be vnto

god we are all at this time in good healthe in owr howsse but Rownd a
bowte vs yt hathe bene all moste in every howsse abowt vs & wholle
howsholdes deyed & yet my frend the baylle doth scape but he smealles
monstrusly for feare & dares staye no wheare for ther hathe deyed this
laste weacke in generall 1603 of the which number ther hathe died of them
of the plage 1135 which hause bene the greatest that came yet & as for
other newes of this & that I cane tealle youe none but that Robart brownes
wife in shordech & all her chelldren & howshowld be dead & heare dores
sheat vpe.' Mrs Browne was one of the players' wives left behind who did
not survive. On 14 August Henslowe wrote: 'your tenantes weax very
power for they cane paye no Reant nor will paye no Rent whill myhellmas
next ... as for newes of the sycknes I cane not seand you no Juste note of
yt be cause there is command ment to the contrary but as I thincke doth
die with in the sitteye and with owt of all syckneses to the nomber of
seventen or eyghten hundreth in one weacke.' Henslowe continued to
send domestic news: 'your beanes are growen to hey headge'. And to
comment about the men on the road: 'we hard that you weare very sycke
at bath & that one of your felowes weare fayne to playe your parte for
you'; 'comend me harteley to all the Reast of your fealowes in generall for
I growe poore for lacke of them therfor haue no geaftes to sende but as
good & faythfull a harte as they shall desyer to haue comen a mongste
them'. By September, when the following letter was sent, it seems that
London nerves were fraying. Henslowe rebuked Alleyn for not writing as
frequently as he should: 'you littell knowe howe we do but by sendinge'.
He referred to Bartholomew Fair, 24 August, which had been allowed,
after protests were made, but severely restricted. His most important
professional news had to do with Pembroke's Men. On the back of this
letter are drawings of four heads and the full length figure of a man.
Another sketch may be a stage drawing. The letter itself is partly damaged.
Several lines are missing at the bottom of the page.

———

Righte wealbeloved Sonne edward allen I & your mother & your sisster
beasse haue all in generall our hartie Comendations vnto you & as for
your wiffe & mowsse she desieres to send heare Comendationes alone
which she sayes Comes ffrome heare very harte but as ffor your wellfare
& heallth we do all Joyne to geather in Joye and ReJoysse ther att & do
all to geather with one consent praye to god longe to contenew the same
now sonne leate vs growe to alyttell vnkindnes with you becausse we cane
not heare from you as we wold do that is when others do & if we cold as
sartenly send to you as you maye to vs we wold not leat to vesete you
often ffor we beinge with in the cross of the lorde you littell knowe howe
we do but by sendinge for yt hath pleassed the lorde to vesette me Rownd
a bowte & almoste alle my nebores dead of the plage & not my howsse

ffree for my two weanches haue hade the plage & yet thankes be to god leveth & ar welle & I my wiffe & my two dawghters I thancke god ar very well & in good heallth now to caste a waye vnkindnes & come to owr newes that is that we hade a very bade market at smyth fylld for no mane wold ofer me a boue fower pownd for your horsse & therfor haue not sowld hime but to saue carges I haue sent him downe in to the contrey ther to be keapte tell you Retorne & as for your clocke cloth ther wasse none sowld by Retaylle for all wasse bowght vp by wholle saylle in to dayes so the fayer lasted but iij dayes & as for your stockings they are deyed & your Joyner hath seate vp your portolle in the chamber & hath brothe you a corte cobert & sayes he will bringe the Reaste very shortley & we beare with hime because his howsse is visited & as for your garden that is very weall your spenege bead & all sowed & as for my lorde a penbrockes which you desier to knowe wheare they be they are all at home an hauffe ben this v or sixe weackes for they cane not saue ther carges with trauell as I heare & weare fayne to pane ther parell for ther carge & when I wasse in smythfell a sellyng of your horsse I meate with owld   [several lines are missing at the foot of the page; the letter continues on the back]   To aske for yt for yf we dead we wold haue sowght yt owt but we never had yt & this I eand praysinge god that it doth pleass hime of his mersey to slacke his hand frome visietinge vs & the sittie of london for ther hath abated this last two weacke of the syckness iiij hundreth thurtie and five & hath died In all betwexte a leven and twealle hundred this laste weack which I hoop In the lord yt will contenew in seasynge euery weacke that we maye ReJoysse agayne at owr meatinge & this with my hartie comendation to thy own seall & lickwise to all the Reast of my felowes In genereall I praye you hartily comende me from london the 28 of september 1593

your asured owne seallfe   your lovinge father & frend to my
tell deathe Jonne allen   power tell death Phillipe Henslowe
comendinge to her mvnshen

your wiffe prayeth you to send her word in your next leater what goodman hudson payes you yerley for his Reante for he hause the sealer and all stille in his hand & as for your tenenantes we cane geat no Rent & as for greges & his wife hath ther comendations vnto you & your sister phillipes & her husband hath bered two or thre owt of ther howsse yet they in good health & doth hartily comend them vnto you

27. December 1593–February 1593/4. Rose Playhouse Receipts.

Nearly eleven thousand Londoners died of plague in the visitation of 1593. Evidently Lord Strange's Men were among the casualties, for when playing resumed they did not return to the Rose. Instead, Sussex's Men, a company that may have been patched together from its own remnants pieced out with the shreds of other companies such as Lord Strange's and the bankrupt Pembroke's Men, opened at Henslowe's playhouse. Their fortunes were slippery, for a new restraint forced them to abandon playing after only seven weeks and thirty performances. They earned £50 9s for Henslowe in that brief run. Sussex's repertoire of twelve plays, though completely different from Strange's repertoire, shows the same range of titles – 'tragical-comical-historical-pastoral' – from what can be guessed as patriotic chronicle (*Huon of Bordeaux, William the Conqueror, King Lud*) to folk romance (*George a Greene the Pinner of Wakefield, The Fair Maid of Italy*) to pious moral (*Abraham and Lot*). None of these plays, except for *George a Greene*, survives. *God Speed the Plough* was entered in the Stationers' Register in 1601 but has also disappeared. *Friar Francis* was named by Thomas Heywood in his *Apology for Actors* (*c.* 1608) in connection with an edifying story about an undated performance of the play by Sussex's Men in Norfolk, during which a woman in the audience, watching the notorious murder enacted, leaped up and confessed to having killed her own husband. At the Rose, Sussex's Men premiered a hugely successful *Titus Andronicus*, playing it with atypical frequency three days out of six. It was entered in the Stationers' Register on 6 February as played by 'the Earle of Darbie' [i.e., Lord Strange], Earle of Pembrooke, and Earle of Sussex their Servants'. *Titus* is almost certainly Shakespeare's, and its identification with the three companies probably improves the assumption that these were the remnant companies that had amalgamated into Sussex's Men. It is tempting to argue that Ned Alleyn had likewise joined this company. The one anomalous title in the repertoire is *The Jew of Malta*, for it is the only play that had been performed at the Rose before. It belonged to Lord Strange's Men. If, when that company disbanded, they split their stock and Alleyn came to possess *The Jew*, he may have offered it to Sussex's collaborative repertoire with himself in the title role. Several other Stationers' Register entries about this time are pertinent: on 7 December, 'the historye of Orlando ffurioso'; on 7 January, ' "a knack to knowe a knave" newlye sett fourth as it hath sundrye tymes ben plaid by NED ALLEN and his companie with KEMPS applauded merymentes of the menn of Goteham'; and on 12 March, 'the firste parte of the Contention of the twoo famous houses of York and Lancaster withe the deathe of the good Duke Humfrey and the banishement and Deathe of the Duke of Suffolk and the tragicall ende of the prowd Cardinall of Winchester with the notable rebellion of Jack Cade and the Duke of Yorkes ffirste clayme vnto the Crowne'. The revels at Court this Christmas season were subdued, perhaps in deference to the crisis newly passed, perhaps because the companies were in utter disarray; only the Queen's Men performed and, by the evidence of their £10 payment, only one play. Henslowe's receipts in this account should be compared to earlier series for Lord Strange's Men (see nos. 11, 16 and 21). Christmas was always lucrative in the playhouse, but even so, these exceptional receipts show audiences were delighted to see players at the Rose again after so long an inhibition. As elsewhere, Henslowe marked the performance weeks with dashes and indicated 'ne' plays; he did not change his calendar to the new year until April.

————

In the name of god Amen begninge th 27 of
desember 1593 the earle of susex his men

	Rd at good spede the plowghe	iij *li* j s
	Rd at hewen of burdoche the 28 desember 1593	iij *li* x s
	Rd at gorge a gren the 29 of desember 1593	iij *li* x s
	Rd at buckingam the 30 of desember 1593	lj s
	Rd at Richard the confeser the 31 of desember 1593	xxxviij s
————	Rd at buckingam the j of Jeneway 1593	lviij s
	Rd at gorg*e* a gren the 2 of Jen*ew*arye 1593	xviij s
	Rd at hewen of burdo*c*kes the 3 of Jeneway 1593	xiiij s
	Rd at william the conkerer the 4 of Jeneway 1593	xxij s
	Rd at god spead the plowe the 5 of Jeneway 1593	xj s
————	Rd at frier frances the 7 of Jeneway 1593	iij li j s
	Rd at the piner of wiackefelld the 8 of Jeneway 1593	xxiij s
	Rd at abrame & lotte the 9 of Jenewarye 1593	lij s
	Rd at buckingam the 10 of Jenewarye 1593	xxij s
	Rd at hewen the 11 of Jenew*ar*ye 1593	v s
	Rd at the fayer mayd of ytale the 12 Jeneway 1593	ix s
————	Rd at frier frances the 14 of Jeneway 1593	xxxvj s
	Rd at gorge a grene the 15 of Jenewarye 1593	xx s
	Rd at Richard the confeser the 16 of Jenewarye 1593	xj s
	Rd at abr*am* & lotte the 17 of Jeneway 1593	xxx s
	Rd at Kinge lude the 18 of Jenewarye 1593	xxij s
————	Rd at ffrier ffrances the 20 of Jenewarye 1593	xxx s
	Rd at the fayer mayd of ytaly the 21 of Jeneway	xxij s
	Rd at gorge a grene the 22 of Jenewarye	xxv s
ne———	Rd at titus & ondronicus the 23 of Jenew*ary*	iij *li* viij s
————	Rd at buckengam the 27 of Jenewarye 1593	xviij s
	Rd at titus & ondronicous the 28 of Jeneway	xxxx s
	Rd at abrame & lotte the 31 of Jeneway 1593	xij s
————	Rd at the Jewe of malta the 4 of febery 1593	l s
	Rd at tittus & ondronicus the 6 of feb*er*y 1593	xxxx s

28. 3 February 1593/4. Privy Council Minute.

This restraint, directed to Sir Cuthbert Buckle, the Lord Mayor, extended until April. The signatories were the Archbishop of Canterbury (John Whitgift), Thomas Buckhurst, the Lord Keeper of the Seal, the Secretary, the Lord Admiral, and the Chancellor of the Exchequer. To judge from the receipts Sussex's Men were collecting at the Rose, the Council's 'infourmation' that 'great multitudes of all sorts of people do daylie frequent & resort to common playes lately again set vp' was indeed 'certein' (see no. 27). The wording of the letter gives a glimpse of how the Queen used language to promulgate the notion of personal rule.

———

After our very hartie commendations to your Lordship. Whearas certein infourmation is given that very great multitudes of all sorts of people do daylie frequent & resort to common playes lately again set vp in & about London whearby it is vpon good cause feared that the dangerous infection of the plague, by Gods great mercy and goodness well slaked, may again very dangerously encrease and break foorth to the great losse and prejudice of hir Maiesties Subjects in generall & especially to those of that Citie of whose safetie & well doing hir Highnes hath alwayes had an especiall regard as by the last years experience by lyke occasions & resort to playes it soddainly encreased from a very little number to that greatnes of mortallitie which ensued. Wee thearfore thought it very expedient to require your Lordship foorthwith to take strait order that thear bee no more publique playes or enterludes exercised by any Companie whatsoever within the compas of five miles distance from London till vpon better lykelyhood and assurance of health farther direction may bee given from vs to the contrary. So wee bid your Lordship very hartily farewell. ffrom the Court at Hampton. the 3. of February. 1593.

Your Lordshippes very louing friends,

John: Canterbury   John Puckering   Charles Howard
Thomas Buckhurst   Robert Cecyll   John Fortescue

To our very good Lord mr. Alderman Buckle Lord Maior of the Citie of London

29. 1 April 1593/4. Rose Playhouse Receipts.

When playing resumed, the Queen's Men had joined Sussex's Men at the Rose, possibly because members of that amalgamated company had decamped: Shakespeare and others may have gone across the river to join Heminges and Phillips at the Theater. This new association lasted for only eight performances before collapsing. Three of their plays had been part of Lord Strange's repertoire; evidence, perhaps, of Alleyn's involvement? *The Fair Maid of Italy* came from Sussex's repertoire, and *The Ranger's Comedy* would next be played by the Admiral's Men (see no. 30). *King Leire*, not Shakespeare's, was entered in the Stationers' Register on 14 May as 'The moste famous Chronicle historye of Leire kinge of England and his Three Daughters'; a printed version, dating from 1605, is extant. Remnants of Lord Strange's Men would have been saddened by the death of their old patron, Ferdinando Stanley, the Earl of Derby, on 16 April. In the accounts, Henslowe dated the first two entries 'marche' then changed them; he still had not altered his calendar to the new year.

——

In the name of God Amen begininge at easter 1593
the Quenes men & my lord of Susexe to geather

Rd at frier bacone the j of Aprell 1593	xxxxiij *s*
Rd at the Rangers comodey 2 of Aprell 1593	iij *li*
Rd at the Jew of malta the 3 of aprell 1593	iij *li*
Rd at the fayer mayd of Italey 4 of aprell 1593	xxiij *s*
Rd at frier bacon the 5 of aprell 1593	xx *s*
Rd at kinge leare the 6 of aprell 1593	xxxviij *s*
——Rd at the Jewe of malta the 7 of aprell 1594	xxvj *s*
Rd at Kinge leare the 8 of aprell 1594	xxvj *s*

30. 14 May 1594. Rose Playhouse Receipts.

Henslowe's accounts this spring show evidence of the struggles of several playing companies to establish themselves in his playhouse. First Sussex's Men, then Sussex's Men with the Queen's Men, and finally the Admiral's Men, opened, only to collapse or be forced to close within days. The three receipts below show the Admiral's Men launching their first Rose season as a newly reorganised company led by Edward Alleyn. Evidently a restraint cut short production, but the Company was permitted to play in tandem with the Chamberlain's Men at Newington Butts from 3 June (see no. 31). By 15 June they had negotiated a return to the Rose. They occupied Henslowe's playhouse continuously thereafter until the summer of 1600. Several entries in the Stationers' Register are important in these weeks: on 2 May, 'A plesant Conceyted historie called "the Tayming of a Shrowe"' was entered for printing. Five more plays were entered on 14 May: 'the Historye of ffryer Bacon and ffryer Boungaye', 'The famous victories of Henrye the ffyft conteyninge the honorable battell of Agincourt', 'The ... historye of Leire', 'John of Gaunte ... with his Conquest of Spaine', and 'a pastorall plesent Commedie of Robin Hood and Little John'. A play on the John of Gaunt story would be written for the

Admiral's Men by Richard Hathaway and William Rankins in 1601, and Anthony Munday perhaps derived from the 'pastorall plesent Commedie' his own Robin Hood plays in 1597 (see no. 62). On 17 May 'the murtherous life and terrible death of the riche Jew of Malta' was entered together with 'The famous Cronicle of Henrye the First, with the life and death of Bellin Dunn the firste theif that ever was hanged in England'. A play on *Henry I* would be performed by the Admiral's Men in 1597, while a play about Bellin Dunn, 'bellendon', entered their repertoire 'ne' on 8 June, 1594 (see no. 31). 'The woundes of Civill warr lively sett forthe in the true Tragedies of Marius and Scilla' was entered in the Stationers' Register as played by the Admiral's Men on 25 May.

———

In the name of god A men begininge the 14 of
maye 1594 by my lord admeralls men

Rd at the Jewe of malta 14 of maye 1594	xxxxviij *s*
Rd at the Rangers comodey the 15 of maye 1594	xxxiij *s*
Rd at Cvtlacke the 16 of maye 1594	xxxxij *s*

31. 3 June 1594. Rose Playhouse Receipts.

Although the order does not survive, a restraint apparently closed the playhouses in mid May. Two weeks later, the Admiral's Men were permitted to play at Newington Butts together with the Chamberlain's Men. Neither company would have been happy with the arrangement. Only twelve months earlier they had been all one company (see nos. 23 and 25), and wounds they had inflicted in parting may not have healed. Besides, each company had filled its ranks with new personnel. The Admiral's Men had Alleyn; the Chamberlain's Men had Richard Burbage. Sharing a stage may not have appealed to either. For everybody, playing at Newington Butts meant inconvenient travelling, or setting up in digs, but the Chamberlain's Men particularly would have found travelling a hardship, for they normally played north of the City at the Theater in Shoreditch. London traffic was no less congested in the sixteenth century than it is today, and the slog through town, across the river and down the Kent road would have been wearying. As it turned out, however, the arrangement at Newington Butts did not last long, for by 15 June the Admiral's Men had apparently won permission to return to the Rose. This is surmise, for Henslowe did not remark upon the transfer; he simply drew a line across his account book after the entry for 13 June, and thereafter his receipts jump dramatically. While the companies were at Newington Butts, production schedules make it unlikely that they were playing as a single amalgamated company. Two of the plays performed came from the Admiral's repertoire, another four belonged to the Chamberlain's Men, and the seventh, a play that opened 'ne' at the Butts, must have been in rehearsal by the Admiral's Men before they left the Rose. To combine companies would have meant sharing play texts – an unlikely situation. It would also have meant re-rehearsing seven plays in the two week interval between the Admiral's Men vacating the Rose and opening with the Chamberlain's Men at the Butts. The players were used to opening new plays every fortnight, but seven plays, though admittedly not rehearsed from scratch, seems unlikely. It seems even more unlikely that the new play, *Bellendon*, which opened on 8 June, would have shared roles between the two companies, for a week later, when the Admiral's Men returned to the Rose, their first performance was of this play. If *Bellendon* were a collaborative production, the Admiral's Men must have recast and re-rehearsed it overnight. Instead of such impossibilities it is probable that the two companies remained intact and played their separate repertoires on alternate days. But why, then, was Henslowe involved? Why did he collect receipt money from either company? They were not using his playhouse so owed him no rent. A look at the receipts themselves shows them to be peculiar. They are extremely low. Was that because audiences were small? (The undated warrant, no. 20, re-opening the Rose, mentions the fact that at Newington 'of longe tyme plaies haue not there bene vsed on working daies', so perhaps people simply did not attend.) Henslowe may, of course, have acted as the companies' agent in renting the Newington Butts playhouse from Peter Hunningborne, its owner, and his costs may have come off the top of his receipts each day, making them modest. Of course, if the players had dealt directly with Hunningborne, Henslowe would have been out of the picture altogether. Even so, they may have been paying Henslowe for some service – influence peddling perhaps – for both companies would have been willing to pawn their best straw-coloured beard to ease the way home to their usual playing place. Henslowe might have been helpful in using his influence at Court and on the South Bank to secure their early return. It is just possible that warrants of all kinds, and the Watermen's Petition (see no. 20) in particular, issued from greased palms.

———

In the name of god Amen begininge at newing
ton my Lord Admeralle men & my Lorde chamberlen
men As ffolowethe 1594

3 of June 1594	Rd at heaster & asheweros	viij *s*
4 of June 1594	Rd at the Jewe of malta	x *s*
5 of June 1594	Rd at andronicous	xij *s*

6 of June 1594		Rd at cvtlacke	xj *s*
8 of June 1594	—ne—	Rd at bellendon	xvij *s*
9 of June 1594		Rd at hamlet	viij *s*
10 of June 1594		Rd at heaster	v *s*
11 of June 1594		Rd at the tamynge of A shrowe	ix *s*
12 of June 1594		Rd at andronicous	vij *s*
13 of June 1594		Rd at the Jewe	iiij *s*

32. 15 June 1594–14 March 1595. Rose Playhouse Receipts (extracts).

The Admiral's Men returned to the Rose and began a season of unprecedented stability that ran without interruption until the following March, when the Company broke for Lent. Only the first four weeks of this season are produced below, to show continuity and change; the Christmas period is given as no. 34. Over the nine months the Company gave 217 performances of thirty-two plays. They opened seventeen new plays at the rate of one every fortnight and revived two old plays – *Tamburlaine* and *Long Meg of Westminster* – that had been so thoroughly revised as to require new licences. Henslowe collected £340 11*s* in receipts that season. Two entries in the Stationers' Register for 19 June are pertinent: 'Godfrey of Bulloigne with the Conquest of Jerusalem' (performed 'ne' by the Admiral's Men a month later on 19 July) and 'The Tragedie of Richard the Third wherein is showen the Death of Edward the ffourthe with the smotheringe of the twoo princes in the Tower with a lamentable end of shores wife and the conjunction of the twoo houses of Lancaster and Yorke'. This version, one of many redactions of the Crookback story, belonged to the Queen's Men and may possibly have inspired Shakespeare's play on the theme. In these receipts, Henslowe continued old habits – marking off performance weeks with dashes and indicating new plays – but he simplified his method of recording the receipts into a more accessible calendar format.

---

15 of June 1594		Rd at bellendon	iij *li* iiij *s*
17 of June 1594		Rd at cutlacke	xxxv *s*
18 of June 1594		Rd at the Rangers comodey	xxij *s*
19 of June 1594		Rd at the Gwies	liiij *s*
20 of June 1594		Rd at bellendon	xxx *s*
22 of June 1594	——	Rd at the Rangers comodey	lviiij *s*
23 of June 1594		Rd at the Jewe	xxiij *s*
24 of June 1594		Rd at cvtlacke	xxv *s*
25 of June 1594		Rd at the masacer	xxxvj *s*

26 of June 1594	—ne—Rd at galiaso	iij *li* iiij *s*
27 of June 1594	Rd at cvttlacke	xxxvj *s*
30 of June 1594	——Rd at the Jewe of malta	xxxxj *s*
2 of Julye 1594	Rd at bellendon	xxxxij *s* vj *d*
3 of Julye 1594	Rd at the masacer	xxxj *s*
4 of Julye 1594	Rd at cvtlacke	xxiiij *s*
5 of Julye 1594	Rd at the Rangers comodey	xviij *s*
6 of Julye 1594	Rd at bellendon	xxxiiij *s*
8 of Julye 1594	——Rd at the masacer	xxvij *s*
9 of Julye 1594	—ne—Rd at the phillipo & hewpolyto	iij *li* ij *s*
10 of Julye 1594	Rd at the Jewe	xxvij *s*
11 of Julye 1594	Rd at bellendon	xxvij *s*
12 of Julye 1594	Rd at galiaso	xxxxvj *s*
13 of Julye 1594	Rd at phillipo & hewpolyto	xxxx *s*

[Receipts continue to March 1595]

33. 3 November 1594. Letter.

The Lord Mayor, Sir John Spencer, wrote to Lord Burghley in some alarm about a new playhouse one Francis Langley intended to build. Henslowe must have felt equal alarm, for the site of the proposed construction was a mere stone's throw away from the Rose in Paris Garden. Langley won. The Swan opened before the summer was out. Spencer's letter is chiefly remarkable for its length. Spencer makes Langley's case the preamble to a recital of all the objections to plays and playhouses that Guildhall repeated so predictably, and this may be because Spencer had just been elected to the mayoralty and was seizing this as the first opportunity for sending the *pro forma* complaint against plays that seems to have been one of the first obligations of new incumbents. The letter is practically a redraft of William Webbe's letter of February 1592 (see no. 13). Langley's decision to build a playhouse shows that the industry had grown up into big business. He would hardly have been interested in it otherwise, for by nature Langley was a profiteer, a land-pirate constructed upon the Cockney model. Spencer's letter calls him an 'alnager' – an official who inspected woollen cloth, the title being derived from 'aulne' = 'ell' – which is right enough. He also called himself a goldsmith, though in Langley's case this was little more than a euphemism for 'money lender'. Given such chemistry it is not surprising that the history of the Swan is filled with accounts of acrimonious disputes and litigation. One of the greatest explosions ever to rock the Elizabethan playhouse was detonated in Langley's Swan (see nos. 53 and 54).

My humble duetie remembred to your good Lordship. I vnderstand that one ffrancis Langley one of the Alneagers for sealing of cloth intendeth to erect a niew stage or Theater (as they call it) for thexercising of playes vpon the Banck side. And forasmuch as wee fynd by daily experience the great inconuenience that groweth to this Citie & the government thearof by the sayed playes I haue embouldened my self to bee an humble suiter to your good Lordship to bee a means for vs rather to suppresse all such places built for that kynd of exercise then to erect any more of the same sort. I am not ignorant (my very good Lordship) what is alleadged by soom for defence of these playes that the people must haue soom kynd of recreation & that policie requireth to divert idle heads & other ill disposed from other woorse practize by this kynd of exercize. Whearto may bee answeared (which your good Lordship for your godly wisedom can far best judge of) that as honest recreation is a thing very meet for all sorts of men so no kynd of exercise beeing of itself corrupt & prophane can well stand with the good policie of a Christian Common Wealth. And that the sayed playes (as they ar handled) ar of that sort & woork that effect in such as ar present and frequent the same may soon bee decerned by all that haue any godly vnderstanding & that obserue the fruites & effects of the same conteining nothing ells but vnchast fables, lascivious divises shifts of cozenage & matters of lyke sort which ar so framed & represented by them that such as resort to see & hear the same beeing of the base & refuse sort of people or such yoong gentlemen as haue small regard of credit or conscience draue the same into example of imitation & not of avoyding the sayed lewd offences. Which may better appear by the qualitie of such as frequent the sayed playes beeing the ordinary places of meeting for all vagrant persons & maisterles men that hang about the Citie, theeves, horsestealers whoremoongers coozeners connycatching persones practizers of treason & such other lyke whear they consort and make their matches to the great displeasure of Almightie God & the hurt and annoyance of hir Maiesties people both in this Citie & other places about, which cannot be clensed of this vngodly sort (which by experience wee fynd to bee the very sinck & contagion not only of this Citie but of this whole Realm) so long as these playes & places of resort ar by authoritie permitted. I omit to trouble your Lordship with any farther matter how our apprentices and servants ar by this means corrupted & induced hearby to defraud their Maisters to maintein their vain & prodigall expenses occasioned by such evill and riotous companie whearinto they fall by these kynd of meetings to the great hinderance of the trades & traders inhabiting this Citie, and how people of all sorts ar withdrawen thearby from their resort vnto sermons & other Christian exercise to the great sclaunder of the ghospell & prophanation of the good & godly religion established within this Realm. All which disorders hauing observed & found to bee true I thought it my duetie beeing now called to this publique place to infourm your good Lordship whome I know to bee a patrone of religion & lover of virtue & an honourable a friend to the State of this Citie humbly beeseaching you to voutchsafe mee your help for the stay & suppressing not only of this which is now intended by directing your lettres to the Justices of peace of Middlesex & Surrey but of all other places if possibly it may bee whear the sayed playes ar shewed & frequented. And thus crauing pardon for this over much length I humbly take my leaue. ffrom London the 3 of November 1594.

Your Lordshippes most humble

To the right honourable my very good Lord the Lord high Treasurer of England.

34. 1 December 1594–15 January 1594/5. Rose Playhouse Receipts (extracts).

These cover the Christmas season – Christmas and Shrovetide were the two most lucrative periods in the playhouse. After opening a new play on 2 December, the Admiral's Men offered no more premieres until 11 February. One explanation might be that since even well-worn plays were money-makers during the holidays, fresh plays could be held in reserve, to lure sluggish new year audiences into the theatre. But from a very different angle, it is possible that the Company simply could not afford to stage another new production that year. Although Christmas week was typically brilliant, Henslowe's receipts at the beginning of December had fallen far short of normal. Indeed, from autumn onward receipts had been low. Audiences may have been distracted by Francis Langley's building project practically next door, though it seems inconceivable that the Swan could have been open and competing with the Rose before summer – unless, of course, the Lord Mayor's letter in November was an objection to a *fait accompli* and the Swan was practically complete by the time he complained about the 'niew stage' Langley 'intendeth to erect' on the premises. No decline in the Company's popularity can be detected by their Court performances this Christmas, for while the Chamberlain's Men appeared at Court either once or twice, the Admiral's Men made either three or four appearances. On New Year's day they gave a public performance in the afternoon, performed at Court that night, and were back at the Rose the next afternoon. Comparing this receipts list to the Company's opening weeks in June (see no. 32) it is interesting to see which plays had survived in the repertoire. *The First Part of Tamburlaine* was brought into the schedule on 28 August; *Part Two* entered on 19 December. Thereafter they played back to back with only one exception. The 'Knacke' of this season is *A Knack to Know An Honest Man*, probably a reworking of *A Knack to Know A Knave* from the Strange's repertoire of 1592. The extracts here are taken from a sequence beginning on 15 June 1594 and ending on 14 March 1595.

———

1 of desember 1594	———	Rd at the gresyan comody	iiij *s*
2 of desember 1594	—ne—	Rd at the wise man of chester	xxxiij *s*
3 of desember 1594		Rd at tasso	vj *s*
4 of desember 1594		Rd at mahemet	xj *s*
6 of desember 1594		Rd at wiseman of weschester	xxxiiij *s*
8 of desember 1594	———	Rd at docterfostus	xv *s*
9 of desember 1594	———	Rd at the Jew	iij *s*
10 of desember 1594	———	Rd at seser	xij *s*
12 of desember 1594		Rd at warlamchester	xv *s*
13 of desember 1594		Rd at the Knaacke	xij *s*
14 of desember 1594	—ne—	Rd at the mawe	xxxxiiij *s*
17 of desember 1594		Rd at tamberlen	xxxj *s*
19 of desember 1594		Rd at the 2 p*a*rte of tamberlen	xxxxvj *s*
20 of desember 1594		Rd at docter fostes	xviij *s*
25 of desember 1594	———	Rd at the greasyane comodey	xxxxvj *s*

S steuen

26 of desember 1594	Rd at the sege of london	iij *li* iij *s*
27 of desember 1594	Rd at Docter fostes	lij *s*
29 of desember 1594 ———	Rd at the wissman of weschester	iij *li* ij *s*
30 of desember 1594	Rd at tamberlen	xxij *s*
j of Jenewary 1594	Rd at the 2 p*a*rte of tamberlen	iij *li* ij *s*
2 of Jenewary 1594	Rd at the seat at mawe	xxiiij *s*
3 of Jenewary 1594	Rd at the frenshe docter	xxj *s*
4 of Jenewary 1594	Rd at valy a for	xj *s*
7 of Jenewary 1594 ———	Rd at the knacke	xxij *s*
9 of Jenewary 1594	Rd at docter fostes	xxij *s*
10 of Jenewary 1595	Rd at the greasyon comodey	xxviij *s*
11 of Jenewary 1595	Rd at tasso	xx *s*
13 of Jenewary 1595 ———	Rd at the Knacke	xxxiij *s*
14 of Jenewary 1594	Rd at the seage of london	xxviij *s*
15 of Jeneway*r*ye 1594	Rd at the wiseman of weaschester	iij *li*

35. 2 January 1594/5. Bond.

Playhouse owners were required to post with the Master of the Revels a £100 bond insuring the maintenance of law and order in their playhouses. This acquittance documents Henslowe's final instalment on his bond to Edmund Tilney.

—

Rd by me, of mr Phillipp Hynsley for my Mr the Master of the Revells this second daie of Januarye 1594 in full payement of a bonde of one hundreth powndes the some of tenn powndes & in full payement of what soever is due from the daie above wrytten vntill Ashwednesdaie next ensuinge after the date hereof. In wittness whereof I have put to my hande/
per me Tho. Stonnard.

36. 14 December 1594-14 January 1595. Company List?

On folio 3 of his Diary, between entries dated in December and January, Henslowe wrote this list of actors' names. It may represent the earliest record of the personnel of the Admiral's Men. E A is Edward Alleyn; then follows the other Company sharers: John Singer, Richard Jones, Thomas Towne, Martin Slater or Slaughter, Edward Juby, Thomas Downton, and James Tunstall (also rendered as Donstone and Donstall). In the left column are, probably, Samuel Rowley, Charles Massey, and Richard Allen who were principal players but only as hired men, not as sharers. Richard Allen was no relation to Edward Alleyn.

—

	E A
	J syngr
same	
	R Jonnes
Charles	
	T towne
alen	
	mr slater
	Jube
	T dowten
	donstone

37. March 1595. Playhouse Repairs Account.

The Admiral's Men had occupied the Rose continuously since June 1594, but in March 1595 playing was apparently restrained in observation of Lent. The Company may have been glad of a holiday: they had been performing six days a week nearly every week for nine months. They broke on 14 March and resumed five weeks later, on 'easter mondaye', 22 April. Henslowe used the interim to make repairs on his playhouse, which he itemised and entered in his Diary. His total, £108 19s, is exactly £100 too much, so he may have been figuring in the maintenance accounts the £100 bond he had been required to post with Tilney (see no. 35). The final disbursement, 'for carpenters worke & mackinge the throne In the heuenes', is particularly interesting. The throne must have been so regular a fixture in plays this Company performed that Henslowe saw good reason to invest in one that was permanently installed and was equipped with machinery to raise and lower it from the heavens. Years later, in the prologue he wrote for the 1616 Folio text of *Every Man In His Humour*, Jonson mocked the old conventions of playwriting and pointed specific ridicule at the hopelessly antiquated 'throne In the heuenes'. The modern playwright scorned

> To make a child, now swaddled, to proceede
> Man, and then shoote up, in one beard, and weede,
> Past threescore yeeres: or, with three rustie swords,
> And helpe of some few foot-and-halfe-foot words,
> Fight over Yorke, and Lancasters long jarres:
> And in the tyring-house bring wounds, to scarres.
> He rather prayes, you will be pleas'd to see
> One such, to day, as other playes should be.
> Where neither Chorus wafts you ore the seas;
> Nor creaking throne comes downe, the boyes to please.

When he wrote these lines, no doubt Jonson had the Rose, its plays and furniture, vividly in mind.

———

A nott what I haue layd owt abowt my playhowsse
ffor payntinge & doinge it a bowt with ealmebordes & other
Repracyones as ffoloweth 1595 in lent

Itm bowght iij hunderd & a quarter of elmebordes	xxiiij s
Itm pd the carpenters ther wages	viij s
Itm geuen the paynter in earneste	xx s
Itm geuen the paynter more	x s
Itm geuen more vnto the paynter	xx s
Itm pd vnto the paynter	x s

Itm pd the carpenters ther wages	xvj s
Itm pd for iij henges	ij s
Itm pd for a borde	ij s ij d
Itm pd for v pownde of spickes	xv d
Itm pd the carpenters	v s iiij d
Itm pd the paynter	v s
Itm pd for ij bundell of lathes	ij s ij d
Itm pd for j lode of sande	xiiij d
Itm pd for hallfe a thowsen of lathe naylles	viij d
Itm pd the paynter	vj s
Itm pd the paynter	iiij s
Itm pd for j lode of lyme	xiiij d
Itm pd for wages	iiij s vj d
Itm pd the paynter	v s
Itm pd the paynter In fulle	xvj s
Itm pd for naylles	ij s iiij d
Itm pd the smyth for naylles In fulle	xij s iiij d

	li	s	d
Some is	108	-19	-00

Itm pd for carpenters work & mackinge the throne In the heuenes the 4 of June 1595   vij *li* ij s

38. 23 April–26 June 1595. Rose Playhouse Receipts (extracts).

The Admiral's Men resumed playing on 'easter mondaye' and continued through June. In ten weeks they gave fifty-seven performances of twenty plays, among them four new plays. Henslowe's receipts totalled £107 8s. *Hercules Part I* entered the repertoire on 7 May; *Part II* premiered two weeks later, and thereafter they normally played back to back. It can be observed in these accounts how the playing schedule was arranged so that two-part plays – *Tamburlaine* is another example in this list – played on consecutive days. Two Stationers' Register entries are relevant to this season: on 1 April, *George a Green* 'the Pynder of Wakefeilde' and on 16 April 'a book or interlude intituled a pleasant conceipte called the owlde wifes tale' were entered for printing. Both plays were by George Peele. This season's receipts, only the first four weeks of which are reproduced here, should be compared to the Company's takings in previous runs (see nos. 32 and 34).

——

easter mondaye 1595 easter	Rd at the ffrenshe doctor	liij s
23 of aprell 1595	Rd at the knacke	lv s

24 of aprell 1595	Rd at the grecian comody	lj s
25 of aprell 1595	Rd at the wissman	lviij s
26 of aprell 1595	Rd at the wisseman of weschester	iij li
27 of aprell 1595	Rd at godfrey of bullen	xxix s
29 of aprell 1595 ———	Rd at warlamchester	xxix s
30 of aprell 1595	Rd at longe mege	xxvij s
31 of aprell 1595	Rd at fastes	xxij s
1 of maye 1595	Rd at longe mege	l s
2 of maye 1595	Rd at seleo & olempa	l s
3 of maye 1595	Rd at frenshe docter	xj s
5 of maye 1595 ———	Rd at the Knacke	xxiij s
6 of maye 1595	Rd at the wiseman	xxxx s
7 of maye 1595 —ne—	Rd at the firste parte of herculous	iij li xiij s
8 of maye 1595	Rd at the venesyon comody	xxx s
9 of maye 1595	Rd at selyo & olympo	xxvj s
10 of maye 1595	Rd at warlam chester	xxix s
12 of maye 1595 ———	Rd at the frenshe comodey	xxviij s
13 of maye 1595	Rd at longe mege	xxviij s
14 of maye 1595	Rd at tasso	xx s
15 of maye 1595	Rd at the wisse man of weschester	xxxvij s
16 of maye 1595	Rd at the greasyan comodey	xxxiij s
17 of maye 1595	Rd at godfrey of bullen	xxij s
19 of maye 1595	Rd at olimpo	xxiij s
20 of maye 1595	Rd at hercolas	iij li ix s
21 of maye 1595	Rd at j part of tamberlen	xxij s
22 of maye 1595	Rd at 2 part of tamberlen	xxv s
23 of maye 1595 —ne—	Rd at 2 part of hercolas	iij li x s
24 of maye 1595	Rd at frenshe docter	xxij s

[Receipts continue to June]

39. 25 August 1595–27 February 1596. Rose Playhouse Receipts (extracts).

The Privy Council minute that ordered the playhouse closure in June has not survived to explain why the restraint was called, but plague was certainly not the reason, for only twenty-nine plague deaths were recorded that summer. Other Council memoranda, however, may fill the gap. They report a series of progressively ugly clashes between apprentices and the authorities about this time, and these would have given the Lord Mayor a stockpile of ammunition to level against the playhouses. On 13 June apprentices threw Southwark market into an uproar by disputing the price of butter. Two days later certain of them attempted to release friends from the Counter in Wood Street, while a brawl ensued elsewhere when hard words between a master and his servant ended with the apprentice hitting the older man over the head. The following day there were more disorders, this time cashiered soldiers inciting the apprentices, and finally, on 23 June, the apprentices ran riot in Billingsgate Market. Having discovered the entire day's catch had been bought up by Southwark fishwives, they pursued the women into the borough and removed the fish – though some said they paid for it fairly. This series of disruptions, though nothing to do with plays or players, would have been cause enough for a restraint to have been ordered: the Lord Mayor could argue prudently that plays gave occasion for large numbers of unruly persons – particularly apprentices – to assemble. But whatever prompted the restraint, while it was in effect, the Admiral's Men toured the provinces; local records show they made stops in Bath and Maidstone. By late August they were permitted to return to London. They resumed playing at the Rose on 25 August and continued for the next twenty-seven weeks, giving 150 performances of thirty plays, among them twelve new plays. Henslowe's share in the receipts amounted to £224 15s. After the final entry dated 27 February Henslowe noted: 'the master of the Revelles payd vntell this time al which I owe hime'. Thereafter, playing stopped until 12 April (see no. 43). Only the first four weeks of this run are given below; the Christmas season, because financially it was such a crucial period in the playhouse, is produced separately as no. 41. A comparison between this and the Company's first season at the Rose (see nos. 32 and 34) shows how the repertoire gradually turned over as older plays dropped out, popular money-makers remained – giving quick-changing players a welcome sense of continuity – and new plays, rehearsed and opened in a fortnight, either worked themselves solidly into the repertoire or were jettisoned. Several of the successes this season had been held over from the previous season, the *Hercules* plays, for example, and *Seven Days of the Week*, new on 3 June. Other plays that were still running strong had first been seen as long before as July 1594: after a fourteen-month run *Godfrey of Boulogne* could still net £1 in receipts for Henslowe. The obvious veteran in the schedule was *Faustus*, still more popular after three years at the Rose than the six-month-old *Long Meg*. Of the remaining plays, the revised version of Marlowe's *Tamburlaine* entered the repertoire in August 1594; *The Knack* and *The French Doctor* appeared in October; in December came *The Wiseman of West Chester* and *The Siege of London*; a month later *Antony and Vallia*; and on 5 March, *Olympio and Eugenio* – an alternative title for *Seleo and Olympio* – opened. By contrast to these survivors, other plays that had opened just weeks before disappeared from the repertoire: the two parts of *Caesar and Pompey*, new on 8 November 1594 and 18 June 1595 respectively, were never performed after 26 June when *Part II* was staged for only the second time. *The Mack* was played only once, on 21 February 1595, though it seems to have been well received: Henslowe's receipt that day, at £3, was respectable for a new play. Equally inexplicable, *The Set at Maw* was performed only four times after opening on 14 December with receipts of £2 4s to Henslowe. One wonders what happened to these plays or what criteria the Company set up for deciding their repertoire. Evidently, preference as well as finance entered the decision. One also wonders how, and when, the Company decided which play they would perform each afternoon. Henslowe's records suggest that the schedule was not known in advance, for he entered his receipts day by day or he listed a column of dates, which he sometimes changed, and filled in the titles later.

———

25 of auguste 1595	Rd at the knacke to know a nonest man	xvij s
26 of auguste 1595	Rd at the wisman of wescheaster	xxxix s
27 of auguste 1595	Rd at the weacke	liij s
28 of auguste 1595	Rd at longe mege	xvij s
29 of auguste 1595 —ne—	Rd at longe shancke	xxxx s
30 of auguste 1595	Rd at the seage of london	xviij s
1 of septmber 1595 ———	Rd at j parte of hercvlos	iij li iiij s
2 of septmber 1595	Rd at 2 parte of hercvlos	iij li
3 of septmber 1595	Rd at the vij dayes of the weacke	lij s
4 of septmber 1595	Rd at olempeo & heugenyo	xviij s
5 of september 1595 —ne—	Rd at cracke me this nvtte	iij li j s
6 of septmber 1595	Rd at valia & antony	xiij s
9 of septmber 1595 ———	Rd at the wise man	xxxxiiij s
10 of septmber 1595	Rd at longshancke	iij li
11 of septmber 1595	Rd at docter fostes	xxx s ij
12 of septmber 1595	Rd at cracke me this nutte	iij li
13 of septmber 1595	Rd at the vij dayes	xxxviij s
[no date]	Rd at longe mege	xvj s
15 of septmber 1595	Rd at j parte of tamberlen	xxj s
16 of septmber 1595	Rd at godfrey of bullen	xx s
17 of septmber 1595 —ne—	Rd at the worldes tragedy	iij li v s
18 of septmber 1595	Rd at the Knacke	xvij s
19 of septmber 1595	Rd at the frenshe doctor	xvj s
20 of septmber 1595	Rd at the sege of london	xvij s

[Receipts continue to February 1596]

40. 13 September 1595. Letter.

In this, the incumbent Lord Mayor, Sir Stephen Slany, issued his version of Guildhall's antique appeal to the Privy Council for the abolition of playing. The letter, sent within days of the playhouses' reopening on 25

August, refers to 'the late stirr & mutinous attempt of those fiew apprentices and other servantes who wee doubt not driew their infection from these & like places'. No doubt Slany was talking about the apprentice disturbances in June (see no. 39). Slany's frequent reiteration of his own and the Aldermen's humbleness – all the while implying the lords' dereliction of duty – is put in perspective by his allusion to the 'refuse sort' of people and gives a cold, clear insight into the frame of reference by which Elizabethan civil government was administered. His careful balancing of accusations and apologies makes it difficult to decide where the galling heart of the matter lay for Slany, whether the playhouses offended because they outraged morality or because they despised and subverted the sweat of hard-working industry. The playhouses smelled to heaven because they gave 'oportunitie' to 'vngodly people' to 'make their matches for all their lewd & vngodly practizes'. But one suspects Slany's nostrils were really snorting at 'oportunitie' of a different flavour: playhouses enabled 'maisterles men & vagabond persons ... to recreate themselves'. This Lord Mayor does not, however, seem to have considered the improbability of 'maisterles men & vagabond persons' having the price of admission to even so inexpensive a recreation as a play.

———

Our humble duty remembred to your good Lordshippes & the rest: Wee haue been bold heartofore to signify to your Honors the great inconvenyenc that groweth to this Cytie by the common exercise of Stage Plaies, whear in wee presumed to be the more often & earnest suters to your Honors ffor the suppressing of the said Stage Plaies aswell in respect of the good government of this Cytie, (which wee desire to be such as her Highnes & your Honors might be pleased thearwithall) as for conscience sake being perswaded (vnder correccion of your Honors Judgment) that neither in policye nor in religion they ar to be permitted in a Christian Common wealthe specially being of that frame & making as vsually they are, & conteyning nothing but profane fables, Lasciuious matters, cozoning devizes, & other vnseemly & scurrilous behaviours, which ar so sett forthe; as that they move wholy to imitacion & not to the avoyding of those vyces which they represent which wee verely think to bee the cheef cause aswell of many other disorders & lewd demeanors which appeer of late in young people of all degrees, as of the late stirr & mutinous attempt of those fiew apprentices and other servantes who wee doubt not driew their infection from these & like places Among other inconveniences it is not the least that the refuse sort of evill disposed & vngodly people about this Cytie haue oportunitie hearby to assemble together & to make their matches for all their lewd & vngodly practizes: being also the ordinary places for all maisterles men & vagabond persons that haunt the high waies to meet together & to recreate themselfes Whearof wee begin to haue experienc again within these fiew daies since it pleased her highnes to revoke her Comission graunted forthe to the Provost Marshall, for fear of whome they retired themselfes for the time into other partes out of his precinct but ar now retorned to their old haunt & frequent the Plaies (as their manner is) that ar daily shewed at the Theator & Bankside: Whearof will follow the same inconveniences whearof wee haue had to much experienc heartofore, ffor preventing Whearof wee ar humble suters to your good Lordships & the rest to direct your lettres to the Justices of peac of Surrey & Middlesex for the present stay & finall suppressing of the said Plaies aswell at the Theator & Bankside as in all other places about the Cytie Whearby wee doubt not but the oportunytie & very cause of so great disorders being taken away wee shalbe able to keepe the people of this Cytie in such good order & due obedienc as that her highnes & your Honors shalbe well pleased & content thearwithall. And so most humbly wee take our Leaue: ffrom London the xiijth of September. 1595.

Your Honors most humble.

To the right honourable the Lords & others of her Maiesties most honourable privy Counsell.

41. 24 November 1595-16 January 1595/6. Rose Playhouse Receipts (extracts).

At Christmas, the Admiral's Men were in the middle of a season that had begun in August (see no. 39) and would continue until the end of February. These receipts should be compared to the Christmas takings of a year earlier (see no. 34). For nearly three weeks in December the Company performed only on alternate days. Langley's Swan was open, with the Chamberlain's Men perhaps installed there, and was doubtless putting pressure on the Rose, perhaps even drawing away sufficient numbers to make daily playing unviable. By all accounts, the Swan was magnificent, and the Little Rose must have looked dowdy in the light of its splendour. Still, the Admiral's Men soldiered on. They seem to have been depending on their new play, *Henry V* – not Shakespeare's – to boost their Christmas receipts, for they repeated that play with uncharacteristic frequency. *Hercules II*, having shown itself consistently less popular than *Part I* from its opening performance, was dropped from the repertoire. On 1 and 4 January (after a public performance on the afternoon of New Year's Day and between performances on the 3rd and 5th) the Admiral's Men appeared at Court; but the Chamberlain's Men were there for four performances, on 26, 27, 28 December and 6 January. At Shrovetide the balance of royal approval was nearly redressed with two performances by the Admiral's Men (again after a public afternoon performance) on Shrove Tuesday and on 24 February, against one by their rivals. The Company had to wait a year, until December 1596, to be paid for any of these Court appearances. Even worse to players who may have been feeling pinched for money by the appearance of a rival playhouse on their doorstep, yet another playhouse was in the offing. On 4 February, James Burbage acquired the lease to the Blackfriars playhouse. His son Richard was with the Chamberlain's Men, who perhaps were at the Swan but who likewise were ambitious for an indoor playing space: they had sought permission to use the Cross Keys Inn as winter quarters. Burbage's new transaction was a potential threat of alarming implications to the outdoor playhouses. If he could convert the Blackfriars into a professional playhouse, some company would have a permanent indoor home. No doubt that company would be the Chamberlain's Men. In this series of receipts, Henslowe continued to mark playing weeks and new plays and also to indicate the date on which he paid the Master of the Revels: he put 'mr pd' against 18 December and 2 January. After the entry for 5 January, he wrote '140-11-0', a subtotal of his receipts to date. The last entry in this list was not dated. The extracts here are taken from a sequence running from August 1595 to February 1596.

———

24 of novmber 1595	——— Rd at j herculos	xx s
25 of novmber 1595	Rd of 2 part of herculos	xvj s
26 of novmber 1595	Rd at longshancke	xviij s
27 of november 1595	Rd at the newes wordles tragedy	xviij s
28 of november 1595	—ne— Rd at harey the v	iij li vj s
29 of novmber 1595	Rd at the welche man	vij s
31 of novmber 1595	——— Rd at the toye to please chaste ladeyes	xij s
2 of desember 1595	Rd at hary the v	xxxv s
3 of desember 1595	Rd at barnardo	vij s
4 of desember 1595	Rd at wonder of A womon	xiiij s
6 of desember 1595	Rd at Crack me this nvtt	xv s
8 of desember 1595	——— Rd at hary the v	xxxxiij s
10 of desember 1595	Rd at prynce longshanke	xxx s
12 of desember 1595	Rd at the new worldes tragedy	xxxj s vj d
14 of desember 1595	——— Rd at the vij dayes	xxiiij s
16 of desember 1595	Rd at hary the v	xxix s
18 of desember 1595	mr pd Rd at j part of herculos	xiij s
22 of desember 1595	——— Rd at the newe worldes tragedie	xx s
25 of desember 1595	S steuens day Rd at the wonder of A womon	iij li ij s
26 of desember 1595	Rd at barnardo	lviij s
28 of desember 1595	——— Rd at harye the v	lvj s
29 of desember 1595	Rd at longshanckes	xxxij s

30 of desember 1595	Rd at the wisman of weschester	xxij s
1 of Jeneway 1595	Rd at the wecke	xxxxij s
2 of Jeneway 1595	mr pd Rd at cracke me this nvtt	ix s
3 of Jenewary 1595	—ne—Rd at chinone of Ingland	l s
5 of Jenewary 1595	Rd at harey the v	xxvj s
6 of Jeneway 1595	Rd at hurculos the j parte	iij li
7 of Jeneway 1595	Rd at a Knack to Know & onest man	xx s
8 of Jeneway 1595	Rd at new worldes tragedie	xviij s
9 of Jeneuery 1595	Rd at the Jew of malta	lvj s
10 of Jenewary 1595	Rd at a toye to please chaste ladeys	xviij s
12 of Jenewary 1595	———Rd at chynon of Ingland	l s
13 of Jenewary 1595	Rd at the sege of london	xv s
14 of Jenewary 1595	Rd at cracke me this nvtte	xxiij s
15 of Jenewary 1595	Rd at the wonder of a womon	xxvij s
16 of Jeneway 1595	—ne—Rd at pethageros	iij li j s
	Rd at wessman of weschester	xviij s

42. 12 April 1596. Rose Licensing Fee.

The weekly playhouse licensing fee payable by Henslowe to Edmund
Tilney had risen to 10s, double the fee in 1592. Blewenson could not sign
his name. He authorised receipt with a mark.

———

Rd for ij weckes paye which was dew vnto the master of the Revelles
frome the 12 of aprell 1596 vnto the 26 of the same moneth xxs I saye Rd

mihell Blvenson
marke

43. 12 April–18[23] July 1596. Rose Playhouse Receipts (extracts).

Having interrupted their season on 27 February, two days after Ash
Wednesday, the Admiral's Men resumed on Easter Monday, 12 April.
Their receipts for the next two weeks, though not exceptional, were
steady enough, and they opened a moderately successful *Julian the Apostate* on 29 April. Henslowe's receipts that day were £2 7s. But by May
Day the Admiral's Men seem to have been in financial trouble, for Edward
Alleyn began negotiating a series of loans from his father-in-law in the
Company's name (see no. 44). The debts were repaid over the summer
(see no. 45). The complete receipts from May Day forward are produced

below so that comparisons between the loans and repayments can be made. Playing was eventually inhibited by a restraint dated 22 July; over the fifteen-week season the Company gave eighty-five performances of twenty-five plays, among them seven new plays. They earned for Henslowe £115 6s. The two parts of *Tambercame* – *Tamar Cham* – had been in the repertoire of Lord Strange's Men in 1592, and the fact that they are marked 'ne' this season probably means that they had been so thoroughly revised as to require relicensing by the Master of the Revels. *Fortunatus* is not Dekker's, but the original revised by Dekker in 1599. The receipt entry against *Chinon* on 1 June is probably a miswriting of shillings for pounds since, as the entries on either side of it show, receipts around the Whitsun holidays usually rose dramatically: *Pythagoras* earned just £1 7s on May 22 but on Whit Monday collected £3. The final play this season was a premiere, *The Tinker of Totnes*, which promised fair at £3; apparently, though, it was never played again at the Rose for the title never reappears in the accounts. In this list Henslowe wrote his date and play title columns separately, and where they got out of alignment he connected them with lines. Toward the end of the calendar he misnumbered his dates; correctly the season finished on 23 July, a day after the restraint fell.

———

[Receipts begin on 12 April]

maye Daye 1596		Rd at wonder of a womon	xxij s
2 of maye 1596	————	Rd at chinon	xx s
3 of maye 1596		Rd at the blinde beger	xxxv s
4 of maye 1596		Rd at pethagorus	xx s
5 of maye 1596		Rd at Docter ffostes	xx s
6 of maye 1596	—ne—	Rd at tambercame	xxxxvij s
7 of maye 1596		Rd at cracke me this nvtte	xviij s
10 of maye 1596	mr pd	Rd at Julian apostata	xxvj s
11 of maye 1596		Rd at fortunatus	xviij s
12 of maye 1596		Rd at tambercame	xxxxv s
13 of maye 1596		Rd at blind beger	xxxx s
14 of maye 1596		Rd at the Jew of malta	xxiiij s
16 of maye 1596	————	Rd at chynone	xxxiij s
17 of maye 1596		Rd at tambercame	xxxxvj s
18 of maye 1596		Rd at beger	xxxxix s
19 of maye 1596	—ne—	Rd at tragedie of ffocasse	xxxxv s
20 of maye 1596		Rd at Julyan apostata	xiiij s
22 of maye 1596	mr pd	Rd at pethagoros	xxvij s
23 of maye 1596		Rd at tragedie of ffocasse	xxxix s
24 of maye 1596		Rd at ffortunatus	xiiij s
25 of maye 1596		Rd at tambercame	xx s

26 of maye 1596	Rd at hary the v	xxiij s
27 of maye 1596	Rd at chinone	ix s
31 of maye 1596	whittsenmvnday Rd at pethagores	iij li
1 of June 1596	Rd at chinone of Ingland	iij s
2 of June 1596	Rd at longshancke	iij li
3 of June 1596	Rd at the blinde beager	xxxxj s
4 of June 1596	Rd at the tragedie of focas	xxxj s
5 of June 1596	Rd at tambercame	xxviij s
7 of June 1596	mr pd Rd at cracke me this nvtte	xxviij s
8 of June 1596	Rd at wisman of weschester	xx s
9 of June 1596	Rd at the chaste ladye	xviij s
10 of June 1596	Rd at tambercame	xxviij s
11 of June 1596	—ne—Rd at 2 parte of tambercame	iij li
12 of June 1596	Rd at Docter fostes	xvij s
14 of June 1596	———Rd at sege of london	xxx s
15 of June 1596	Rd at pethagores	xxiij s
16 of June 1596	Rd at ffocase	xx s
17 of June 1596	Rd at hary the v	xxvij s
19 of June 1596	mr pd Rd at j parte of tambercame	xxvj s
20 of June 1596	Rd at 2 parte of tmbercame	xxxv s
21 of June 1596	Rd at Jew of malta	xiij s
22 of June 1596	Rd at focas	l s
22 of June 1596	—ne—Rd at troye	iij li ix s
23 of June 1596	Rd at cracke me this nvtt	xij s
25 of June 1596	———Rd at the beager	xix s
26 of June 1596	Rd at j parte of tambercame	xxx s
27 of June 1596	Rd at 2 parte of tambercame	xx s
1 of July 1596	—ne—Rd at paradox	xxxxv s
2 of Julye 1596	Rd at troye	xxiiij s
3 of July 1596	Rd at fostes	xiiij s
5 of July 1596	mr pd Rd at focasse	xxij s
6 of July 1596	Rd at sege of london	xv s
7 of July 1596	Rd at wisman of weschester	xvj s
8 of July 1596	Rd at 2 part of tambercame	xxiiij s
4 of July 1596	Rd at frenshe dacter	xiiij s
5 of July 1596	Rd at the beager	xvij s
7 of July 1596	———Rd at troye	xxix s
8 of July 1596	Rd at j parte of tambercame	xiiij s
9 of July 1596	Rd at longshancke	xv s
10 of July 1596	Rd at hary the v	xiiij s
11 of July 1596	Rd at bellendon	xxxv s
12 of July 1596	mr pd Rd at the toye	x s
14 of July 1596	Rd at pethagores	xxij s
15 of July 1596	Rd at hary v	xxij s

16 of July 1596	Rd at troye	xxj *s*
17 of July 1596	Rd at focas	xxix *s*
18 of July 1596	—ne—Rd at the tyncker of totnes	iij *li*

44. 2 May-?July 1596. Loan Account.

The loans Henslowe made to the Admiral's Men on this occasion were all in substantial lump sums, which probably means that while the Company was able to meet its day-to-day running costs, they were finding it difficult to amass sufficient funds to set against future productions, a single costume for which might cost over £15. A company could not scrimp on such expenditures, for costumes were the richest scenic effect on the Elizabethan stage, but they were enormously expensive, some costing three or four times what a tradesman expected to earn in a year. The £11 the Admiral's Men borrowed on 2 May possibly went toward costuming *Tamar Cham*, a revival which opened four days later. By 25 May, a week after *Phocas* opened, the Company stood £21 13s 4d in debt, but they had likewise been making repayments in dribs and drabs over these same weeks, so that, by 25 May, they had already given Henslowe £25 10s in repayments. They actually stood in credit (see no. 45). Two undated costume purchases at the bottom of the loan account may relate to *Troy* (new on 23 June) and *The Paradox* (opened 1 July). The £7 6s 8d 'Tvrned over from my sonne' was the surplus Henslowe had accumulated out of the repayments and was reimbursing the Company. This loan-repayment scheme evidently satisfied both parties, for it eventually settled into a permanent pattern in the relationship between Henslowe and the Company. Some readers of Henslowe's Diary have viewed this turn of events grimly, seeing in it Henslowe's attempt to achieve an economic stranglehold around a company of players who, lured into debt, were thereafter shackled to his playhouse and enslaved to his management. But Henslowe's accounts, the very food to this reading, likewise starve it of validity. Henslowe's interest was in making money out of the playhouse, not in slave-driving a company he had first lured into bankruptcy. He demonstrated this clearly enough by making very sure on this first adventure into loan accountancy that his debtors could clear themselves, and the pattern of future loan arrangements is to be seen in the Company's repayment credit this May. From the Company's side, the shortcoming of the sharer system was that it could not provide expansion capital: it could only keep pace with the daily receipts and could not underwrite risks such as a gamble on a spectacular extravaganza that would bring lapsed audiences thronging back to the Rose. Henslowe's loans could provide just this sort of capital by supplying advances upon profits. From his settled role as landlord at the Rose, Henslowe was required to change slowly into bank manager to the Admiral's Men, and as such was probably only so ambiguous a figure as modern bank managers who willingly underwrite hopes but insist on cold cash back and who, though intimidating, gain nothing from forfeited debts.

———

lent vnto my sonne edwarde allen	*li* *s* *d*
as ffoloweth for the company 1596	21-13-04

Itm lent the 2 of maye 1596	xj *li*
Itm lent the 10 of maye 1596	liij *s* iiij *d*
Itm lent the 13 of maye 1596	iij *li*
Itm lent the 15 of maye 1596	xxx *s*
Itm lent the 16 of maye 1596	xxxx *s*
Itm lent the 25 of maye 1596 to paye marcvm	xxx *s*
	21-13-04

lent vnto my sonne for the company to by a new sewte of a parell	vij *li* x *s*
lent vnto my sonne to feneshe vp the blacke veluet gowne	iij *li*
Tvrned over frome my sonne the some of	vij *li* vj *s* viij *d*

45. 10 May–8 July 1596. Loan Repayments.

These repayments should be compared to Henslowe's receipts on each of these dates as a way of establishing where the repayment money was coming from (see no. 43). In every case the Admiral's Men repaid Henslowe slightly more than Henslowe collected in receipts, and this suggests that they were turning over to him their half of the gallery money to match his portion in the takings. The slight discrepancy is to be accounted for in payments to gatherers, those playhouse employees who collected the admission fees. After the 25 May entry Henslowe figured a marginal subtotal, '025-10-00' and against 2 July recorded another subtotal, '36-07-00'. These repayments were entered at the foot of the same page Henslowe used to record the loans.

———

Receued agayne of my sonne EA of
this deate abowe written as foloweth

Rd the 10 of maye 1596	xxx *s*
Rd the 11 of maye 1596	xx *s*

			Rd the 12 of maye 1596	xxxxvj *s*
			Rd the 13 of maye 1596	xxxxvj *s*
			Rd the 14 of maye 1596	xxvj *s*
			Rd the 15 of maye 1596	xxiiij *s*
			Rd the 16 of maye 1596	xxxvj *s*
			Rd the 17 of maye 1596	l *s*
			Rd the 18 of maye 1596	liij *s*
			Rd the 22 of maye 1596	xxviij *s*
			Rd the 23 of maye 1596	xxxx *s*
			Rd the 24 of maye 1596	xxij *s*
li	*s*	*d*	Rd the 25 of maye 1596	xxv *s*
025-10-00			Rd the 11 of June 1596	iij *li* iiij *s*
			Rd the 23 of June 1596	iij *li* xiij *s*
			Rd the 25 of June 1596	xxj *s*
			Rd the 26 of June 1596	xxx *s*
			Rd the 27 of June 1596	xxj *s*
li	*s*	*ds*	Rd the 1 of July 1596	xxxxvij *s*
36-07-00			Rd the 2 of July 1596	xxv *s*
			Rd the 5 of July 1596	xxiij *s*
			Rd the 6 of July 1596	xvij *s*
			Rd the 8 of July 1596	xxij *s*

46. Summer 1596. *Ex Observationibus Londonensibus.*

Johannes de Witt, visiting London from Utrecht this summer, toured the city and made notes of his observations. His famous sketch of the interior of the Swan playhouse, which survives only in a copy a friend entered in his own commonplace book, is the single extant drawing of the interior of an Elizabethan playhouse. Significantly, the Rose gets only a passing glance from de Witt who dwells instead on the magnificent playhouse, the rival playhouse, next door. De Witt makes one thing quite clear: by 1596 the playhouse industry was solidly established on the South Bank.

———

There are four amphitheatres in London of notable beauty, which from their diverse signs bear diverse names. In each of them a different play is daily exhibited to the populace. The two more magnificent of these are situated to the southward beyond the Thames, and from the signs suspended before them are called the Rose and Swan ... Of all the theatres, however, the largest and most magnificent is that one of which the sign is a swan, called in the vernacular the Swan Theatre; for it accommodates in its seats three thousand persons, and is built of a mass of flint stones (of which there is a prodigious supply in Britain), and supported by wooden columns painted in such excellent imitation of marble that it is able to deceive even the most cunning.

47. 22 July 1596. Privy Council Minute.

The lords, for once, were succinct in wording their playhouse restraint. While the order was in effect, the Admiral's Men toured the provinces where local records of appearances in Coventry, Bath, Gloucester and Dunwich survive. The same day the restraint fell, the Lord Chamberlain – Henry Carey, Lord Hunsdon – died, but although all the players, and particularly the Chamberlain's Men (who reverted to 'Hunsdon's Men' under patronage of the new Lord, George Carey) would have mourned so sympathetic an overseer of their profession, there was no connection between the restraint and the death. Hunsdon was replaced by Lord Cobham, a man of untried sympathies, but a man – ominously – who did not retain a cry of players. His appointment was received with misgiving among the players, and when in September a bored Thomas Nashe wrote to William Cotton complaining about having to cool his heels in London while a commission he had been waiting for did not materialise because the players were forced to be elsewhere, he related the players' insecurity about the new Lord Chamberlain: 'Sir this tedious dead vacation is to mee as vnfortunate as a terme at Hertford or St Albons to poore cuntry clients or *Jack Cades* rebellion to the lawyers, wherein they hanged vp the Lord cheife *justice*. In towne I stayd (being earnestly inuited elsewhere) vpon had I wist hopes, & an after harvest I expected by writing for the stage & for the presse, when now the players as if they had writt another Christs tears, ar piteously persecuted by the Lord Maior & the aldermen, & howeuer in there old Lords tyme they thought there state setled, it is now so vncertayne they cannot build vpon it.' The players perhaps breathed easier when Lord Cobham died after only eight months in office. George Carey, son of the 'old Lord' Chamberlain, not only succeeded his father as Lord Hunsdon and continued the patronage of the players but was given his father's office as Chamberlain in March 1597.

———

Lettres to the Justices of middlesex and Surrey to restrayne the Players from shewing or using any plaies or Interludes in the places usuall about the Citty of london, for that by drawing of muche people togeather increase of sicknes is feared.

48. 14 October 1596–25 March 1597. Loan and Repayment Account.

When the restraint was lifted the Admiral's Men returned to the Rose and, as Henslowe's receipts show, were ready to reopen on 27 October (see no. 49). First, though, they needed financial help from Henslowe to get the season started. From 14 October onward they began borrowing money, possibly because their resources as a company had been depleted: the first items in the account refer to additional players being 'feached', and the fourth relates to a playbook the Company was buying from the dramatist Thomas Heywood. The arrangement of these accounts on the page is bewilderingly disjointed, which seems to indicate that the transactions were pretty much *ad hoc*. Henslowe certainly extended more loans than he had anticipated or planned for. Originally he intended to confine them to a single page, for he began listing them on a right-hand page in his Diary, and when he ran out of space there he had to continue on another page – the left-hand. The two pages of loans lie facing each other, but they run back to front, and Henslowe's final reckoning of the loans, 'deliuered vnto the company the 25 of marche', is placed at the head of the account. Further confusion is caused by Henslowe's having conflated the loans with the repayments (which should be compared to Henslowe's receipts for those dates (see no. 49) where *Jeronimo* on 7 January earned Henslowe £3 while the Company in this repayment account gave him an additional £7 out of their own profits). From November, the Company borrowed money nearly exclusively for costumes: *Vortigern*, i.e., *Valteger*, opened 4 December, *Captain Stukeley* ('stewtleyes hosse') 11 December, and *Guido* 14 March. But they also bought a Harry Porter play in December. Between December and March the Company did not need to borrow, possibly because the Court money that had been owing to them for performances before the Queen the *previous* Christmas was finally paid, a sumptuous £40. Company sharers referred to in the account are Edward Alleyn, Martin Slater, James Tunstall and Edward Juby; Steven Magett was the tireman; Thomas Hunt and Robert Browne were actors. Fleacher cannot be identified confidently. It is not likely that he is the Lawrence Fletcher later associated with the Chamberlain's Men. Outside the accounts, two events bearing on the Rose and her tenants occurred: on 9 November the playwright George Peele, whose *Battle of Alcazar* the Company had performed, died. That same month the inhabitants of the Blackfriars successfully petitioned the Privy Council to refuse James Burbage permission to convert rooms in that precinct into a playhouse for the Lord Chamberlain's Men. The Admiral's Men may have accepted the two events philosophically: lose some, win some. Their account with Henslowe printed below is organised chronologically instead of back to front as it stands in the Diary. Two attempts by Henslowe to reckon the 'some' of the debt were crossed out; they appear in square brackets.

———

A note of Suche money as I haue
lent vnto thes meane whose names
follow at seaverall tymes edward alleyn
martyne slather Jeames donstall & Jewbey

all this lent sence the 1596 14 of october

lent vnto martyne to feache fleacher	vj s
lent vnto theme to feache browne	x s
lent vnto my sonne for thomas honte	vj s 8 d
lent vnto them for hawodes bocke	xxx s
lent vnto them at a nother tyme	l s
lent vnto marteyn at a nother tyme	xxx s
lent vnto the tayller for the stocke	xxx s
lent them to by a boocke	xxxxx s
lent the company to geue fleatcher/& the hauepromysed me payement who promysed me is marten donston Jewby	xx s
Rd in part of payment the 29 of october 1596	xx s
Rd in part of payment of al holanday 1596	xx s
[Rd in part of paymente the 13 of desember 1596	xxxx s]

[Some is vij li] [viij li xs]   ttottalles ... 31 li 15 s-00 d
Some ix li

Rd at the second time of playinge that wilbe shalbe the 4 of Janeway 1597 the some of	xxxx s
Rd at Joronymo the 7 of Janeway 1597 in parte of payment	vij li
Rd at elexsander & ladwicke the 14 of Janewarye the fyrste time yt wasse playde 1597 in parte	v li
Rd at a womon hard to please the 27 of Janewary 97	iiij li

lente vnto my lord admerall players at severall
tymes in Redey money as foloweth 1596

lent vnto Jeames donstall for to by thinges for the playe of valteger	v li
lent vnto marten slater to by coper lace & frenge for the playe of valteger the 28 of novmber 1596	xxxx s
lent vnto marten slather the 29 of novmber 1596 to by for the play of valteger lace & other thinges	xxv s
dd vnto steuen the tyerman for to delyver vnto the company	iij li x s

for to bey a headtier & a Rebata & other thinges the 3 of
desember 1596

lent vnto my sonne to by the saten dublet with syluer lace	iiij *li*

the wholl some of this & the other syd is
22 li–15 s–00 d

Lente more the 8 of desember 1596 for stewtleyes hosse	iij *li*
lent donston & marten the 11 of desember 1596	xxxx s
lent marten the 14 of desember 1596	xx s
dd vnto mr porter the 16 of desember 1596	v *li*
payd vnto the carman for fetcheng your wagen	ij s
lent vnto mr porter the 7 of marche 1597	iiij *li*
lent vnto my sonne for to by sylckes & other thing*es* for gvido the 14 of marche	iiij *li* ix s

deliuered vnto the company the 25 of marche beinge good frydaye
1597 the some of fyve pownd & fortenshelyngs which mackes vp the
some of thirtie powndes as her vnder writen maye be sene which
they owe vnto me I saye..............xxx *li* wittnes edward allen

49. 27 October 1596–18 July 1597. Rose Playhouse Receipts (extracts).

Having negotiated their loans, the Admiral's Men reopened at the Rose
on 27 October. They continued without interruption until the following
summer, but at the end of January Henslowe changed his method of
entering the receipts to a new system that has never been satisfactorily
explained; thus, from January onward his receipts can no longer be
identified with certainty, although the play titles, playing calendar and
hence the repertoire are still listed straightforwardly. In the eleven weeks
that the old system prevailed, the Company gave fifty-seven performances
of fifteen plays, five of them new plays and one a revival. Henslowe's
receipts totalled £70 11s. The season overall – including the period covered
by the new accounting system – produced 193 performances in thirty-five
weeks of thirty-one plays. Twelve new plays appeared. The startling fact
about this season is that half the plays performed between October and
January (when receipts are clearly recorded) earned Henslowe under £1.
The Christmas season was disastrous: sixteen plays in thirty-three days
took less than £1 for Henslowe, and even worse, only three plays between
Christmas and Twelfth Night earned more than £3. New plays showed
poorly: *Vortigern*, £2 10s; *Stukeley*, £2; *What Will Be Shall Be*, £2 10s;
Alexander and Lodowick, £2 15s. *Nebuchadnezzar* had the worst opening
performance of any play in the history of the Rose and only showed

respectably in the brief flutter around Christmas. An air of desperation hangs around these new plays: they were thrust on to the stage with unprecedented haste – a week between *Vortigern* and *Stukeley*, another week between *Stukeley* and *Nebuchadnezzar* – as though the Company was trying to find something, anything, that would work with audiences. Significantly, one of the Company's only £3 plays this season was a revival of *The Spanish Tragedy* ('Joronymo'), a standby in the Rose repertoire since 1592. Henslowe marked it 'ne' then crossed that out, so presumably the play had been revised and relicensed, but even so, the unavoidable implication is that playwrights currently employed by the Admiral's Men were producing precious little to excite audiences and so the Company had to dredge up, and dress up, an old standby. *Alexander and Lodowick*, marked 'ne' on 14 January, was 'ne' again on 11 February (see no. 50), which may mean that the play had been fully revised, relicensed and reproduced. The erratic playing schedule at the end of November gave way to more regular performances after mid-December, but the Company was still repeating plays with deadening frequency. The repertoire was bound to go stale if new plays were not taking off. Disappointing receipts over these weeks perhaps explain why the Company's borrowing stretched on (see no. 48). Again, competition from Langley's playhouse may have been responsible for dark days at the Rose, particularly if Hunsdon's Men, soon to reclaim their more prestigious title when their patron assumed his father's office as Lord Chamberlain, were playing the Swan and new plays by Shakespeare. The Admiral's Men did not appear at Court this year: another dismal sign. Every royal performance was given by the Chamberlain's Men. In the accounts, the hiatus between 15 and 25 November is no sure indication that the Company was not performing, for there is evidence that Henslowe had taken to entering his receipts in batches, and the gap after the 15 November entry, which comes near the bottom of a page, is exactly the space he would have required to enter a batch of ten titles that he either neglected or lost. However, a new account heading, 'beginynge the 25 of november' stands at the top of the next page. If the receipts run continuously, that is, if there were no ten-day interruption, one wonders why Henslowe found it necessary to write this new heading.

In the name of god Amen
begynynge one simone & Jewdes daye
my lord admeralles men as ffoloweth

1596

27 of october 1596	Rd at chynon	lij *s*
28 of october 1595	Rd at doctore foster	xxvij *s*

29 of october 1596	Rd at the frenshe docter	xv *s*
1 of novmber 1596	Rd at longe meage ... al holanday	xxxxvij *s*
2 of novmber 1595	Rd at chinone of Ingland	xvij *s*
3 of novmber 1596	Rd at the cnacke to knowe	xv *s*
4 of novmber 1596	Rd at the doctor fostes	xvij *s*
5 of novmber 1596	Rd at longe meage	v *s*
6 of novmber 1596	Rd at the beager	xxx *s*
8 of novmber 1596	——Rd at the toye	xiij *s*
9 of novmber 1596	Rd at the frenshe docter	xiiij *s*
10 of novmber 1596	Rd at chinon	x *s*
11 of novmber 1596	Rd at the vij dayes	xxxv *s*
12 of novmber 1596	Rd at the beager	xvj *s*
13 of novmber 1596	Rd at tambercame	xvij *s*
15 of novmber 1596	——Rd at the vij dayes	xij *s*

In the name of god amen beginynge the
25 of novemb*e*r 1596 as foloweth
the lord admerall players

25 of novmber 1596	Rd at long meage	xj *s*
26 of novmber 1596	Rd at weake	xvij *s*
27 of novmber 1596	Rd at the toye	xj *s*
2 of desember 1596	Rd at the beager	xx *s*
4 of desember 1596	—ne-Rd at valteger	l *s*
8 of desember 1596	——Rd at valteger	xxxv *s*
10 of desember 1596	Rd at the beager	x *s*
11 of desember 1596	—ne-Rd at stewtley	xxxx *s*
12 of desember 1596	Rd at the vij dayes	ix *s*
14 of desember 1596	——Rd at stewtley	xxxx *s*
16 of desember 1596	Rd at valteger	xxxv *s*
17 of desember 1596	Rd at *d*octerfostes	ix *s*
19 of desember 1596	—ne-Rd at nabucadonizer	xxx *s*
21 of desember 1596	Rd at valt*e*ger	xxv *s*
22 of desember 1596	Rd at nabucadonizer	xxvj *s*
23 of desember 1596	Rd at the beager	iij *s*
24 of desember 1596	Rd at valteger	xij *s*
27 of desember 1596	*crisma*s day Rd at nab*u*cadonizer	iij *li* viij *s*
28 of desember 1596	Rd at stewtley	iij *li* iiij *s*
29 of desember 1596	Rd at valteger	xxij *s*

[Receipts continue to July 1597]

50. 1 February–22 March 1597. Rose Playhouse Receipts (extracts).

This is a sample of Henslowe's new accounting system (see no. 49). After the 12 February entry Henslowe drew a line across the page. A two-week interruption followed. He had entered 'Shrove mvnday' and 'Shrove tewesday' in the margin against 7 and 8 February, so the gap might be explained as a general restraint in observation of Lent. It is much more likely, however, that only the Admiral's Men were affected, and that the closure was forced upon them by crippling internal problems. Some time during February two of the Company's leading players – Thomas Downton and Richard Jones – defected and joined a newly organised Pembroke's Men who had just moved into Langley's Swan (the Chamberlain's Men having gone elsewhere) and who opened around 21 February. How the remaining Admiral's Men responded to the defection can be gauged by Henslowe's receipts list when after the fortnight hiatus the records resume on 3 March opposite Henslowe's marginal note, 'begynyng in leant'. (This note would seem to discount the argument that the Rose had closed for Lent on 12 February.) The calendar shows that the Company had replaced their absent colleagues in a full schedule of old productions and were able to open a new play on 19 March. They played mostly alternate days through March and closed for Easter week, which, if any official restraint had been ordered, would have been the obvious time. By April the schedule returned to normal. The daily receipts continue through July; as usual, Henslowe marked performance weeks, new plays, and payments to the Master of the Revels.

ffebreary	01	tt at womones hard to pleasse	01	05	02	11–02
1597	2	tt at what wilbe shalbe	01	18	01	03–00
Candle-maseday	3	tt at oserycke	01	09	03	02–01
	4	tt at womon hard to pleasse	01	08	04	03–00
	5	tt at valteger	01	09	05	13–09
Shrove mvnday	7 ———	tt at oserycke	00	14	07	16–00
Shrove tewesday	8	tt at womon hard to please	01	09	01	02–01
	9	tt at Joronymo	00	17	04	15–02
	10	tt at stewtley	00	18	01	01–00
	11 —ne-tt	at elexsander & lodwecke	03	05	00	17–00
	12	tt at elexsander & lodwicke	01	14	09	13–00

begynyng	3	tt at what wilbe shalbe	oo	o9	oo	16–oo
in leant	5	tt at elexsander & lodwicke	o1	15	oo	13–oo
marche 1597	7 ——tt at A womon hard to pleasse		o1	o5	o6	o2–o1
	8	tt at JoRonymo	o1	o1	oo	o3–o4
[not pd]	9	tt at lodwicke	o1	16	o7	o4–oo
	12	tt at valteger	oo	18	o9	o1–o4
pd	14 ——tt at the beager		oo	18	o3	oo–oo
	15	tt at stewtley	o1	o5	oo	oo–oo
	19 —ne–tt at gvido		o2	oo	oo	o3–o1
	20	tt at elexsander & lodwicke	oo	17	oo	o4–o2
	21	tt at nabucadnazer	oo	o5	oo	oo–o3
	22	tt at gvido	o1	o4	oo	o3–oo

[Receipts continue to July 1597]

51. 3 June 1597. Stage Plot.

The Admiral's Men played *Frederick and Basilea* for the first time on 3 June; this plot almost certainly belongs to that performance, for on 18 July, Martin Slater – Theodore in this production – left the Company. A stage plot outlined a play's entrances and gave some stage directions. It was copied, in studiously legible handwriting, on heavy paper about the weight of modern poster board, and was hung backstage. It served as a road map through the production for players who performed different plays, with several doubles, every day of the week and who must have found it necessary to check their stage movements frequently. The casting requirements of this play stretched the Company's resources to the limits: even the gatherers – the men and women who collected admission money at the playhouse doors – were brought on stage to make up the numbers. Major casting was distributed as follows: Prologue, Frederick: Richard Allen; King: Edward Juby; Basilea: 'Dick'; Sebastian: Edward Alleyn; Theodore: Martin Slater; Myronhamec: Thomas Towne. James Tunstall doubled as the Governor and the Fryer; Thomas Hunt and Black Dick (reinforced by the gatherers) covered the servant/attendant/messenger parts; Charles Massey played a Moor and Thamar; Sam Rowley was Heraclius. The other major woman's role, Leonora, was played by another boy apprentice, 'Will'. 'Griffin', as Anthanasia, and 'Ed. Dutton his boy' (i.e., the boy player apprenticed to Dutton) each appeared in one scene, but Pigg, Edward Alleyn's boy, took a man's role, Andreo, in this production. The remaining parts (Phillipo, Pedro, lords, gaolers) were filled by 'Ledbetter', Dutton, and members of the Company as available. The play *Frederick and Basilea* does not survive. Mistakes the playhouse scribe made in the plot and later crossed out have been placed in square brackets.

THE PLOTT OF FFREDERICK & BASILEA

Enter Prologue: Richard Alleine

Enter Frederick Kinge: Mr Jubie R Allenn To them
Basilea seruant Black Dick, Dick.

Enter Gouernor Athanasia Moore: Mr Dunstann. Griffen
Charles, To them Heraclius Seruants. Tho: hunt black Dick

Enter Leonora, Sebastian, Theodore, Pedro, Philippo Andreo
Mr Allen, well, Mr Martyn. Ed. Dutton. ledbeter, Pigg:
To them King frederick Basilea Guarde. Mr. Juby. R Allen
Dick Tho. Hunt, black Dick.

Enter Myron=hamec, lords. Tho: Towne. Tho Hunt ledbeter
To them Heraclius, Thamar, Sam Charles.

Enter Gouernor Mr Dunstann, To hym Messenger Th: Hunt
To them Heraclius Sam, To them Myranhamec goliors

Enter ffrederick, Basilea, R Allen Dick, To them Kinge
Mr Jubie To them Messenger Black Dick, To them
Sebastian, Heraclius, Theodore, Pedro, Philippo Andreo
Thamar. Mr Allen, Sam: Mr Martyn. leadb: Dutton Pigg.
To them Leonora, Will,

Enter ffrederick Basilea, R Allen: Dick. To them
Philippo, Duttonn, To her King ffrederick, Mr Jubie
R Allenn:

Enter, Myron=hamec Sebastian, Pedroe lords
Tho: Towne. Mr Allenn, ledbeter. Attendaunts

Enter King Theodore ffrederick, Mr Jubie, Mr Martyn
R Allenn. To them Philipo Basilea E Dutton his boye Guard
Tho: Hunt. [Black Dick] Gatherers. To them messenger
Black Dick. To them Sebastian Myron=hamec
leonora Pedroe Andreo. Mr Allen: Tho Towne
will: Leadbeter Pigg guard gatherers.

Enter ffrederick Basilea To them Pedro confederates
Robt: leadb: Black Dick Gatherers.

Enter ffrederick Guard. Mr Juby R Allen
Th: [Tow] Hunt &c. To them Sebastian [leonora]
Theodore Myranhamec Guard Mr Allen. Martyn
To them Pedro Basilea vpon the walls. come downe
Pedro Basilea. Ledb: Dick.

Enter Theodore Andreo. Mr Martyn Pigg To hym
Thamar Heraclius Sam charles.

Enter ffrederick, Basilea, ffryer, R Allen: Dick
Mr Dunstann.

Enter Heraclius, Thamar, Andreo, Sam. Charles
Pigg. To them ffryer. Mr Dunstann, To them
Theodore Martynn

Enter ffrederick Basilea R Allen. Dick, To them
ffryer Mr Dunstann, To them Heraclius Sam

Enter Leonora Myronhamec, Sebastian Goliores
Will: Mr Towne, Mr Allen. Tho Hunt black Dick

To the queen Theodore Martynn.

Enter Heraclius Thamar sam charles To him
Theodore ffryer Dunstan Martynn To them
[... line missing ...]

Enter King Basilea ffrederick messenger
Mr Juby R Allen Dick Black Dick. To them
Sebastian Leonora Myronhamec Thamar Goliors
Mr Allen will Tho Towne Charles. Tho: Hunt
Black Dick gatherers.

Epilogs R Allenn Finis:/

52. 28 July 1597. Letter.

Documents nos. 52, 53 and 54 must be read alongside one another because
they deal with a problematic and consistently misinterpreted period in the
history of the Elizabethan playhouse. July was a troubled month at the
Rose. Two Admiral's Men had left the Company in the spring (see no.

Documents of the Rose Playhouse

50); another departed now. Henslowe noted in the margin of his receipts accounts, 'marten slather went for the company of my lord admeralles men the 18 of July 1597', and thereafter, until the 28th, he recorded only three performances. Then the daily receipts entries stop. That same day, the Lord Mayor and Court of Aldermen issued the following letter, a redraft of previous statements (see nos. 13, 33 and 40). It is merely a coincidence, though a vexing one, that this letter bears the same date as the following document, the Privy Council's order that all the London playhouses were to be plucked down, for the accident of a date has misled historians of the playhouse into supposing that the lords were acting upon the Mayor's demands. The letter contains only one novel appeal, and it is a strange, if ingenious, one: that plays are to be abolished in London because they are 'Contrary to the rules & art prescribed for the makinge of Comedies eaven amonge the Heathen'.

Our humble dutyes remembred to your good Lordships & the rest. Wee haue signifyed to your Honors many tymes heartofore the great inconvenience which wee fynd to grow by the Common exercise of Stage Playes. Wee presumed to doo aswell in respect of the dutie wee beare towardes her highnes for the good gouernment of this her Citie, as for conscience sake, beinge perswaded (vnder correction of your Honors judgment) that neither in politie nor in religion they are to be suffered in a Christian Commonwealth, specially beinge of that frame & matter as vsually they are, conteining nothinge but prophane fables, lascivious matters, cozeninge devises, & scurrilus beehaviours, which are so set forth as that they move wholie to imitation & not to the auoydinge of those faults & vices which they represent. Amonge other inconveniences it is not the least that they give opportunity to the refuze sort of euill disposed & vngodly people that are within and abowte this Cytie to assemble themselves & to make their matches for all their lewd & vngodly practices; being as heartofore wee haue fownd by th'examination of divers apprentices & other seruantes whoe have confessed vnto vs that the said Staige playes were the very places of theire Randevous appoynted by them to meete with such otheir as wear to joigne with them in theire designes & mutinus attemptes, beeinge allso the ordinarye places for maisterles men to come together & to recreate themselves. ffor avoyding wheareof wee are now againe most humble & earnest sutours to your honours to dirrect your lettres aswell to our selves as to the Justices of peace of Surrey & Midlesex for the present staie & fynall suppressinge of the saide Stage playes, as well at the Theatre Curten and banckside as in all other places in and abowt the Citie, Wheareby wee doubt not but th'opportunitie & the very cause of many disorders beinge taken away, wee shalbee more able to keepe the worse sort of such evell & disordered people in better order then heartofore wee haue been. And so most humbly wee take our leaves. From London the xxviijth of Julie. 1597.

Your *Honors* most humble.

The inconueniences
that grow by Stage
playes abowt the
Citie of London.

1. They are a speaciall cause of corrupting their Youth, conteninge nothinge but vnchast matters, lascivious devices, shiftes of Coozenage, & other lewd & vngodly practizes, being so as that they impresse the very qualitie & corruption of manners which they represent Contrary to the rules & art prescribed for the makinge of Comedies eaven amonge the Heathen, who vsed them seldom & at certen sett tymes, and not all the year longe as our manner is. Whearby such as frequent them beinge of the base & refuze sort of people or such young gentlemen as haue small regard of credit or conscience, drawe the same into imitacion and not to the avoidinge the like vices which they represent.

2. They are the ordinary places for vagrant persons, Maisterles men, thieves, horse stealers, whoremongers, Coozeners, Cony-catchers, contrivers of treason, and other idele and daungerous persons to meet together & to make theire matches to the great displeasure of Almightie God & the hurt & annoyance of her *Maiesties* people, which cannot be prevented nor discovered by the Gouernours of the Citie for that they are owt of the Citiees jurisdiction.

3. They maintaine idlenes in such persons as haue no vocation & draw apprentices and other seruantes from theire ordinary workes and all sortes of people from the resort vnto sermons and other Christian exercises to the great hinderance of traides & prophanation of religion established by her highnes within this Realm.

4. In the time of sicknes it is fownd by experience, that many hauing sores and yet not hart sicke take occasion hearby to walk abroad & to recreat themselves by heareinge a play. Whearby others are infected, and them selves also many things [*sic* for 'times'?] miscarry.

53. 28 July 1597. Privy Council Minute.

This manuscript is one of the most enigmatic of all documents relating to the Elizabethan playhouse. Year after year, the Privy Council received the Court of Aldermen's demands for the closure of the playhouses, and year after year they disregarded them, issuing instead their own restraints as necessary, usually during the summer months when outbreaks of plague could be expected. This year the lords made a sharp *volte face*: when they issued their standard injunction, they linked it to an order that all the playhouses in and around London should summarily be pulled down. The order was signed by eight members of the Council, most notably the Lord Admiral, the Lord Chamberlain and Mr Secretary Cecil. The order cannot have been made in sympathy with the Lord Mayor's letter dated the same day (no. 52) for the Privy Council could not have received it before writing their own letter. Unless, of course, the Aldermen had felt the contents of their letter so pressing as to have sent a messenger post haste from Guildhall to Greenwich, where the lords were convened. Nothing in the letter suggests such urgency; rather, the matter seems to have been purely routine. No mention is made of any specific outrage or cause of concern; indeed, parts of the letter are copied word for word from earlier drafts, drafts that had produced no effect whatsoever. Moreover, the Court of Aldermen's meeting on 28 July was a regular session, their only business to swear in a new alderman and to post the letter of complaint. Thereafter they adjourned until 28 August. Evidently, they were not waiting for the lords to reply, perhaps knowing that they could not expect much co-operation because they were already out of favour with the Council over musters for the current expedition against Spain: only ten days earlier they had been severely rebuked for failure to supply the requisite numbers of soldiers. What then prompted the Privy Council's extraordinary com-mandment, a commandment which in fact was not enforced? That, too, is an enigma whose explanation is complicated by the events of the following week: on 8 or 9 August, Richard Topcliffe, the veteran recusant hunter and infamous torturer, wrote to Mr Secretary Cecil that he had received information about a seditious play, later named as *The Isle of Dogs*, and that he had arrested three men, the playwright Ben Jonson and two players, Gabriel Spencer and Robert Shaa. The arrests must have been made on 7 or 8 August. Topcliffe himself did not know much about the matter; he was relying upon his informant's evidence. In a vaguely worded letter of 15 August (no. 54), the Privy Council – no doubt acting upon Robert Cecil's instructions – gave Topcliffe authority to investigate. But what seems quite clear from this series of events is that the assumption most theatre historians have taken as an article of faith – that a perform-ance of *The Isle of Dogs* so infuriated the Privy Council that they acted in co-operation with the Court of Aldermen and ordered the playhouses demolished – is untenable. In fact, the Council seems not to have known of the play's existence until 15 August. The play text is lost. It is impossible to reconstruct its contents – a fact too many writers have ignored. But it is less likely that the matter was 'sedycioos', as Topcliffe claimed, than that the whole charge was trumped up by a necessitous informant anxious to ingratiate himself, for although the Privy Council ordered interroga-tions, the accusations were quietly dropped some weeks later. Jonson, Shaa and Spencer were released on 3 October. While such narrow mazes were being trod at Court, men of the playhouse put their own construc-tions on events: before 10 August, Henslowe had made no connection between the ill-fated performance and the restraint, but in a Diary entry that day he linked them. He was wrong, but probably drew that conclusion because the arrests had just been made (see no. 55). Thomas Nashe, one of the collaborating playwrights who fled London and Topcliffe when he learned his rooms had been searched, wrote ruefully about the event two years later (see no. 54). Of the Privy Council's order of 28 July nothing more was heard. No playhouses were pulled down; when playing resumed in October, only Langley's Swan, refused a licence, remained shut. This tracing of events does nothing to illuminate the Privy Council's method or madness in issuing an order they seem not to have intended should be carried out.

———

A lettre to Robert Wrothe, William ffleetwood, John Barne, Thomas ffowler and Richard Skevington, Esquires, and the rest of the Justices of middlesex nerest to London. Her Maiestie being informed that there are verie greate disorders committed in the common playhouses both by lewd matters that are handled on the stages and by resorte and confluence of bad people, hathe given direction that not onlie no plaies shalbe used within London or about the Citty or in any publique place during this tyme of sommer, But that also those play houses that are erected and built only for suche purposes shalbe plucked downe namelie the Curtayne and the Theatre nere to Shorditch or any other within that County. Theis are therfore in her Maiesties name to Chardge and Commaund you that you take present order there be no more plaies used in any publique place within three myles of the Citty untill Alhallowtide next and likewyse that you do send for the owners of the Curtayne, Theatre or anie other common playhouse, and Injoyne them by vertue hereof forthwith to plucke downe quite the stages, Gallories and Roomes that are made for people to stand in, and so to deface the same as they maie not be ymploied agayne to suche use, which yf they shall not speedely performe you shall advertyse us that order maie be taken to see the same don according to her Maiesties pleasure and commaundment. And hereof praying you not to faile, we, &c.

The like to Mr Bowier, William Gardyner and Bartholomew Scott, Esquires and the rest of the Justices of Surrey; Requiring them to take the like order for the playhouses on the Banckside, in Southwarke or elswhere in the said county within iij^e miles of London.

54. 15 August 1597. Privy Council Minute.

This letter, which gave Richard Topcliffe authority to interrogate players apprehended in *The Isle of Dogs* affair, is suspiciously vague: evidently, the Privy Council did not know the names of the players, the play, or the playhouse in which it had been performed. Vague, too, is the phrase 'wee caused some of the Players to be apprehended', for only by stretching a point could the Council claim to have 'caused' arrests that Topcliffe, without their knowledge, had made days earlier. It was not until Topcliffe informed Robert Cecil, both of the 'mutynous' events and the arrested players, that Cecil alerted the rest of the lords. The playwright Nashe, whose rooms were searched and papers confiscated, probably had no reason to fear interrogation: the charge of sedition was groundless and was ultimately dropped. But Nashe had been a friend of Marlowe's and knew how Kyd had been tortured in connection with that shadowy investigation (see no. 25) by 'the cruellest Tyrant of all England, Topcliffe, a man most infamous and hatefull to all the realm for his bloody and butcherly mind'. Jittery nerves caused Nashe to flee to Yarmouth where, still bewildered, he wrote of the 'straunge turning of the Ile of Dogs, from a commedie to a tragedie two summers past'. The play, he said, was 'an infortunate imperfit Embrion' which he protested he did not father: 'hauing begun but the induction and first act of it, the other foure acts without my consent, or the least guesse of my drift or scope, by the players were supplied, which bred both theire trouble and mine to'.

——

A *lettre* to Richard Topclyfe, Thomas ffowler and Ri*ch*ard Skevington, esqu*ires*, doct*our* ffletcher and mr. Wilbraham. Vppon Informac*ion* given us of a lewd plaie that was plaied in one of the plaie howses on the Bancke side contaynge very seditious and sclanderous matter, wee caused some of the Players to be apprehended and comytted to pryson; whereof one of them was not only an Actor, but a maker of p*arte* of the said Plaie; ffor as moche as yt ys thought meete that the rest of the Players or Actors in that matter shalbe apprehended to receave soche punyshment as theire leude and mutynous behavior doth deserve; These shalbe therefore to Re*quire* you to examine those of the plaiers that are comytted, whose names are knowne to you, mr. Topclyfe, what ys become of the rest of there fellowes that either had theire p*artes* in the devysinge of that sedytious matter, or that were Actors or plaiers in the same, what copies they have given forth of the said playe, and to whome, and soch other pointes as you shall thincke meete to be demaunded of them, wherein you shall re*quire* them to deale trulie as they will looke to receave anie favour. wee praie you also to p*eruse soch papers as were fownde in Nash his lodgings, which Ferrys a messenger of the Chamber shall delyver vnto you, And to certyfie vs th'examynac*ions* you take. So, &c.

55. July–August 1597. Players' Bonds.

Before the 28 July inhibition fell, attempts were being made to replace personnel the Admiral's Men had lost when Downton and Jones defected and Martin Slater retired. Henslowe negotiated a two-year contract with one Thomas Herne to serve the Company as a hired man at set wages per week. The bond was entered in the Diary on 27 July. The next day, the Privy Council ordered playing restrained until All Hallows (1 November) and all the London playhouses demolished. Henslowe behaved as though he had not heard the news or did not believe it: he signed a contract with John Helle, 'the clowne', on 3 August, stipulating that he was 'to contenew with me at my howsse in playnge tylle srafte tyd next'. On whose authority Henslowe was acting in these negotiations is unclear: he referred to 'my company' and said the men were 'to searve me'; moreover, Henslowe signed all the witnesses' names, so what looks like company authorisation is spurious, falling short of forgery only in that Henslowe made no attempt to imitate the players' handwriting. This means that the Company may not even have been privy to the bonds. Throughout August Henslowe continued to defy or to remain undeterred by the Privy Council. He wrote out more bonds, dating them 'from mihelmase next' (29 September) as though oblivious even to the lords' order that playing was not to resume until All Hallows. In the next three bonds, it becomes evident that the Admiral's Men were picking up the pieces of the company – Pembroke's Men – that had been shattered by the debacle at Langley's Swan. Richard Jones and Robert Shaa were the first to bind themselves. Jones had been with the Admiral's Men until the spring defection, and he may have signed for Shaa because Shaa was unavailable: in hiding, perhaps, or already arrested with Jonson and Spencer by Topcliffe and his henchmen. If Jones failed to give Henslowe his friend's current address as the Marshalsea, his neglect is understandable: all the companies would be panicked when they heard the news of Topcliffe on the prowl against players, and Pembroke's unfortunate players would be scrambling for jobs – they certainly could not expect to return to the Swan. In this climate, who would want to contract an accused player? Four days later, another refugee from the Swan, William Bird or Borne, signed on with the Admiral's Men, possibly having brought Henslowe news of the arrests. Only then did Henslowe connect 'this Re straynt' to the 'playinge' of 'the Iellye of dooges'. Again, Henslowe signed for the witnesses. Just how binding these agreements were on the Company is therefore debatable. Henslowe may have been acting purely out of self-interest, his object not to meddle with the Company's internal management but to proffer some tough-looking, though ineffectual, gesture as a landlord to ensure that his playhouse would not stand empty as Langley's was. The sum of the forfeiture – either £40 or 100 marks – was an enormous figure, but less than half the amount Langley required Pembroke's Men to put their names to in bonds at the Swan (see no. 59). An assumpsit (rendered '& asumsette' or 'a somsette' by Henslowe) is a promise or contract.

Memorandom that the 27 of Jeuley 1597 I heayred Thomas hearne with
ijd pence for to searve me ij yeares in the qualetie of playenge for fyue
shellynges a weacke for one yeare & vjs viijd for the other yeare which he
hath couenanted hime seallfe to searue me & not to departe frome my
compane y tyll this ij yeares be eanded wittnes to this

       John synger
       Jeames donston
       thomas towne

lent John Helle the clowne the 3 of aguste 1597 in Redey money the some
of ....xs
at that tyme I bownd hime by ane a sumsett of ijd to contenew with me at
my howsse in playnge tylle srafte tyd next after the date a boue written yf
not to forfytte vnto me fortipowndes wittneses to the same

  EAlleyn   John synger   Jeames donstall
  edward Jubey samewell Rowley

Memorandom that the 6 of aguste 1597 I bownd Richard Jones by & a
sumsett of ijd to contenew & playe with the company of my lord admeralles players frome mihelmase next after the daye a bowe written vntell
the eand & tearme of iij yeares emediatly folowinge & to playe in my
howsse only knowne by the name of the Rosse & in no other howse a
bowt london publicke & yf Restraynte be granted then to go for the tyme
into the contrey & after to retorne agayne to london yf he breacke this a
sumsett then to forfett vnto me for the same a hundreth markes of lafull
money of Ingland wittnes to this EAlleyn & John midelton

more over Richard Jones at that tyme hathe tacken one other ijd of me
vpon & asumset to forfet vnto me one hundrethe markes yf one Robart
shaee do not playe with my lordes admeralles men as he hath covenanted
be fore in euery thinge & tyme to the oter meste wittnes/EAlleyn/John
              midellton/

Memorandom that the 10 of aguste 1597 william borne came & ofered
hime sealfe to come and playe with my lord admeralles mean at my
howsse called by the name of the Rosse setewate one the back after this
order folowinge he hathe Receued of me iijd vpon & A sumsette to
forfette vnto me a hundrethe marckes of lafull money of Ingland yf he do
not performe thes thinges folowinge that is presentley after libertie beinge
granted for playinge to come & to playe with my lorde admeralles men at
my howsse aforsayd & not in any other howsse publicke a bowt london
for the space of iij yeares beginynge Imediatly after this Re straynt is
Recaled by the lordes of the cownsell which Restraynt is by the menes of
playinge the Ieylle of dooges yf he do not then he forfettes this asumset
afore or ells not wittnes to this

        EAlleyn & Robsone

56. 3 October 1597. Privy Council Warrant.

Spencer, Shaa and Jonson had been detained since 8 August. Upon release they joined the Admiral's Men.

———

A warrant to the Keeper of the Marshalsea to release Gabriell Spencer and Robert Shaa Stage players, out of prison, who were of lat comitted to his custodie.

The like warrant for releasing of Benjamin Johnson.

57. 6 October 1597. Player's Bond.

Thomas Downton had been a member of the Admiral's Men but had left the Company the previous February to join the Swan venture. Henslowe signed for the witnesses.

———

*Memoran*dom that the 6 of octob*er* 1597 Thomas dowten came & bownd hime seallfe vnto me in xxxx *li* in & a somesett by the Receuing of iij *d* of me before wittnes the covenant is this that he shold frome t*h*e daye a bove written vntell sr*a*f*t*id next come ij yeares to playe in my howsse & in no other a bowte London pvblickeley yf he do w*i*th owt my consent to forfet vnto me this some of money a bove writt*e*n wittnes to this

EAlleyn	Robarte shawe
Wm borne	John synger
dick*e* Jonnes	

58. 11 October–30 December 1597. Rose Playhouse Receipts.

In spite of the Privy Council's July ultimatum, Henslowe's playhouse was not only standing but was open for business in the second week of October – closer to Michaelmas, Henslowe's date in the players' bonds, than to All Hallows, the lords' date for lifting their restraint. Shaa, Spencer and Jonson had been released from prison barely a week earlier and had joined the Admiral's Men. For a few days after the Company resumed playing, Henslowe recorded receipts in his familiar five-column format but then went over to a new system of entering only weekly totals. One consequence of his decision for modern readers is that the Diary no longer provides a calendar of play titles and performance dates. Playing in these first weeks was erratic, but the wonder is that plays were staged at all, for if Downton joined the Company around 6 October and the hapless trio who performed in Topcliffe's farce arrived soon after the 3rd, a third of the Admiral's Men would have been available for only ten days' rehearsal before opening on the 11th. The repertoire was as unsettled as the Company. Plays from the separate schedules were recast. *Hardicanute* and *Bourbon* transferred from the Pembroke repertoire, and *Friar Spendleton* was a new play altogether. That this patched up company whose feet were not yet steady underneath them would attempt a new production while trying to reconstruct several old productions says as much about the cold facts of playhouse economics as about their pluck: audiences might be sympathetic to their plight in the past months but would not rush to see old plays, even if the beards were stuck on different faces, for audiences demanded novelty. There were many more demands than guarantees in this profession; specifically, there were no guarantees that amalgamations would work out, even though in this case Henslowe had tried to manufacture some in binding the refugee players to forfeitures so exorbitant as to be ludicrous (see no. 55). His cooler judgement upon the partnership was perhaps expressed in his account heading where he styled the companies separately, 'my lord admeralles & my lord of penbrocke'. In the Diary, the two series of receipts produced below are entered on pages remote from each other; here, they are juxtaposed because where they overlap they may provide someone a clue for breaking Henslowe's so-far impenetrable five-column accounting code. The weekly totals, on the face of it, appear less puzzling, yet it still remains to discover what they mean: did they simply replace Henslowe's daily entry of his receipts, turning his laborious accounting system into a neat weekly reckoning of his share in the galleries, or had Henslowe abandoned entering his receipts altogether and were these weekly amounts repayments against the Company's debt handed over in sums the Admiral's Men could afford week by week? If so, what was their source? From what pocket was the Company removing this money? Answers can be found to these questions only by turning years ahead in the Diary. From July 1598 forward Henslowe collected weekly payments from the players which he described as 'the wholle gallereys' (see no. 69). In October 1599 he totalled those 'wholle gallereys' as '358 – 03 – 00' and declared that, having 'Reconed with the company ... yt doth a peare that I haue Receued of the deate which they owe vnto me iij hunderd fiftie & eyght pownds'. That is, he figured the entire £358 against the debt, which means that by 'wholle gallereys' Henslowe was referring to the *players'* entire share in the gallery money, for had it included his own share, he would have subtracted that portion before arriving at the Company's reckoning. Those 'whole gallereys' that are reproduced as document 69 look very much like the weekly receipts below – doubled. Perhaps, then, from 21 October 1597 to 8 July 1598 (see nos. 61 and 67) the Admiral's Men were repaying debts to Henslowe by handing over half of their gallery money on a weekly basis, and he, having discontinued his daily receipts accounts, entered that amount instead. Thus, to calculate the entire weekly gallery at the Rose in these months one would multiply the receipts below by four; to arrive at the analogue to Henslowe's daily receipts (which, it will be remembered, were equal shares of the gallery money with the players) figured as a weekly total, one would multiply by two. In the week of 21 October, then, Henslowe would have taken over £10 in receipts from the Rose in addition to collecting some £5 from the Company against their debt.

———

the xj of october	11	tt at Joroneymo	[illegible] 01-13-00
be gane my lord admerals & my		tt at the comodey of vmers	[illegible] 00-19-0
lord of penbrockes men to playe at		tt at docter fostes	o.
my howsse 1597		tt at	
		tt at	
	19	tt at	
		tt at hardicute	00 16 00-00-1-
october	31-ne-	tt at fryer spendelton	02 00 01-014-00
november 1597	2	tt at burbon	00 16 30-12-00
	3	tt at knewtus	00 10 00-14-00
	4	tt at vmers	00 16 03-00-14
the mr payde the	5	tt at fryer spendelton	00 14 01-14-00
26 of novmber 1597 for iiij weckes the some of xxxxs			

A Juste a cownte of all Suche monye
as I haue Receued of my lord
admeralles & my lord of penbrocke men
as foloweth be gynynge the 21 of october 1597

Rd the 21 of october 1597	v li j s xj d
Rd the 28 of october 1597	iij li xj s x d
Rd the 30 of october 1597	iij li
Rd the 5 of novmber 1597	lviij s x d
Rd the 12 of novmber 1597	xxxxvij s
Rd the 19 of novmber 1597	xxxxviij s viij d
Rd the 26 of novmber 1597	xxxxiiij s
Rd the 3 of desember 1597	xxxxiiij s
Rd the 10 of desember 1597	xxvj s

Rd the 17 of desember 1597   xxxxix *s*
Rd the 30 of desember 1597 binge crysmas weacke   vij *li* xvj *s*

59. 11 October–28 December 1597. Loan Account.

The newly amalgamated company, named individually in this account
heading and styled collectively 'my lord admeralles players', opened their
season at the Rose by asking their landlord for money. Henslowe began
entering the loans in his typically unsystematic fashion on folio 37 of the
Diary, but when in December he was still lending the Company money,
he must have realised the arrangement was to be more permanent than he
had allowed for. He turned to empty territory in his Diary, wrote a formal
account heading, transcribed all the entries from f. 37, and continued with
more loans. Why the Company required the loans is obvious from a check
of Henslowe's weekly receipts (see no. 58). But why the receipts should
have fallen so disastrously at a time when the Swan was offering no
competition is probably to be explained by the fact that the Company had
lost its principal player and star attraction with audiences; Edward Alleyn
had retired. Although Alleyn continued to live among the players on the
Bankside and to witness their transactions with Henslowe, he had left the
Admiral's Men, possibly while the amalgamation was solidifying (he is
not named among the players in the account heading below), but certainly
by December. Into retirement with Alleyn went a group of plays he had
made famous: *Tamar Cham*, *The Jew of Malta*, *Faustus*. This meant that
the new Admiral's Men had to replace not just a player but a repertoire.
The loan accounts show them doing precisely that. They bought plays by
Munday, Drayton, and 'yonge harton' – William Haughton – and, having
seen Ben Jonson's 'plotte', commissioned a play from him 'w*h*ich he
promysed to *deliver* vnto the company at cryssmas' three weeks later.
Branholt and *Alice Pierce*, named in costume payments around the first
week of December, were new plays probably set to open in the following
week, for by the time costumes were purchased a play was in the final
stages of production. Another payment for a costume that might have
been intended either for *Alice* or *Branholt* raises interesting speculation.
When Henslowe originally entered the 1 December expenditure for
'bornes gowne' on f. 37, he described it as 'for bornes womones gowne'.
William Borne (or Bird) was an adult player, and if he took a woman's
role, perhaps even the leading woman's role, in one of those new plays,
this stray reference in a costume payment may open up the possibility that
female roles were not monopolised by boy players. It is impossible to
guess how many of the other 'gownes' Henslowe recorded were like
'bornes womones gowne', but it is not difficult to imagine casting men in
preference to boys in many female roles: Shakespeare's Volumnia, Juliet's

Nurse, Cleopatra, Lady Macbeth, Paulina, and Mistresses Overdone and Quickly are cases in point. Outside the accounts, several events would have affected the Company. On 22 October, their patron Charles Howard, the Lord Admiral, was created Earl of Nottingham; formally, his company became Nottingham's Men and assumed new prestige, but Nottingham remained Lord Admiral, and the Company remained the Admiral's Men to Henslowe in the Diary. He finally changed their title in 1599. The Company, under whatever name, had certainly not heard the last of Francis Langley, for in November a series of cross suits were filed between the Swan owner and the players, now among the Admiral's Men, who had leaped off his sinking ship and feared reprisals. Shaa, Jones, Downton, Bird and Spencer had all signed bonds to play exclusively at the Swan back in February when they first decided to combine as Pembroke's Men; the forfeitures were each in the sum of £100 to Langley. But after the Privy Council ordered the general restraint of 28 July, and *The Isle of Dogs* subsequently landed Pembroke's Men in particular trouble, and Langley's Swan was refused a licence to reopen in the autumn, the players could hardly honour their contract to Langley. Still, there was the uncomfortable matter of the £100 bonds, and in November the players decided to sue to prevent Langley collecting on what amounted to technical forfeitures. They claimed that, once the July restraint was lifted, they went to Langley 'and offered them selves to playe in the howse of the said De*fendant* according to the Condi*ci*on of their obliga*ci*on', but, learning that the Swan had not been licensed for reopening, 'sayd that they durst not play ... wi*t*hout lycence, And that yt was to their vndoeinge to Contynue in Idlenes And that Phillipp Henslowe ... had obtayned lycens for his hous'. Langley was reported to have replied that the players were 'best to goe to him' – meaning Henslowe. But when they did, they discovered Langley intended to prosecute their bonds. Hence their attempt to block that suit. The players also described a financial arrangement with Langley analogous to the Admiral's Men with Henslowe, whereby Langley disbursed money for costumes and properties and the Company repaid him from receipts. However, when Langley accused them of reneging on payments to the tune of £300, they countercharged him with withholding costumes that belonged to the Company, and even of converting 'the same to his best pro*f*ytt by lending the same to hyre'. Evidently there was some basis to this last accusation, for in September 1598 the Admiral's Men paid £35 in settlement 'A bowt the agrement betwext langley & them', and eventually managed to 'feche home a Riche clocke wh*i*ch they had of mr langleyes'. Even so, the players could hardly have been sincere in claiming that they had offered to resume their playing contract with Langley, for by the time they would have had to have presented themselves to him – as they stated in their suit – they had already bound themselves to play with Henslowe. The cross-fire with Langley continued through the following spring (in March, Henslowe loaned William Bird £1 'to descarge the areaste betwext langley & hime') before being settled in favour of the players that May. In December, the Admiral's Men appeared at Court for one performance, as against three performances by the Chamberlain's Men; not an even showing, but certainly an improvement over the previous Christmas when they did not appear at all. They did not receive payment for this performance until the following December.

———

> A Juste a cownt of All suche money as I haue
> layd owt for my lord admeralles players begynyng
> the xi of october whose names ar as foloweth
> borne gabrell shaw Jonnes dowten Jube towne
> synger & the ij geffes   1597

layd owt vnto Robarte shawe to by a boocke for the companey the 21 of october 1597 the some of called the cobler wittnes   EAlleyn xxxx *s*

lent vnto Robarte shaw to by a boocke of yonge harton the 5 of novmber 1597 the some of
wittnes EAlleyn x *s*

lent vnto Robarte shaw for the company to bye viij yardes of clothe of gowlde for the womones gowne in bran howlte the 26 of novmber 1597 the some of iiij *li*

lent vnto Robarte shawe to geue the tayller to by tynssell for bornes gowne the j of desember 1597 ix *s*

layd owt for the companye to by tafetie & tynssell for the bodeyes of a womones gowne to playe allce perce which I delivered vnto the littell tayller the 8 of desember 1597   wittnes EAlleyn xx *s*

layd owt for mackynge allce perces bodeyes & A payer of yeare sleaues the some of vj *s* vij *d*

lent vnto Bengemen Johnson the 3 of desember 1597 vpon a boocke which he showed the plotte vnto the company which he promysed to dd vnto the company at cryssmas next the some of xx *s*

lent vnto Robart shawe to by copper lace of sylver for a payer

hosse in alls perce the 10 desember 1597 xvj *s*
    wittnes *willia*m borne Jube & gabrell spenser

layd owt for ij gyges for the companey to ij yonge men the 12
of desember 1597 the some of vj *s* 8 *d*

layd owt the 22 of desember 1597 for a boocke called mother
Read cape to antony monday & drayton iij *li*

layd owt the 28 of desember 1597 for the boocke called mother
Read cape to antony mondaye v *s*

60. 8 December 1597. Player's Bond.

Henslowe contracted another hired man (the entry and signature were
written by Alleyn) and 'bowght' a boy player: this meant that William
Augusten, himself a player, was transferring James Bristow's apprenticeship indentures to Henslowe, who would now take over the boy's maintenance and training, though the practical training in the playhouse was
undoubtedly under someone else's hand.

———

*Memorandum tha*t this 8th of december 1597 my father philyp hinchlow
hiered as A Covenaunt servant willyam kendall for ij years after The
statute of winchester *with* ij single penc A to geue hym for his sayd servis
everi week of his playng in london x *s* & in *th*e Cuntrie v *s*: for the which
he covenaunteth for *th*e space of those ij years To be redy att all Tymes to
play in *th*e howse of the sayd philyp & in no other during the sayd Terme
                   wittnes my self the writer
                      of This   EAlleyn
Bowght my boye Jeames brystow of william agusten player the 18 of
desember 1597 for viij *li*

61. 7 January–4 March 1597/8. Rose Playhouse Receipts.

These weekly totals of receipts, which represent half of the players' gallery
money handed over to Henslowe to balance against their loan account,
continue directly from no. 58. Henslowe wrote the figure '65-16-07' at
the foot of this account to total the receipts from October.

———

Rd the 7 of Janeway 1597   xxx *s*
Rd the 14 of Jeneway 1597   l *s*
Rd the 21 of Jeneway 1597   iij *li* ix *s*

Rd the 28 of Janewary 1598   xxviij *s* ix *d*
Rd the 4 of febreary 1598   v *li*
Rd the 11 of febreary 1598   lvj *s* 4 *d*
Rd the 18 of febreary 1598   iij *li* ix *s*
Rd the 25 of febrearye 1598   iiij *li* xv *s*
Rd the 4 of marche 1598   v *li* xj *s* iiij *d*
    li   *s*   *d*
so*m* 65–16–07

62. 5 January–8 March 1597/8. Loan Accounts.

In the same period covered by the weekly receipts accounts (see no. 61), the Admiral's Men borrowed some £34, itemised in the following account and split four ways: £24 15s on plays, £6 9s on costumes, 9s on licences, and £3 on miscellaneous costs. The Company probably bailed Thomas Dekker out of the Counter in the Poultry because they needed him to finish a play for them, and they may have wanted £1 10s 'when they fyrst played dido at nyght' to smarten themselves up for a private performance in the house of a nobleman. These loan accounts provide a wide range of information about the Admiral's Men and about the men who worked for them: the accounts name the non-acting personnel who made wigs, costumes, head tires, properties, beards; they name the Company's playwrights and show with whom they collaborated, how much they were paid, how quickly they worked (Munday finished *Mother Redcap* on 5 January, submitted the finished script of another play, *Robin Hood Part I*, on 15 February, and proposed *Part II* on 20 February); they indicate how the machinery of production worked non-stop (Dekker delivered the final instalment of *Phaeton* on 15 January; the play was probably licensed as one of 'ij boockes' Henslowe mentioned in an undated entry immediately after the 15 January payment; and it was well into production by 26 January when 'a sewte for phayeton' was bought). The patterns of collaboration the loan accounts display are revealing indicators of theatre practice. The playing company commissioned plays by inspecting a plot or a few sheets of writing; thereafter, most playwrights submitted scripts piecemeal, collecting payment in instalments until the last pages were handed over and the standard £6 payment was made in full. This payment system, however, obscures one striking fact, that most plays of the Diary were collaborations. Of the eighty-nine plays whose composition for the Admiral's Men is documented from first instalment to 'pd in full' by Henslowe's entries, fifty-five were collaborations while only thirty-four were single-author plays. Looking at individual entries, though, it is by no means clear whether collaborators are at work or not, since playwrights frequently submitted their contribution independently of the rest of the syndicate, and since some collaborations were *ad hoc* arrangements that organised themselves as the work was in progress. For example: *Robin Hood Part I* in the account below was Munday's sole work, and Munday began the sequel. But on 25 February, Henry Chettle turns up in a payment for that play – an unexpected collaboration. This case is relatively straightforward, but in other instances when as many as five collaborators are contributing instalments and collecting payments, the Diary must be read patiently. It yields the information, but grudgingly. Some syndicates are named in the first instalment and appear together in all subsequent payments; other teams pick up writers along the way; some drop playwrights. Occasionally, dramatists work alone, as Dekker on *Phaeton* and *The Triplicity of Cuckolds*. Syndicate playwriting raises questions about organisation and supervision. How were plots developed and work apportioned? Who was responsible for editing or smoothing the joins between scenes? How was continuity ever achieved, for if playwrights were submitting scenes piecemeal instead of waiting to assemble a full script, would it not have been possible that one collaborator was creating a character, another developing him, and a third killing him off – without ever seeing each other's work? Henslowe's records demonstrate that collaborative playwriting was not forced upon the dramatists out of economic necessity; it was the preferred method of working, possibly because it allowed each playwright to exploit his best talents. By the same token, syndicate playwriting probably explains why some plays of this period are so uneven. The signatures attached to this loan account are autograph and document the membership of the Admiral's Men at this date. Humphrey Jeffes and his brother Antony held a share between them, while Massey and Rowley, hired men in the Company for some three years, had graduated to sharer status. The Admiral's Men appeared at Court in the Shrovetide revels on 28 February, two days after the Chamberlain's Men. They were not paid for this performance until the following December.

———

layd owt for my lord admeralles meane as foloweth 1597
1597

pd vnto antony monday & drayton for the laste payment of the Boocke of mother Readcape the 5 of Jenewary 1597 the some of

lv s

Layd owte for copper lace for the littell boye & for a valle for the boye A geanste the playe of dido & enevs the 3 of Jenewary 1597

xxix s

Lent vnto thomas dowton the 8 of Jeneway 1597 twenty shillinges to by a boockes of mr dickers lent — xx s

lent vnto the company when they fyrst played dido at nyght the
some of thirtishillynges which wasse the 8 of Jenewary 1597 I
saye — xxx s

lent vnto the company the 15 of Jeneway 1597 to bye a boocke
of mr dicker called fayeton fower pownde I saye lent — iiij li

lent vnto Thomas dowton for the company to paye the mr of
the Reuells for lysensynge of ij boockes xiiij s a bated to dowton
v s so Reaste — ix s

lent vnto Thomas dowton for the company to bye a sewte for
phayeton & ij Rebates & j fardengalle the 26 of Jenewary 1598
the some of three pownde I saye lent — iij li

lent vnto Thomas dowton the 28 of Janewary 1598 to bye a
whitte satten dublette for phayeton forty shyllenges I saye lent — xxxx s

lent vnto the companey the 4 of febreary 1598 to dise charge mr
dicker owt of the cownter in the powltrey the some of fortie
shillinges I saye dd to thomas dowton — xxxx s

layd owt vnto antony monday the 15 of febreary 1598 for a
playe boocke called the firste parte of Robyne Hoode — v li

lent vnto Robarte shawe the 18 of febreary 1598 to paye vnto
harton for a comodey called A womon will haue her wille the
some of — xx s

lent vnto thomas dowton the 20 of febreary 1598 to lende vnto
antony mondaye vpon his seconde parte of the downefall of
earlle huntyngton surnamed Roben Hoode I saye lent the some
of — x s

Layd owt vnto Robarte lee the 22 of febreary 1598 for a boocke
called the myller some of — xx s

lent vnto thomas dowton the 25 of febreary 1598 to geue vnto
chettell in part of paymente of the seconde parte of Robart
hoode I saye lent — xx s

Lent vnto antony mondaye the 28 of febreary 1598 in *p*arte of
paymente of the second *p*arte of Roben Hoode   v *s*

lent vnto Thomas dowten & Robart shaw & Jewebey the j of
marche 1598 to bye a boocke of mr dickers called the treplesetie
of cockowlles the some of fyve powndes I say lent   v *li*

Lent vnto Robart shawe the 8 marche 1598 in full payment of
the seconde *p*arte of the booke called the downf*a*ll of Roben
hoode the some of   iij *li* v *s*

JSinger		
P me Thomas Downt*o*n		
P me william Birde		Charles massye
Robt Shaa	Richard Jones	Samuell Rowlye
Gabriell Spenser		
Thomas towne		
Humfry Jeffes		

Thes men dothe a knowlege this deat to be dewe by them by seatynge of
ther handes to yette

63. 9 February 1598. Statute (extracts).

This 'Acte for punyshment of Rogues Vagabonds and Sturdy Beggars'
repealed all former statutes. In no provision was the new act more lenient
than previous legislation had been; indeed, for players, it was becoming
increasingly difficult to avoid infringing the law because restrictions upon
those allowed to patronise and protect them were being tightened. Before
1572 any gentleman in England could exercise the privilege of patronising
a company; in 1572 the privilege was confined to 'any Baron of this
Realme, or any other honorable Personage of greater Degree'. That statute
was being reiterated now in 1598, but officially the Privy Council was on
record as wanting to narrow restrictions even further. A letter of 19
February makes it clear that the number of authorised playing companies
was to be limited to two (see no. 64). But while the lords issued draconian
orders, they took no effectual steps to enforce them.

———

2. All Fencers Bearewardes common Players of Enterludes and Min-
strelles wandring abroade (other than Players of Enterludes belonging to
any Baron of this Realme, or any other honorable Personage of greater
Degree, to be auctoryzed to play, under the Hand and Seale of Armes of
such Baron or Personage) ... shalbe taken adjudged and deemed Rogues

Vagabondes and Sturdy Beggers, and shall susteyne such Payne and Punyshment as by this Acte is in that behalfe appointed.

3. Every person which is by this presente Acte declared to be a Rogue Vagabonde or Sturdy Begger, which shalbe ... taken begging vagrant wandering or mysordering themselves in any part of this Realme ..., shall uppon their apprehension ... be stripped naked from the middle upwardes and shall be openly whipped untill his or her body be bloudye, and shalbe forthwith sent from Parish to Parish by the Officers of every the same, the nexte streighte way to the Parish where he was borne ...

4. Yf any of the said Rogues shall appeare to be dangerous to the inferior sorte of People where they shalbe taken, or otherwyse be such as will not be reformed of their rogish kinde of lyfe by the former Provisions of this Acte, ... it shall and may be laufull to the said Justices ... to commit that Rogue to House of Correccion, or otherwyse to the Gaole of that County, there to remaine untill their next Quarter Sessions to be holden in that County, and then such of the same Rogues so committed, as by the Justices of the Peace then and there presente or the most parte of them shalbe thought fitt not to be delivered, shall and may lawfully by the same Justices or the more parte of them be banysshed out of this Realme ... And if any such Rogue so banyshed as aforesaid shall returne agayne into any part of this Realme or Domynion of Wales without lawfull Lycence or Warrant so to do, that in every such case such Offence shalbe Felony, and the Party offending therein suffer Death as in case of Felony.

64. 19 February 1598. Privy Council Minute.

This letter refers to an order which has not survived but which apparently limited the number of licensed playing companies to two. The order was violated, and the lords here took steps to suppress a third company, who may have been Worcester's Men or a new Pembroke's Company recon-stituted out of the remnant players who had not affiliated themselves with the Admiral's Men. Both the order and this letter seem to be canards – airy nothings – for they were never enforced. They fit into the same bureaucratic pigeon-hole as the order of 28 July 1597 calling for the demolition of all the London playhouses (see no. 53). An inquiry into the Privy Council's motives and methods is legitimate: were the lords issuing directives they had no intention of seeing carried out and if so why; had they initiated a policy and then changed their minds; were they putting on the statute book orders they might usefully hold in abeyance now but invoke at some later date? Such alternatives seem possible.

A lettre to the Master of the Revelles and Justices of Peace of Middlesex & Surrey. Whereas licence hath bin graunted vnto two Companies of Stage Players retayned vnto vs the Lord Admyral and Lord Chamberlain, to vse and practise Stage Playes, whereby they might be the better enhabled and prepared to shew such plaies before her Majestie as they shalbe required at tymes meete and accustomed, to which ende they have bin Cheefelie licensed and tollerated as aforesaid: And whereas there is also a third Company who of late (as wee are informed) haue by waie of intrusion vsed likewise to playe, having neither prepared any plaie for her Majestie nor are bound to you the Masters of the Revelles for perfourming such orders as haue bin prescribed, and are enjoyned to be observed by the other two Companies before mencioned; Wee have therefore thought good to require you uppon receipt heereof to take order that the aforesaid third company may be suppressed, and none suffered heereafter to plaie, but those two formerlie named belonging to us, the Lord Admyrall and Lord Chamberlaine, vnles you shall receaue other direccion from vs. And so, etc.

65. 10 March 1598. Playhouse Inventories (now lost).

The Admiral's Men took stock of their costumes, properties and play-books in the spring of 1598. These inventories, which Edmond Malone discovered among a bundle of Henslowe's loose papers and published in 1790, have since disappeared, but they were doubtless genuine. Two other costume inventories, dated 13 March and 'sence the 3 of April' 1598, are not reproduced here. One contains ten items, the other eighty-seven items, mostly doublets, cloaks and hose. Among them are 'Tamberlynes cotte with coper lace', 'Tasoes robe', 'Harye the v. velvet gowne' and 'a robe for to goo invisibell'. Many of the items inventoried below can be identified with specific productions or players. In the 'Gone and loste' category, for example, 'longe-shanckes sewte' and 'Harey the fyftes dublet' belonged to plays that opened on 29 August 1595 and 28 November 1595 respectively. Among the 'Clownes Sewtes and Hermetes Sewtes' are green coats for *Robin Hood* (licensed for performance on 28 March 1598); a 'fierdrackes' – dragon – suit for an unidentified player, Dobe; Hercules's limbs (new on 7 May 1595); four Turks' heads (possibly for *The Battle of Alcazar*, the plot of which calls for dead men's heads, in 1597); and Branholt's bodice (a woman's gown for that play was purchased on 26 November 1597). A 'red sewt of cloth for pyge' was meant for John Pigg, the boy player apprenticed to Edward Alleyn, but 'Will. Sommers sewte', for an actor impersonating Henry VIII's famous clown, cannot be linked to any known Admiral's play at this date. The same list includes a ghost's suit and bodice; Merlin's gown (perhaps for *Uther Pendragon*, new on 29

April 1597); Eve's bodice; a fool's coat, cap and bauble; a hobbyhorse; and a small orchestra. Costumes 'Leaft above in the tier-house' include 'Lord Caffes gercken' – maybe, as Malone suggested, 'Caiaphas' – and 'hosse for the Dowlfen' – the Dauphin in *Henry V*? The jerkin for *Vortigern* (new on 4 December 1596), the anticks' coats for *Phaeton* (which the Company bought from Dekker on 15 January 1597/8), and the 'payer of bodeyes for Alles Pearce' (in production by December 1597) can all be identified confidently. It is important to remember that none of these would have been 'period' costumes. Neither, of course were they strictly 'Elizabethan', for the inventories and a contemporary illustration of *Titus Andronicus* reveal that theatrical costume marked a world apart from the man in the street. The very act of putting on costumes for a performance placed the players ambiguously with respect to social convention and law, for costumes of satin or velvet 'layd thycke with gowld lace' were garments the statutes on apparel accorded only to the nobility. Hence the moralisers' outrage at 'proude players' who '*jet* vnder gentlemens noses in sutes of silke'. The inventory of properties prompts a different reflection: that the Elizabethan stage was not as bare as has sometimes been argued. The Admiral's Men owned a veritable forest – two moss banks, a bay tree, a tree with dead limbs, Tantalus's tree, a tree of golden apples – as well as a small zoo: snakes, lions, a 'great horse with his leages', a boar's and a bull's head, a black dog, a bear skin, and a herd of dragons, both in a 'chayne' and in menacing isolation: 'j dragon in fostes'. The inventory of mortuary effects included three tombs, a hell mouth, two coffins and a 'frame for the *be*heading in Black Jone'; the cauldron for *The Jew of Malta*; and an assortment of dismembered bodies – 'owld Mahemetes' head, Phaeton's limbs, Kent's wooden leg (probably for *The Wise Man of West Chester*, new in December 1594). The number of targets, foils, swords, shields, visors and spears was balanced by the array of mitres, scepters, globes and crowns (imperial, plain and ghost). But most impressive among these properties are structures that sound like modern sets: stairs for *Phaeton*, a steeple with a chime of bells, a wooden canopy, Bellendon's stable (*Bellendon* was new in June 1594), a rock and a cage, a wheel and frame in *The Siege of London* (which premiered on 26 December 1594), and – magnificently – 'the sittie of Rome'. Like the rainbow and 'the clothe of the Sone & Mone', the City of Rome was probably painted on canvas that was stretched over wooden frames as a backdrop but was stored rolled up. One play, Dekker's *Phaeton*, is mentioned over and over in these inventories, and a look at the properties it required suggests that it was a highly 'theatrical' production, dependent on visual effects and sophisticated machinery. All the playbooks listed in the final inventory except 'Sturgflaterey' can be traced through the Diary. The following words that occur throughout the inventories have never been explained: Orlates, Cathemer, mawe, asane, Nabesathe, and hecfer;

additional notes to the inventories can be consulted in Foakes and Rickert, *Henslowe's Diary*, 314–24.

———

The booke of the Inventary of the goods of my Lord Admeralles men, tacken the 10 of Marche in the yeare 1598.

Gone and loste.

Item, j orenge taney satten dublet, layd thycke with gowld lace.
Item, j blew tafetie sewt.
Item, j payr of carnatyon satten Venesyons, layd with gold lace.
Item, j longe-shanckes sewte.
Item, j Sponnes dublet pyncket.
Item, j Spanerd gyrcken.
Item, Harey the fyftes dublet.
Item, Harey the fyftes vellet gowne.
Item, j fryers gowne.
Item, j lyttell dublet for boye.

The Enventary of the Clownes Sewtes and Hermetes Sewtes, with dievers other sewtes, as followeth, 1598, the 10 of March.
Item, j senetores gowne, j hoode and 5 senetores capes.
Item, j sewtte for Nepton; Fierdrackes sewtes for Dobe.
Item, iiij genesareyes gownes, and iiij torchberers sewtes.
Item, iij payer of red strasers, and iij fares gowne of buckrome.
Item, iiij Herwodes cottes, and iij sogers cottes, and j green gown for Maryan.
Item, vj grene cottes for Roben Hoode, and iiij knaves sewtes.
Item, ij payer of grene hosse and Andersones sewte. j whitt shepen clocke.
Item, ij rosset cottes, and j black frese cotte, and iiij prestes cottes.
Item, ij whitt sheperdes cottes, and ij Danes sewtes, and j payer of Danes hosse.
Item, The Mores lymes, and Hercolles lymes, and Will. Sommers sewtte.
Item, ij Orlates sewtes, hates and gorgetts, and vij anteckes cootes.
Item, Cathemer sewte, j payer of cloth whitte stockens, iiij Turckes hedes.
Item, iiij freyers gownes and iiij hoodes to them, and j fooles coate, cape, and babell, and branhowlttes bodeyes, and merlen gowne and cape.
Item, ij black saye gownes, and ij cotton gownes, and j rede saye gowne.
Item, j mawe gowne of calleco for the quene, j carnowll hatte.
Item, j red sewt of cloth for pyge, layed with whitt lace.
Item, v payer of hosse for the clowne, and v gerkenes for them.
Item, iij payer of canvas hosse for asane, ij payer of black strocers.
Item, j yelow leather dublett for a clowne, j Whittcomes dublett poke.
Item, Eves bodeyes, j pedante trusser, and iij donnes hattes.
Item, j payer of yelow cotton sleves, j gostes sewt, and j gostes bodeyes.

Item, xviij copes and hattes, Verones sonnes hosse.

Item, iij trumpettes and a drum, and a trebel viall, a basse viall, a bandore, a sytteren, j anshente, j whitt hatte.

Item, j hatte for Robin Hoode, j hobihorse.

Item, v shertes, and j serpelowes, iiij ferdingalles.

Item, vj head-tiers, j fane, iiij rebatos, ij gyrketruses.

Item, j longe sorde.

The Enventary of all the apparell for my Lord Admiralles men, tacken the 10 of marche 1598. – Leaft above in the tier-house in the cheast.

Item, My Lord Caffes gercken, & his hoosse.

Item, j payer of hosse for the Dowlfen.

Item, j murey lether gyrcken, & j white lether gercken.

Item, j black lether gearken, & Nabesathe sewte.

Item, j payer of hosse, & a gercken for Valteger.

Item, ij leather anteckes cottes with basses, for Fayeton.

Item, j payer of bodeyes for Alles Pearce.

The Enventary tacken of all the properties for my Lord Admeralles men, the 10 of Marche 1598.

Item, j rocke, j cage, j tombe, j Hell mought.

Item, j tome of Guido, j tome of Dido, j bedsteade.

Item, viij lances, j payer of stayers for Fayeton.

Item, ij stepells, & j chyme of belles, & j beacon.

Item, j hecfor for the playe of Faeton, the limes dead.

Item, j globe, & j golden scepter; iij clobes.

Item, ij marchepanes, & the sittie of Rome.

Item, j gowlden flece; ij rackets, j baye tree.

Item, j wooden hatchett; j lether hatchete.

Item, j wooden canepie; owld Mahemetes head.

Item, j lyone skin; j beares skyne; & Faetones lymes, & Faeton charete; & Argosse heade.

Item, Nepun forcke & garland.

Item, j crosers stafe; Kentes woden leage.

Item, Jerosses head, & raynbowe, j littell alter.

Item, viij viserdes; Tamberlyne brydell; j wooden matook.

Item, Cupedes bowe, & quiver; the clothe of the Sone & Mone.

Item, j bores heade & Serberosse iij heades.

Item, j Cadeseus; ij mose banckes, & j snake.

Item, ij fanes of feathers; Belendon stable; j tree of gowlden apelles; Tantelouse tre; jx eyorn targates.

Item, j copper targate, & xvij foyles.

Item, iiij wooden targates; j greve armer.

Item, j syne for Mother Readcap; j buckler.

Item, Mercures wings; Tasso picter; j helmet with a dragon; j shelde, with iij lyones; j eleme bowle.

Item, j chayne of dragons; j gylte speare.

Item, ij coffenes; j bulles head; and j vylter.

Item, iij tymbrells, j dragon in fostes.

Item, j lyone; ij lyon heades; j great horse with his leages; j sack-bute.

Item, j whell and frame in the Sege of London.

Item, j paire of rowghte gloves.

Item, j poopes miter.

Item, iij Imperial crownes; j playne crowne.

Item, j gostes crown; j crown with a sone.

Item, j frame for the heading in Black Jone.

Item, j black dogge.

Item, j cauderm for the Jewe.

A Note of all suche bookes as belong to the Stocke, and such as I have bought since the 3d of March 1598.

Blacke Jonne.	Woman will have her will.
The Umers.	Welchmans price.
Hardicanewtes.	King Arthur, life and death.
Borbonne.	1 part of Hercules.
Sturgflaterey.	2 parte of Hercoles.
Brunhowlle.	Pethagores.
Cobler quen hive.	Focasse.
Frier Pendelton.	Elexsander and Lodwicke.
Alls Perce.	Blacke Battman.
Read Cappe.	2 part black Battman.
Roben Hode, 1.	2 part of Goodwine.
Roben Hode, 2.	Mad mans morris.
Phayeton.	Perce of Winchester.
Treangell cockowlls.	Vayvode.
Goodwine.	

66. 25 March 1598. Players' Bonds.

Between 4 March and 2 April the Rose may have been closed: Henslowe did not record any receipts. But the Company was not inactive. More players were put under contract. Richard Allen, though only a hired man, had been a major actor with the Admiral's Men for years. Thomas Heywood was known to the Company as a playwright. The witnesses' signatures are not autograph; Henslowe supplied them.

me*morandum* that this 25 of marche 1598 Richard alleyne came &
bownde hime seallfe vnto me for ij yeares in & asumsette as a hiered
servante with ij syngell pence & to continew frome the daye aboue written
vnto the eand & tearme of ij yeares yf he do not performe this couenant
then he to forfette for the breache of yt fortye powndes & witnes to this

> wm borne
> Thomas dowton
> gabrell spencer
> Robart shawe
> Richard Jonnes

me*morandum* that this 25 of marche 1598 Thomas hawoode came &
hiered hime seallfe with me as a covenante searvante for ij yeares by the
Receuenge of ij syngell pence acordinge to the statute of winshester & to
beginne at the daye a boue written & not to playe any wher publicke a
bowt london not whille thes ij yeares be exspired but in my howsse yf he
do then he dothe forfett vnto me the Receuinge of these ijd fortie powndes
& wittnes to this Antony monday   wm Borne
       gabrell spencer   Thomas dowton
       Robart shawe   Richard Jonnes
       Richard alleyn

67. 2 April – 8 July 1598. Rose Playhouse Receipts.

These weekly totals continue, after a month-long interruption, from no.
61. Henslowe entered a marginal subtotal, '56-11-10', opposite 31 June.
That same month, a scandalous play shown in Brussels was agitating the
English Privy Council. Lord Burghley's private papers contain information about it, including a synopsis of a dumb show representing the French
King, nominally a Protestant, and the Catholic Cardinal who had long
opposed him. In this scenario, the two end their civil war and fall to a
treaty. A lady appears. She pries into the business and fawns upon the
French King, hoping to flatter his attentions away from the treaty. She is
discovered to be the Queen of England. A rout of fellows dressed as boors
disrupt the proceedings. They are shown to be 'boors of Holland' –
Protestants, like Elizabeth – and they are scoffed at while the Cardinal
indicates that when his negotiations give him leisure he will hang them.
The English Privy Council issued a protest against this play: not only were
they edgy about the political situation it enacted but they were angry that
Her Majesty had been demeaned by presentation on the public stage.
Their political anxieties had foundation, for in a surprise move, Henry IV
of France negotiated a secret peace with Philip of Spain, upsetting the
delicate balance that Europe had painfully erected over the international

question of religion. Concluded in late April, the perfidious French peace was broadcast to England by 12 July when a printed version of 'The articles and conditions of peace betweene the high and mightye prynces Phillip kynge of Spayne, and Henrye the IIIJth the Ffrench Kynge, in Anno 1598' was entered in the Stationers' Register. The figures below represent half of the players' gallery money, totalled on a weekly basis, which the Company was handing over to Henslowe to balance against their loan account (see no. 58).

——

Receued as ffolowethe of the company of my lorde admeralles mean *from* the 2 of aprrell 1598 at diuers tyme as foloweth

Rd the 2 of Aprell 1598	xxvj *s*
Rd the 9 of Aprell 1598	iij *li* vij *s* vj *d*
Rd the 14 of Aprell 1598	lvij *s*
Rd the 22 of Aprell 1598	vj *li* iij *s* vj *d*
Rd the 29 of Aprell 1598	lij *s* vj *d*
Rd the 6 of aprell 1598	iiij *li* ij *s* vj *d*
Rd the 14 of [aprell] maye 1598	v *li* ij *s*
Rd the 20 of maye 1598	iiij *li* vj *s*
Rd the 27 of maye 1598	iij *li* iiij *s* vj *d*
Rd the 3 of June 1598	lij *s* vj *d*
Rd the 10 of June 1598	v *li* xvj *s* vij *d*
Rd the 17 of June 1598	iij *li* xvj *s*
Rd the 24 of June 1598	v *li* vij *s*
Rd the 31 of June 1598	v *li* xviij *s* iij *d*
Rd the 8 of July 1598	lj *s* vij *d*

68. 13 March – 28 July 1598. Loan Account (extracts).

Even more significantly than the players' bonds of 25 March, the loans extended in the first three weeks of this account document Company activity at a time when the Rose was probably closed and they were not performing (see no. 66). Having reckoned the Company debt on 8 March Henslowe opened a new account with them five days later and, in the next four months, made sixty-two payments in their name: £84 toward sixteen new and five old playbooks, £37 7s 4d for costumes, 5s for properties, £1 15s for play licences, and 13s for miscellaneous items. About two-thirds of the payments are reproduced below, edited to include every reference to any given play so that the steps in production – from commissioning to licensing to costuming – can be followed unbroken. This way it is possible to watch the progress of, for example, *Black Batman of the North*. Chettle was paid £1 for a plot or a treatment or perhaps a few scenes of *Black Batman* around 6 May; on the 22nd, the completed script was turned over to the Company by Wilson, Drayton, Dekker and Chettle, who shared the £6 fee. By 13 June the play had evidently been licensed and was into production, for the Company was buying costumes for it, a total of £8 'to bye divers thinges for blacke batmane' on the 13th and 14th. Two weeks later, Chettle was offering to write a sequel. By then, Drayton and Dekker had dropped out of the playwriting team. Chettle wrote the lion's share of *Part II* (he collected £4 15s in three payments), while Wilson picked up the crumbs. This second play, finished on 14 July, may have been among three unnamed plays the Company licensed on 24 July. The *Black Batman* entry for 26 June sees Harry Porter standing surety for Chettle to Henslowe: 'he hath geven me his worde for the performance of the same & all so for my money'. Robert Shaa made a similar vouch for Chettle on 14 July, promising 'eather to deliver the playe or els to paye the mony with in one forthnyght'. Such guarantees are tell-tale, for responsible playwrights had no need of them. Their word was sufficient surety. Chettle, though he behaved dependably over *Black Batman*, was normally one of the least reliable playwrights the Company employed. Shaa may have wondered whether he would live to rue his promise. Porter probably did not give it a second thought: he and Chettle were dyed in the same wool, the colours brave but apt to fade, and necessity figuring more prominently in their dealings than conscience. Chettle, for one, was quick to propose plots and to accept initial payments on scripts, but he was slower to deliver a finished play. He was also constantly in debt to the Admiral's Men (see, for example, the entry of 24 June), who, in later years, would bail him out of the Marshalsea and discharge his arrest for debt. The Company was used to discounting his plays in consideration of his debts or to turning over part of his fee to some other party to whom he owed money. On one occasion they had to pay 'mr bromflde' – the mercer from whom they bought cloth – £1 to retrieve 'the playe which harey chettell Layd vnto hime to pane'. His productivity record was anything but brilliant: he defaulted on twelve plays out of forty-five he proposed to the Admiral's Men in the Diary, and he frequently proposed untitled projects. So did other playwrights. But in Chettle's case the suspicion arises that these nameless plays may have been spurious, sleights of hand that would wind up in his own pocket clutching a few shillings. In this respect, at least, Harry Porter was more honourable. Although he was constantly begging loans and even prevailed upon the Company to hand over cash without any writing to show for it, he did finish four of the five plays he proposed. He survived for only two impoverished years in the Diary – he could hardly grow rich writing two plays a year – after which he is no longer traceable. He must have proved a trial to the players' patience, and the fact that they tolerated him at all may have been for old times' sake: Porter had been among the first to write for the Admiral's Men. Another playwright, George Chapman, was not exactly a new-comer to the Admiral's playwriting stable, for his *The Blind Beggar of Alexandria* and *A Humorous Day's Mirth* ('the comodey of vmers') were premiered by the Company, on 12 February 1595/6 and 11 May 1597 respectively. But he was not exactly a 'regular'. By comparison, if Chettle and Porter were beggarly wolves in moth-eaten sheep's clothing, Chapman at thirty-eight years of age was something of a donkey, content to plod along, solitary, while the young veteran Thomas Dekker (only twenty-six) was the stable's sociable farmyard cock, perpetually scratching around for more work. The same month Chapman was working on a single play, and finding it difficult to produce even a title for it, Dekker was involved in six plays, all of them collaborations. Dekker's habits are typified in the last two entries in this loan account: in one, he picked up his final instalment payment on *Hannibal*; in the next, he collected a first instalment at 'the same time vpon the next boock called perce of winschester'. He and his collaborators finished *Pierce* two weeks later. Clues as to how collaborators organised themselves and their work can be gathered across the shifting pattern of payments for a play such as *Richard Coeur de Lion*. A different sort of clue is provided by play titles, which, though never to be relied upon to convey the sense of lost plays – how reckless it would be to distinguish between *The Old Wive's Tale* and *The Winter's Tale* on titles alone – do at least name the current Admiral's repertoire and suggest its range of possibilities. If taste was changing, perhaps the evidence of new public demand lies in these play titles. The loan accounts that follow reveal as much about the Admiral's Men themselves as about their plays and playwrights. Authorisations for individual payments possibly show various members of the Company emerging in specific management functions: Thomas Downton seems to have been mainly responsible for costumes at this time. Payments for 'good cheare' at 'the sonne in new fyshstreate' point to the auspices and the mood in which the Company gathered to read new plays, on these occasions, *Henry I* and *Earl Goodwin*. Their mood would have been different when, having 'played in fleatstreat pryvat', their 'stufe was loste'. One wonders how much the Company was set back when a hamper full of costumes went missing. Perhaps that loss was compensated for in May when they arranged to retrieve five old playbooks that Martin Slater had taken away as his share in joint company stock when he retired in July 1597, particularly as there seems to have been some argument about these scripts. Undoubtedly Slater possessed them rightfully, but he may have been threatening to sell them to another company when, in March, William Bird, Thomas Downton and Gabriel Spencer borrowed money from Henslowe to pursue 'the sewt be twext marten & them'. Slater finally surrendered the fifth manuscript, of *Alexander and Lodowick*, on 18 July, but if blackmail was his object, he was probably disappointed: he was paid only £8 for the five plays. Other plays that have been entirely edited from the following extracts include five finished works: *King Arthur* (Hathaway, 12 April); *A Woman Will Have Her Will* (Haughton, 18 February–6 May); *Love Prevented* (Porter, 30 May); *The Madman's Morris* (Wilson, Drayton, Dekker, 31 June–10 July); and *Hannibal and Hermes* (Wilson, Drayton, Dekker, 17 July). *Valentine and Orsen* was probably completed, for Hathaway and Munday collected a substantial payment of £5 for it on 19 July, but after that the play disappears. *Pierce of Exstone* (Drayton, Dekker, Wilson, c. 30 March) may have been abandoned. At the end of this account, Henslowe totalled the loans as £120 15s 4d and immediately below opened a new repayment account, declaring that 'frome this daye' he was to 'Receue the wholle gallereys' from the Company to balance against their debts.

———

Lent vnto drayton & cheatell the 13 of marche 1598 in parte of paymente of a boocke wher in is a parte of a weallche man written which they haue promysed to delyuer by the xx day next folowinge I saye lent Ready money   xxxx s

lent vnto the company to paye drayton & dyckers & chetell ther full payment for the boocke called the famos wares of henry the fyrste & the prynce of walles the some of   iiij li v s

lent at that tyme vnto the company for to spend at the Readynge of that boocke at the sonne in new fyshstreate   v s

pd vnto the carman for caryinge & bryngyn of the stufe backe agayne when they played in fleatstreat pryvat & then owr stufe was loste   iij s

layd owt for the company to bye a boocke of mr drayton & mr dickers mr chettell & mr willsone which is called goodwine & iij sones fower powndes in part of paymet the 25 of marche 1598 in Redy mony I saye   iiij li

layd owt the same tyme at the tavarne in fyshstreate for good cheare the some of   v s

Layd owt the 28 of marche 1598 for the licencynge of ij

boocke to the master of the Revelles called the ij partes
of Robart hoode

xiiij s

lent vnto the companey the 30 of marche 1598 in full
payment for the boocke of goodwine & his iij sonnes I
saye lent

xxxx s

Lent vnto thomas dowton the 11 of aprell 1598 to bye
tafitie to macke a Rochet for the beshoppe in earlle
goodwine

xxiiij s

lent vnto the companey the 29 of aprell 1598 to bye a
bvgell dvblett & a payer of paned hoosse of bugell panes
drane owt with clothe of sylver & cangones of the same

xxxxvj s viij d

Lent vnto cheattell vpon the playe called blacke batmone
of the northe the some of wittnes thomas dowton

xx s

lent vnto mr cheattell & mr dickers the 6 of aprell 1598
vpon ther boocke of goodwine the 2 part the some of

xx s

Lent vnto mr Chapmane the 16 of maye 1598 in earneste
of a boocke for the companye wittnes wm Birde

xxxx s

Lente vnto the company the 16 of maye 1598 to bye v
boockes of martine slather called ij partes of hercolus
& focas & pethagores & elyxander & lodicke which
laste boocke he hath not yet delyuerd the some of

vij li

Bowght of mr willsones drayton & dickers & cheattell
for the companey a boocke called blacke battmane of
the northe the 22 of maye 1598 which coste sixe powndes
I saye layd owt for them

vj li

lent vnto wm birde the 23 of maye 1598 which he lent
vnto mr chappman vpon his boocke which he promised
vs

xx s

lent vnto thomas dowton the 6 of June 1598 to leand
vnto drayton I saye leante for the 2 part of goodwine

x s

lent vnto the companey the 10 of June 1598 to paye vnto
mr drayton willson dickers & cheattell in full paymente
of the second parte of goodwine l s as foloweth drayton
30s & willson x s & cheattell x s some is

l s

lent vnto mr willsone the 13 of June 1598 vpon A bocke
called Richard cordelion funeralle   v s

lent vnto thomas dowton the 13 of June 1598 to bye
divers thinges for black batmane of the northe the some
of fyve pownd I saye lent   v li

lent vnto thomas dowton the 14 of June 1598 to bye
divers thinges for blacke batmane of the northe the some   iij li

lent vnto cheattell the 14 of June 1598 in earneste of A
boock called Richard cordeliones funeralle   v s

lent vnto Cheattell the 15 of June 1598 in earneste of
ther boocke called the funerall of Richard cvrdelion   v s

lent vnto cheattell willsone & mondaye the 17 of June
1598 vpon earneste of ther boocke called the funerall of
Richard cordelion   xv s

Lent vnto mr cheattell the 21 of June 1598 in earneste of
a boocke called the fenerall of Richard cvrdelion the
some of I saye xxv s wittnes wm birde   xxv s

lent vnto antony mvnday the 23 of June 1598 in earneste
of a boocke called the fenerall of Richard cvrdelion the
some of   xx s

lent vnto mr drayton the 24 of June 1598 in earneste of
a boocke called the funerall of Richard cordelion the
some of   xxx s

lent vnto mr cheattell the 24 of June 1598 the some of
x s I saye   x s
all his parte of boockes to this place are payde which
weare dew vnto hime & he Reastes be syddes in my
Deatte the some of xxx s

Lent vnto mr willson the 26 of June 1598 the some of
xx s which is in full paymente of of his parte of the
boocke called Richard cordelion funerall   xx s

lent vnto Thomas dowton the 26 of June 1598 to by
satten to macke ij dubleattes for the 2 parte of goodwine
the some of   v li

Lent vnto Cheattell the 26 of June 1598 in earneste of A
boocke called the 2 parte of blacke battman of the north
& mr harey porter hath geven me his worde for the
performance of the same & all so for my money   xx s

Lent vnto mr Cheattell the 8 of July 1598 vpon A Boocke
called the 2 parte of blacke battman the some of   iij li

Lent vnto mr willsones the 13 of July 1598 in part of
payment of a boocke called the 2 part of blacke battman
the some of   x s

lent vnto mr wilsone the 14 of July 1598 in part of
payment of a boock called the 2 part of black battman
the some of   xv s

pd vnto mr cheattell the 14 of July 1598 in fulle paymet
of a boock called the 2 part of black battmane the some
of   xv s

Lent vnto Harey Cheattell the 14 of July 1598 vpon a
boocke called the playe of A womons Tragedye the
some of v li which Robart shawe willed me to delyuer
hime I saye   v li
eather to dd the playe or els to paye the mony with in
one forthnyght

lent vnto Thomas dowton the 16 of July 1598 for to bye
A Robe to playe hercolas in the some of   xxxx s

pd vnto the master of the Revelles man for the licensynge
of iij boockes the 24 of July 1598 the some of   xxj s

pd vnto mr drayton & mr deckers the 28 of July 1598 in
full payment of a boocke called haneball & hermes
other wisse called worsse feared then hurte   x s

lent vnto mr deckers the same time vpon the next boock
called perce of winschester   x s

   120 li–15s–4d

69. 29 July–29 September 1598. Rose Playhouse Receipts.

The Admiral's Men, £120 in debt to Henslowe on 28 July, had discovered that their borrowing was outstripping their ability to repay him out of half their weekly gallery money. They therefore began turning over to Henslowe all their galleries. This state of affairs continued for the next eight months, but the Company was not heading for bankruptcy nor was Henslowe reaching an economic strangle-hold around the organisation, for although the total debt was growing, the Company's rate of borrowing was not escalating. Over ten weeks in 1596 they had borrowed nearly £40, or £4 per week; from October to March 1597, about £50, or £2 per week; and from October to July 1598, £166, or just over £4 per week. In the next three months – the period covered by the loan account reproduced as no. 70 – the figure jumped to £152: more than £10 each week. But then it dropped again, £115 in six months to July 1599, once more just over £4 weekly. Perhaps in July 1598 the Admiral's Men knew they had expensive months ahead and were budgeting for them by depositing their 'wholle gallereys' with Henslowe. Henslowe, too, may have been checking his credit in July: not on the balance sheet but in the community, for he had evidently been visited by a vestry committee from St Saviour's, Southwark, who deemed his playhouse a blight upon the parish and wanted it removed. A vestry meeting on 19 July resolved 'that a petition shal be made to the bodye of the councell concerninge the play houses in this pareshe, wherein the enormeties shal be showed that comes therebye to the pareshe, and that in respect thereof they may be dismissed and put down from playing, and that iiij or ij of the churchwardens, Mr Howse, Mr Garlonde, Mr John Payne, Mr Humble, or ij of them, and Mr Russell and Mr Ironmonger, or one of them, shall prosecute the cause with a collector of the Boroughside and another of the Bankside.' So, it seemed, Francis Langley would be visited, too. But where Langley probably met them with cudgels – such was the story of his life – Henslowe undoubtedly smoothed their way. He was, after all, a man of some status in the community: a tax assessor for the subsidies collected in 1593, 1594 and 1598, a Groom of Her Majesty's Chamber, a vestryman by 1608 and a churchwarden the following year. Moreover, Garland, Ironmonger and Russell were all friends and fellow businessmen who could possibly weigh 'enormeties' against economics and decide that Henslowe's playhouse was more of a benefit than a threat to life on the Bankside. On 4 August, Lord Burghley, the Lord Treasurer and the kingpin of Elizabeth's Privy Council, died. The Queen was disconsolate, not only because she saw in Burghley's death intimations of her own mortality but because she would miss him as a friend; he was the last of the old guard who had served her from her coronation; he was the last of her contemporaries: the Privy Council was filling up with young men, Burghley's son Robert Cecil and, fatefully, Robert Devereux, the Earl of Essex. Later in August, on the 15th, George Chapman's play, 'The blynde begger of Alexandrya' was entered in the Stationers' Register, and Francis Meres's *Palladis Tamia: Wit's Treasury* was entered on 7 September. In this treatise Meres acclaimed Shakespeare as 'the most excellent in both kinds', comedy and tragedy, 'for the stage', but he also recognised the merits of several Rose playwrights: 'our best for Tragedie' included 'The Lorde Buckhurst, Doctor Leg of Cambridge, Doctor Edes of Oxford, Master Edward Ferris, the author of the *Mirror for Magistrates*, Marlow, Peele, Watson, Kid, Shakespeare, Drayton, Chapman, Decker, and Beniamin Johnson'. 'The best for Comedy amongst vs bee Edward, Earle of Oxforde, Docter Gager of Oxforde, Master Rowley, once a rare scholler of learned Pembrooke Hall in Cambridge, Maister Edwardes, one of Her Maiesties Chappell, eloquent and wittie John Lilly, Lodge, Gascoyne, Greene, Shakespeare, Thomas Nash, Thomas Heywood, Anthony Mundye, our best plotter, Chapman, Porter, Wilson, Hathway, and Henry Chettle.' 'Wittie Wilson' is said to have inherited Tarlton's mantle as the king of extemporal wit and to have worn it 'to his great and eternall commendations, ... in his challenge at the Swanne on the Banke Side'. Edward Alleyn had been invited to stand challenger in one such contest of the player's art when one 'W.P.' wrote to him of a wager between two 'gentlemen', one claiming that Bentley, famous as a Queen's Man in the 1580s, was player non-pareil, the other urging Alleyn as surpassing even Bentley. Perhaps Wilson's challenge was a similar contest. The 'wholle gallereys' that follow should be compared to nos. 58, 61 and 67 for an assessment of the season's success.

Here I Begyne to Receue the wholle gallereys
frome this daye beinge the 29 of July 1598

Rd the 29 of July 1598	x *li* xiiij *s*
Rd the 6 of aguste 1598	vij *li* x *s*
Rd the 13 of aguste 1598	ix *li* ix *s*
Rd the 19 of aguste 1598	viij *li* xij *s*
Rd the 26 of aguste 1598	viij *li* ij *s*
Rd the 2 of [aguste] september 1598	viij *li* xiiij *s*
Rd the 10 of september 1598	ix *li* iij *s*
Rd the 17 of september 1598	vj *li* xviij *s*
Rd the 24 of september 1598	viij *li* ij *s*
Rd the 29 of september 1598	v *li* xiiij *s*

70. 30 July–29 September 1598. Loan Account (extracts).

In all, Henslowe made twenty-seven payments for the Admiral's Men this summer: £36 19s toward eight plays, £45 5s for costumes, and £35, possibly also for costumes, in settlement of claims the Company had been making against Francis Langley since November 1597 (see no. 59). Henslowe noted that this loan was 'Lent vnto the company ... A bowt the agrement betwext langley & them'. A new playwright had appeared on the scene in the person of John Day; Ben Jonson, of whom nothing had been heard since he showed his 'plotte vnto the company' on 3 December 1597 and promised them a play by Christmas, resurfaced, working on a collaboration that, when he published his collected *Works* in 1616, he would decline to admit he wrote. Anthony Munday apparently had second thoughts about the 'comodey for the corte' he promised to supply 'with in one fortnyght' for that entry was cancelled from the Diary and the advance repaid. Dekker's and Drayton's new play, *The First Civil Wars in France*, would eventually run to three parts, which, when no more sequels could be spun out, would be enlarged with a fourth play *introducing* the civil wars. The insatiable demand for these plays would be explained if Dekker and Drayton were taking their material from the current French civil wars that had ended only in April with the secret peace treaty that was published to dumbfounded Londoners in July (see no. 67). Two other plays that have been edited from the following extracts are Chettle's *Brute* and Chapman's *Fount of New Fashions*; both were completed. A third play, *Catiline's Conspiracy*, was commissioned from Wilson and Chettle but was evidently abandoned. 'Worse a feared then hurte' was first given as an alternate title to *Chance Medley*. In three payments edited from these extracts, an additional £4 was spent for costumes for *Vayvode* by 29 August.

———

Lent the companey the 30 of July 1598 to bye A boocke of John daye called the con queste of brute with the firste fyndinge of the bathe the some of   xxxx s

Lent vnto the company the 8 of aguste 1598 to paye mr drayton willsone & dickers in parte of payment of A boocke called perce of winschester the some of   l s

[lent vnto antony monday the 9 of aguste 1598 in earneste of A comodey for the corte called   the some of   x s
mr drayton hath geuen his worde for the boocke to be done with in one fortnyght wittnes

                                  Thomas dowton]

Lent vnto the company the 10 of aguste 1598 to paye mr drayton
willsone & dickers in fulle payment for a boocke called perce
of winschester the some of   l s

lent vnto the company the 18 of aguste 1598 to bye a Boocke
called hoote anger sone cowld of mr porter mr cheattell &
bengemen Johnson in full payment the some of   vj li

Lent vnto the company the 19 of aguste 1598 to paye vnto mr
willson monday & deckers in parte of payment of A boock
called chance medley the some of iiij li v s in this maner willson
xxx s cheattell xxx s mondy xxv s I saye   iiij li v s

Lent vnto Thomas dowton the 21 of aguste 1598 to by A sewte
& a gowne for vayvode the some of tene pownde I saye lent   x li
                    wittnes mr willsone

pd vnto mr drayton the 24 of aguste 1598 in fulle payment of A
Boocke called chance medley [or worse a feared then hurte the]
some of   xxxv s

lent vnto Robart shaw the 25 of aguste 1598 to paye the lace
manes byll ij li xvj s vj d & the tayllers bylle xxviij s vj d some is iiij li v s
                    for vayvode

Lent vnto the company the 19 of septmber 1598 in Redy money
A bowt the agrement betwext langley & them the some of   xxxv li

Lent vnto the company the the 23 of septmber 1598 to bye
diuers thinges for perce of winchester the some of x li dd vnto
thomas dowton I saye   x li

Lent vnto thomas dowton the 28 of septmber 1598 to bye diuers
thinges for pearce of winchester the some of   xxxx s

Lent vnto thomas dowton the 29 of septmber 1598 to [feche
home a Riche clocke which they had of mr langleyes the some
of] to bye divers thinges for perce of winchester   xij li

Lent vnto the companey the 29 of septmber 1598 to by A boocke
of mr drayton & mr dickers called the firste syvell wares in
france   vj li

71. 26 September 1598. Letter.

Henslowe wrote to Alleyn, who was visiting family friends in Sussex, with troubling news. First: of Henslowe's still unsuccessful bid to extend his profits in London entertainment by securing the Mastership of the Royal Games of Bears and Bulls, a tidy monopoly in a sport that would have earned him some hundreds of pounds a year; sounding almost mournful at the anticipated disappointment, he wanted Alleyn's presence 'Rather ... then your leatters'. Secondly: of a killing, in a duel, 'of one of my company' which 'hurteth me greatley'. Gabriel Spencer had joined the Admiral's Men in 1597. Jonson – called 'bricklayer' in this letter – was known to the Company as a player and a playwright. In August he had been collaborating with Porter and Chettle on *Hot Anger Soon Cold* for the Admiral's Men, and at one time he had taken first steps to join the Company. He made an initial payment toward a share in July 1597. Henslowe's epithet is bitter and intentionally demeaning. Jonson's own version of events, reported by William Drummond in the *Conversations* (1619), turns the killing into something of a heroic flourish in which Spencer was the challenger and he the victor over unequal odds, who 'being appealed to the fields ... killed his adversarie, which had hurt him in the arme & whose sword was 10 Inches Longer than his, for the which he was Emprissoned & almost at the Gallowes'. The hangman was no idle threat, for Jonson was indicted of manslaughter, a felony, and only escaped the gallows by latinising his neck verse. That is, he claimed benefit of clergy. From medieval times, clerics arraigned of a felony could claim exemption from trial by a secular court, referring the crime instead to the spiritual court, which did not pass death sentences. They proved they were clerics by reading – literacy being the first mark of the calling – a Latin verse from the Bible printed in black letter, usually the beginning of the Fifty-first Psalm: 'Have mercy on me, O God, according to thy loving-kindness: according unto the multitude of thy tender mercies blot out my transgressions. Wash me thoroughly from mine iniquity, and cleanse me from my sin.' By Jonson's time benefit of clergy virtually meant the exemption from sentencing on the first conviction of anyone who could read the neck verse, which was fortunate for Ben Jonson and the Elizabethan playhouse since the indictment made it clear that he was indisputably guilty, having 'feloniously and wilfully struck and assaulted the same Gabriel Spencer with a certain sword of iron and steel called in English a Rapier, costing 3s, which he had and held in his right hand then and there drawn, giving to the same Gabriel Spencer then and there with the said sword in and upon the right side of the very Gabriel a mortal wound of a depth of six thumbs [i.e., inches] and a width of one thumb ...'. Spencer 'instantly died', and the deponents 'upon their sacrament' swore again that Jonson 'did kill and murder' 'feloniously and wilfully'.

In consequence, while he hung on to his life, Jonson forfeited all his goods. His career with the Admiral's Men was damaged, but not permanently. Though in October George Chapman took over the writing of 'A tragedie of bengemens plotte', by August 1599 Jonson was again submitting scripts to the Company.

———

ssonne Edward alleyn I haue Rd your leatter the which you sent vnto me by the careyer wher in I vnderstand of both your good healthes which I praye to god to contenew and forther I vnder stand you haue considered of the wordes which you and I had betwene vs consernynge the beargarden & acordinge to your wordes you and I and all owr frendes shall haue as mvch as we cane do to bring yt vnto a good eand therefore I wold willingeley that you weare at the bancate for then with our losse I shold be the meryer therfore yf you thincke as I thincke yt weare fytte that we weare both her to do what we mowght & not as two frends but as two Joyned in one therfor ned I love not to mack many great glosses & protestaciones to you as others do but as a poore frend you shall comande me as I hoope I shall do you therfore I desyer Rather to haue your company & your wiffes then your leatters for ower laste talke which we had abowte mr pascalle assuer you I do not for geatte now to leat you vnderstand newes I will teall you some but yt is for me harde and heavey sence you weare with me I haue loste one of my company which hurteth me greatley that is gabrell for he is slayen in hoges den fylldes by the hands of bengemen Jonson bricklayer therfore I wold fayne haue alittell of your cownsell yf I cowld thus with hartie comendations to you & my dawghter & lyckwise to all the Reast of our frends I eande from london the 26 of september 1598

> Your assured frend
> to my power
>
> Phillippe Henslowe

[addressed]
To my welbeloude ssonne
mr Edward alleyne at
mr arthure langworthes
at the brille in
susex giue this

72. 7 October–30 December 1598. Rose Playhouse Receipts.

Henslowe continued to collect the Company's entire share in the gallery money in repayment of the loans that were accruing over the same period. These receipts follow directly from no. 69. On 4 November the news reached England that Philip II of Spain had died on 13 September. On 3

December 'in the forenone. At the Court at Whitehall', a warrant 'to pay vnto Robert Shaw and Thomas Downton, servants to the Erle of Nottingham' a total of £20 for performances before the Queen the previous Christmas was signed. The Company appeared at Court this year two days after Christmas, probably playing *Robin Hood* which, an entry in the Company's loan account makes clear, was being revised 'for the corte' (see no. 73). They were paid for their performance in October 1599. On about 28 December the Burbages, who had been negotiating acrimoniously for a new ground lease on the property upon which the Theater stood, finally pulled the playhouse down. With Peter Street, the carpenter, and others, they carried the dismantled building across the Thames to the South Bank where they erected a new playhouse, the Globe, open by the autumn of 1598. John Stowe, in his *Annals*, reported that the Thames was frozen that Christmas, solidly between the 15th and 18th and again after the great snowfall on 28 December. How satisfying it would be to one's sense of drama if one could imagine Richard Burbage and his company, including of course William Shakespeare, transporting 'the great globe itself' across the ice.

———

Rd the 7 of october 1598	vj *li* iij *s*
Rd the 14 of october 1598	vij *li* xv *s*
Rd the 21 of october 1598	x *li* xiiij *s*
Rd the 28 of october 1598	v *li* xix *s*
Rd the 5 of novmber 1598	viij *li* ij *s*
Rd the 12 of novmber 1598	v *li* iij *s*
Rd the 19 of novmber 1598	vj *li* xvj *s*
Rd the 24 of novmber 1598	iiij *li* xvj *s*
Rd the 2 of desember 1598	vj *li* xvj *s*
Rd the 9 of desember 1598	vij *li* xvj *s*
Rd the 16 of desember 1598	iiij *li* iij *s*
Rd the 23 of desember 1598	iiij *li* v *s*
Rd the 30 of desember 1598	xij *li* x *s*

73. 1 October–30 December 1598. Loan Account (extracts).

Over a period in which they repaid Henslowe some £92 from their gallery receipts, the Admiral's Men took loans of £142 in thirty-seven payments. They spent nearly twice as much on costumes (£88 1s) as on playbooks (£45 10s), partly because they had finally reached an agreement with Francis Langley about the costumes he had evidently been withholding since Pembroke's Men decamped from the Swan in the summer of 1597, partly because they 'exsepted into the stocke' two expensive cloaks that had been in pawn since the previous November, and partly because they spent heavily on costumes for Drayton and Dekker's *Civil Wars in France* trilogy: in the second week of October, £10 for *Part I* and in late November, £20 for *Part II* just about the time *Part III* was being commissioned. Lavish costumes were likewise bought for Chapman's *Fount of New Fashions*, a play that has been edited from these extracts but that was commissioned in September, completed on 12 October, and into production by 8 November when the first payment 'to bye dyvers thinges for the playe called the fownte of new faciones' was made. By 14 November £17 had been spent to costume that play. Some of these costumes were enormously costly. Langley's 'Riche clocke' cost £19. But the Company likewise spent a modest £1 4s 'to macke cottes for gyantes' in *Brute*, a play Chettle had completed on 22 October and which probably opened soon after the giants' coats were paid for. Besides costumes, the Company bought instruments: a total of £4 for 'a sackebute of marke antoney' and 'a basse viall & other enstrementes'. Several payments in this account widen understanding of playwrights' workaday lives. There are first of all Dekker's several sequels to the *Civil Wars* which show dramatists tuned to the mood of an audience their Company could play upon. Next there is Chapman's payment for 'ij ectes of A tragedie of bengemens plotte'. Jonson was probably estranged from the Admiral's Men over the murder of Gabriel Spencer (see no. 71), and may even have been in prison under indictment, so his 'plotte' was turned over to Chapman who proceeded to flesh it out. This was an unusual sequence of events that may have owed something either to the Company's desire for revenge or to the quality of Jonson's plot – the Company refusing to abandon it even though the playwright was perhaps in jail – for partially completed plays in the Diary were almost never salvaged by replacement dramatists. If instalments had been paid on a play before the project fizzled out, the Company kept the writing, and the playwright his payment to date, but new dramatists were not enlisted to finish the work. Evidently the Company did not expect every commission to bear fruit, but for this reason, it may have been a slap in the face to Jonson that his plot was handed over to Chapman. Finally, there is the payment of 10s to Chettle on 18 November 'vpon the mendynge of the firste part of Robart hoode'. By 'mendynge' Henslowe meant revising or 'alterynge', a job that was undertaken only under specific conditions, one a revival, the other a Court performance. This December the Admiral's Men appeared at Court on 27 December and probably played *Robin Hood*, for a further payment on 25 November indicates that Chettle's 'mendinge of Roben Hood' was 'for the corte'. Some sort of etiquette seems to have prevailed among revisers. Nearly every time they can be seen at work in the Diary, they have been called in to refurbish a play they originally wrote. Here Chettle, the junior collaborator with Anthony Munday on *The Death of Robert Earl of Hunting-*

ton, alias *Robin Hood*, probably supplied a prologue and epilogue to compliment the royal audience. Three entries around the middle of November show how the playhouse might be used when the players were on holiday. 17 November was the Queen's Accession Day, a time of national celebration; the receipts lists between 1592 and 1597 demonstrate that the playhouse was usually closed for a few days this week, but closed maybe only to play-goers, the stage being given over to tumbling and vaulting. This year one 'mr haslette' was paid in advance 'A gaynest his valtinge' and 'James cranwigge ... playd his callenge' at the Rose. The proceeds of such events were evidently split three ways: Henslowe and the Company both took a cut, as he shows by complaining, 'I shold haue hade for my parte xxx s which the company hath Received & oweth yt to me'. Two additional plays edited from the following extracts are *Mulmutius Donwallow* by a new playwright, William Rankins, who apparently did not finish this first play, and *Conan Prince of Cornwall*, completed by Drayton and Dekker between 16 and 20 October. The impecunious Harry Chettle extracted a half dozen personal loans from the Company over these weeks, including 'ij s vj d for to arest one with lord lester'. He did not finish *Tis No Deceit to Deceive the Deceiver*.

———

Bowght for the company the 1 of october 1598 A whitte saten womanes dublett & A Blacke tynsell valle for   xx *s*

Layte *v*nto the company the 4 of october 1598 to by a Riche clocke of mr langley which they had at ther a grement the some of   xix *li*

Lent vnto Thomas dowton to feache ij clockes owt of pane the 2 of november 1597 the some of xij *li* x *s* the one clocke was & ashecolerd velluet embradered with gowld the other a longe black velluet clocke layd with sylke lace which they exsepted into the stocke the 28 of septmber 1598 some   xij *li* x *s*

Lent vnto thomas dowton the 8 of october 1598 to bye divers thinges for the playe called the firste sevelle warres of france the some of   vj *li*

Lent vnto Thomas dowton the 11 of october 1598 to bye diuers thinges for the play called the first syvell wares of france the some of   iiij *li*

payd for the company the 12 of october 1598 vnto the lace man for the playe of perce of winchester the some of   v *li* ij *s*

Lent vnto Robart shawe & Jewbey the 23 of october 1598 to
lend vnto mr Chapmane one his playe boock & ij ectes of A
tragedie of bengemens plotte the some of iij li

Layd owt for the company the 3 of novmber 1598 to mr drayton
& mr dickers for A Boocke called the second parte of the syvell
wares of france the some of vj li

Lent vnto thomas dowton the 10 of novmber 1598 to bye a
sackebute of marke antoney for xxxx s

[Lent vnto Robart shawe & Thomas dowton the 15 of novmber
1598 to lend to mr haslett the some of xx s which wm whitte
hathe geuen his word for yt xx s]

[Lent vnto Robart shawe & Thomas dowton the 16 of novmber
1598 to lend to mr haslette A gaynest his valtinge which wm
whitte hathe geuen his word for yt the some of xx s]

James cranwigge the 4 of november 1598 playd his callenge in
my howsse & I sholde haue hade for my parte xxxx s which the
company hath Rd & oweth yt to me xxxx s

Lent vnto Robarte shawe the 18 of novmber 1598 to lend vnto
mr dickers in earneste of A boocke called the 3 parte of the
syvell wares of france some xx s

Lent vnto Robarte shawe the 18 of novmber 1598 to lend vnto
mr Cheattell vpon the mendynge of the firste part of Robart
hoode the some of x s

Lent vnto Robart shaw & Jewbey the 19 of novmber 1598 to
bye diuers thinges for the playe called the 2 part of the syvelle
wares of france x li

Lent vnto Jewby the 24 of november 1598 to bye divers thinges
for the playe called the 2 parte of the syvell wares of france the
some of x li

Lent vnto harey Chettell at the Requeste of Robart shawe the
25 of november 1598 in earneste of his comodey called tys no
deseayt to deseue the deseuer for mendinge of Roben hood for
the corte x s

Lent vnto Robarte Shawe the 6 of desember 1598 to bye A
Boocke called ware with owt blowes & love with owt sewte of
Thomas hawodes some of   iij *li*

Dd vnto same Rowley the 12 of desember 1598 to bye divers
thinges for to macke cottes for gyantes in brvtte the some of   xxiiij *s*

Lent vnto Richard Jonnes the 22 of desember 1598 to bye a
basse viall & other enstrementes for the companey   xxxx *s*

Lent vnto thomas dowton the 22 of desember 1598 to bye A
boocke of harey poorter called the 2 parte of the 2 angrey
wemen of abengton   v *li*

Pd vnto mr drayton & mr dickers the 30 of desember 1598 for
A Boocke called the 3 parte of the syvell wares of france the
some of   v *li*

74. 16 November 1598. Players' Bonds.

Charles Massey and Samuel Rowley had been members of the Admiral's
Men since 1594. The witnesses' signatures are not autograph: Henslowe
signed the names.

———

Memorandum that this 16 of novmber 1598 I hired as my covenente
Servantes Charlles massey & samewell Rowley for A yeare & as mvche
as to sraftide begeninge at the daye A bove written after the statute of
winchester with ij syngell pence & for them they haue covenanted with
me to playe in my howes & in no other howsse dewringe the thime
publeck but in mine yf they dooe with owt my consent yf they dooe to
forfett vnto me xxxx *li* a pece wittnes thomas dowton Robart shawe wm
borne Jubey Richard Jonnes

75. 3 August–22 December 1598. Personal Loan Account.

This list of advances Henslowe made to William Borne (alias Bird) shows
the variety of expense a player was likely to incur in his professional life.
There was litigation to contest with the ever-vexatious Francis Langley,
a widow to entertain, and, on one state occasion, status to gloss with new
apparel or with ready money in the purse. More typically, players laid out
money on costumes. Sometimes they paid for personal flourishes the
Company would not subsidise, like Borne's 'payer of sylke stockens' or

the embroidery on his hat 'for the gwisse', probably a revival of Marlowe's *Massacre at Paris*. Borne had to pawn a cloak to raise the cash to 'Imbrader his hatte', but for him the expense may have been justifiable: the phrase 'to playe the gwisse in' suggests that he had landed the title role. Sometimes, too, players bought costumes as a personal investment that could be sold to the Company upon retirement. Borne's silk stockings might come under that heading. At £2 they were wildly expensive. Thomas Pope, whom Borne was suing, had been a member of Lord Strange's Men until that company disbanded in 1593 but was now with the rival Chamberlain's Men. 'My wiffe' refers to Agnes Henslowe; 'mrs Reues' is unidentified.

———

lent wm borne by my wiffe the 3 of aguste 1598   v s

lent wm borne to folowe sewt agenste Thomas poope the 30 of aguste 1598 by my wiffe   x s

lent vnto wm borne the 9 of agust 1598 the some of viij s which thomas towne feched for hime I saye   viij s

Lent wm borne the 27 of septmber 1598 when he Reade to croyden to ther lorde when the quene came thether   v s

lent wm birde ales borne the 27 of november to bye a payer of sylke stockens to playe the gwisse in   xx s

lent vm borne to bye his stockens for the gwisse   xx s

Lent vnto wm Borne the 19 of november 1598 vpon a longe taney clocke of clothe the some of xij s which he sayd yt was to Imbrader his hatte for the gwisse   xij s

Lent vnto wm Birde ales borne the 22 of desember 1598 when the widow came to mrs Reues to super In Redey money the some of   x s

76. 7 January–24 February 1598/9. Rose Playhouse Receipts.

A direct continuation from no. 72, these receipts, which represent that full share in the galleries the players were paying Henslowe to offset their loans, look much healthier than earlier takings. Perhaps the Christmas season was responsible for the upturn, but a stronger repertoire would also have boosted receipts. Playing was interrupted for a month after 24 February, probably in observation of Lent. Henslowe's note, interlined between the entries for 24 February and 26 March, reads 'dew 233 *li*–17 *s*– 17 *d*', and calculates the difference between the loans to date (£481 0*s* 17*d*) and the repayments (£247 3*s* 0*d*). The Admiral's Men were at Court on 18 February, followed two days later by the Chamberlain's Men; they were paid for these performances in October 1599. On 21 February the formal lease of the site on which the Globe playhouse was to be erected was executed; the lessor was Nicholas Brend.

———

Rd the 7 of Janewary 1598	vij *li* xvij *s*
Rd the 14 of Janewary 1598	viij *li* xj *s*
Rd the 21 of Janewary 1598	viij *li* xiij *s*
Rd the 28 of Janewary 1598	vij *li* vj *s*
Rd the 4 of ffebreary 1598	x *li* xvij *s*
Rd the 11 of ffebreary 1598	vij *li* x *s*
Rd the 18 of ffebreary 1598	vij *li* x *s*
Rd the 24 of ffebreary 1598	——dew 233^{li}–17^{s}–17^{d}——xv *li* iiij *s*

77. 4 January–31 March 1598/9. Loan Accounts (extracts).

In the first quarter of the new year, Henslowe disbursed £67 7*s* in twenty-nine payments on the Admiral's account. The Company made partial payments worth £42 on fourteen plays; they spent £23 5*s* on costumes and £2 2*s* on play licences. Their playwrights were a source of aggravation: Chettle had to be bailed out of the Marshalsea; Dekker had to be discharged 'frome the a reaste of my lord chamberlenes men' at a daunting cost of £3 10*s*; and Harry Porter had finally to be placed under contract to the Company, he giving Henslowe 'his faythfulle promyse that I shold haue alle th*e* boockes w*hic*h he writte ether him sellfe or w*i*th any other'. This bond, like one Chettle would sign on 25 March 1601/2, was not a strong-arm tactic to coerce the exclusive services of a successful playwright. Just the opposite, it was a rather feeble attempt to make an unreliable playwright more serviceable. Porter, like Chettle, was constantly in debt to the Admiral's Men. Since neither had any collateral but his craft to offer against the loans, this agreement would have been one way – perhaps the only way – of convincing anyone that the money would be paid back. The bond guaranteed Porter's debts, not his services, an interpretation which finds support in the fact that Chettle and Porter were the only playwrights the Admiral's Men ever put under contract. Henslowe was the 'I' of the bond, but he affixed Downton's and Shaa's names to it, for this was Company business: Porter was, of course, contracted to the Company, not to Henslowe. These accounts show Chapman having as much trouble as ever titling his plays. His 'iij ackes of A tragedie' remained nameless even when the final instalment was delivered, and his 'world Rones A whelles', which was not finished until July, went under that title until the very last payment, when it became *All Fools*. The title to Heywood's *Joan As Good As My Lady* was also left blank; it was filled in later, in a space too small, so Henslowe crowded part of the title into the margin. *Alexander and Lodowick*, for which 'divers thinges' were bought at the end of March, was a revival, the original production having opened at the Rose in January, 1597. *Vayvode* too was 'old', it being last summer's play. It had come into Edward Alleyn's private possession, probably as part of his retirement settlement with the Company. Alleyn here sold it back to the Admiral's Men who may have returned it to the active repertoire. The payments for *The Two Angry Women of Abingdon Part II* are curious in showing Porter being paid 'in fulle' for the play on the same date that costumes were ordered. Either Porter had already submitted the manuscript (he was paid a lump sum of £5 for *The Two Angry Women Part II* in December) and was late collecting the final payment, or the Company was anticipating the Master of the Revels' willingness to license the play. In March, when the Company seems not to have been playing at the Rose, most of the payments were for licences; evidently a backlog of plays was being lined up in advance of reopening. *The Four Kings* is a play known only by this reference to it among the books licensed. The four unnamed plays the Master of the Revels approved may have been *Joan*, *Two Angry Women Part II*, *Troy's Revenge*, and *Friar Fox*. These last two – the first Chettle's, completed between 16 and 27 February; the second anonymous, submitted on 10 February – are among plays edited from the following extracts. The Company also bought *The Spencers* (Chettle and Porter, 4–22 February) and *War Without Blows* (Heywood, 6 December–26 January). Drayton abandoned *William Longsword* after collecting a £2 instalment on 20 January. Dekker, having completed three parts to *The Civil Wars in France* began work on a *First Introduction* to the epic; his collaborators so far on the project having dropped from exhaustion, Dekker attempted this fourth play solus. He did not complete it.

———

Lent vnto mr chapman the 4 of Jeneway 1598 vpon iij ackes of
A tragedie which thomas dowton bad me dd hime the some of

called   iij li

Lent vnto Robarte Shawe the 8 of Janewary 1598 to paye mr
chapman in fulle payment for his tragedie the some of

called   iij li

Lent vnto Thomas downton the xvij of Janewary 1598 to lend vnto
harey chettell to paye his charges in the marshallsey the some of xxx s

Lent vnto wm Jube the 20 of Janewary 1598 to lend mr dickers
in earneste of his playe called the firste Intreducyon of the syvell
wares of france the some of iij li

pd vnto my sonne Edward alleyn the 21 of Janeway for the playe
of vayvod for the company the some of xxxx s I saye pd 1598 xxxx s

Lent vnto thomas downton the 22 of Janewary 1598 to Leand
vnto mr Chapman in earneste of A Boocke called the world
Rones A whelles the some of iij li

Lent vnto Thomas downton the 30 of Janewary 1598 to descarge
Thomas dickers frome the a reaste of my lord chamberlenes men
I saye lent iij li x s

Lent vnto Thomas dowton the 31 of Janewary 1598 to bye tafetie
for ij womones gownes for the ij angrey wemen of abengton the
some of ix li

Lent vnto Thomas dowton the 10 of febreary 1598 to bye A
boocke of mr hewode called Jonne as good as my ladey the some
of iij li

Lent vnto Thomas downton the 12 of·febreary 1598 to paye mr
hawode in full payment for his boock called Jonne as good as my
Ladey the some of ij li

Lent vnto Thomas downton the 12 of feberye 1598 to pay mr
poorter in fulle payment for his boock called the 2 parte of the
angrey wemen of abington the some of ij li

Lent vnto Thomas downton the 12 of febreary 1598 to by divers
thinges for the playe called the 2 parte of the angrey wemen of
abington ij li

Lent vnto mr Chapman the 13 of febreary 1598 in part of payment
of his boocke called the world Ronnes A whelles xx s

Lent vnto harey porter at the Requeste of the company in earneste
of his boocke called ij mery wemen of abenton the some of
fortyshellengs

& for the Resayte of that money he gaue me his faythfulle
promysse that I shold haue alle the boockes which he writte ether
him sellfe or with any other which some was dd the 28 of febreary
1598 I saye thomas downton Robart shawe   xxxx s

Lent vnto Thomas downton the 8 of marche 1598 to paye vnto
the mr of the Reuelles for the lysencenge of ij playes the some   xiiij s

pd vnto the mr of the Revelles the 18 of marche 1598 for the
lysensynge of ij boockes some of   xiiij s

pd vnto the mr of the Reueulles man for the lysansynge of A
boocke called the 4 kynges   vij s

pd vnto the mr of the Revelles man for the lycensynge of A
boocke called brute grenshillde the some of   vij s

lent vnto Jewbe the 31 of marche 1598 to bye divers thinges for
elexander & lode wicke the some of   v li

78. 25 January 1599. Draft Contract (unexecuted).

Thomas Downton was taking a leading role in company management
and seems to have attained either the status or the wealth to hire his own
servant, a younger player who would double as personal servant for
Downton and spear carrier for the Admiral's Men. Henslowe drafted this
contract. Though it seems never to have been executed and was eventually
cancelled from the Diary, the contract shows the changing status of
employment in the playhouse by including a wage clause to cover periods
when the theatre was closed. If the Company had to 'lye stylle' more than
a fortnight, this hired man was to receive half wages until playing resumed.

Thomas downton the 25 of Janewary 1599 ded hire as his couenante
servante
                                            for ij yers
to be gyne at shrofe tewesday next & he to geue hime viij s a wecke as
longe as they playe & after they lye stylle one fortnyght then to geue hime
hallfe wages wittnes P H & edward browne & charlles masey

79. Undated. Letter.

This message, sent to Edward Alleyn by William Bird, may belong to a
date much later than the spring of 1600 and may refer not to the Rose but

to the Fortune: the Admiral's Men moved into their new playhouse in the autumn of 1600 and a decade later John Russell was living in a tenement nearby on Golding Lane. That Bird addressed the letter to Alleyn rather than Henslowe tends to support the later date since gatherers were appointed by playhouse owners and Alleyn, who was not a shareholder in the Rose, was co-owner of the Fortune. Even so, John Russell held property in Southwark that Henslowe managed for him in the 1590s. It is therefore possible that he was among those gatherers who collected entrance money to the Rose. Bird's letter establishes another playhouse job, the 'nessessary atendaunt on the stage' who might also 'mend our garmentes, when he hath leysure'.

———

Sir there is one Jhon Russell, that by yowr apoyntment was made a gatherer with vs, but my fellowes finding often falce to vs, haue many tymes warnd him ffrom takinge the box. And he as often, with moste damnable othes, hath vowde neuer to touch, yet not with standing his execrable othes, he hath taken the box, & many tymes moste vnconsionablye gatherd, for which we haue resolued he shall neuer more come to the doore yet for your sake, he shall haue his wages, to be a nessessary atendaunt on the stage, and if he will pleasure himself and vs, to mend our garmentes, when he hath leysure, weele pay him for that to, I pray send vs word if this motion, will satisfye you; for him his dishonestye is such we knowe it will not,

Thus yealding our selues in that & a farr greater matter to be comaunded by you I committ you to god

> your loving
> ffrend to comaund
> W Birde

[addressed:]
To his loving ffrend mr Allin Giue these

80. 26 March 1598/9–3 June 1599. Rose Playhouse Receipts.

Resuming after a month's interruption, these receipts comprise the Company's entire share of the gallery money that they were turning over to Henslowe to balance against their loans (see no. 76). The disastrous receipts in March and early April are probably to be accounted for in one of two ways: either the playhouse, after a month's closure for part of Lent, was open for only short performance weeks until Easter (which fell on 16 April this year), or the Admiral's Men were playing to empty houses, their audience having gone elsewhere. The 'elsewhere' could have been the Globe, described as 'de novo edificata' by one Thomas Brand in

May and situated – gallingly – midway between Henslowe's house and the Rose. The first rush of enthusiasm for the new playhouse (if that is what is reflected in the receipts) damaged trade at the Rose for a few giddy weeks before things returned to normal; but the receipts in May and June are deceptive. The Rose never fully recovered, and the Chamberlain's Men at the Globe increasingly took control of the Bank.

———

Rd the 26 of marche 1598	iij *li* xviij *s*
Rd the j of Aprell 1598	iij *li* ij *s*
Rd the 8 of Aprell 1598	iij *li* viij *s*
Rd the 15 of Aprell 159[8]9	xiij *li* vij *s*
Rd the 22 of Aprell 159[8]9	xiij *li* xvj *s*
Rd the 29 of aprell 1599	xj *li* v *s*
Rd the 6 of maye 1599	viij *li* x *s*
Rd the 13 of maye 1599	ix *li*
Rd the 20 of maye 1599	xj *li* xj *s*
Rd the 27 of maye 1599	x *li* viij *s*
Rd the 3 of June 1599	xvj *li* xij *s*

81. 7 April–8 June 1599. Loan Account (extracts).

For nearly six weeks between mid-April and the end of May, the Admiral's Men did not borrow any money from Henslowe. They authorised sixteen disbursements in the three weeks before and after those dates: £11 15s was contributed toward three plays; £45 was spent on costumes, £30 on *The Spencers* alone; 7s went to license a play; and £3 was paid for miscellaneous items such as travel expenses 'to the corte vpon ester euen'. Chettle and Dekker were the only playwrights much occupied in these months. Their 'tragede of Agamemnon' at first glance appears to be simply an alternate title for 'Troyelles & cresseda', a play they should have been close to completing by mid-April. Henslowe was confused by the titles, for he first wrote 'troylles' in the entry for 26 May but then had to cross it out since, after having submitted £4 worth of instalments on a *Troilus* play, the collaborators had evidently discovered their true tragic subject in Agamemnon. They abandoned the Trojan, settled happily among the Greeks, and produced a script in four days. The play was licensed before the week was out. Presumably Rose audiences saw the tragic *Agamemnon* over the summer, and one wonders whether Shakespeare was among that audience – whether he stood riddled with doubts, thinking the playwrights had got it all wrong. Perhaps reaction to that *Agamemnon* produced the cerebral and cynical version of the Troy story the Chamberlain's Men were acting two years hence. In these accounts,

Henslowe ran out of room in the section of the Diary he was using to record them, so, after the entry for 16 April, he turned several pages, wrote a new account heading, 'Layde owt for the company ...', and continued entering the loans. He styled the Company 'lord of notingame men' for the first time, although they had been Nottingham's Men since October 1597 when Charles Howard was elevated to the Earldom. Outside the playhouse, there was bustle at Court as the Earl of Essex, whose commission to assume command of the Irish wars against Tyrone had finally been dispatched on 12 March, received his final instructions and sailed for Ireland at the end of the month. He was commanded specifically not to waste ordnance; not to confer knighthoods except for 'notorious' service; and not to accept any but unconditional surrender from the rebels. Before the summer was out, he had broken every command. England's Icarus was spiralling toward his doom. On 4 June, by order of the Archbishop of Canterbury, a public book burning at Stationers' Hall threw Marlowe's *Elegies* into the flames and consumed *The Scourge of Villainy*, *Skialetheia*, and *The Snarling Satires*. (It was in Gilpin's 'Satire V' of the *Skialetheia* that the Rose received mention: 'Perswade me to a play, I'le to the Rose,/Or Curtaine, one of Plautus Comedies,/Or the Patheticke Spaniards Tragedies'; by contrast to the Rose's bustling entertainments, the 'vnfrequented Theater' stood 'in darke silence, and vast solitude'.) All of Nashe and Harvey's books were ordered confiscated wherever they were for sale and no more of their books were to be printed. Seven of the eleven banned titles satirised unmistakable personages, though under feigned names. On 8 June Henslowe calculated the Company's debt. The 'ttottales' debt carried forward was £586 12s 7d but repayments brought the 'Reste dewe' down to £262 12s 7d.

———

aprell 7 daye 1599	Lent vnto Thomas downton to lende vnto mr dickers & harey cheattell in earneste of ther boocke called Troyeles & creasse daye the some of	iij *li*
Aprell 7 daye 1599	Lent vnto Thomas Towne & Richard alleyn to go to the corte vpon ester euen the some of	x s
	Lent vnto Thomas downton the 9 of Aprell 1599 to bye dyvers thinges as 4 clathe clockes & macke vp a womones gowne the some of for the spencers	x *li*
	Lent vnto Thomas downton the 14 of Aprell 1599 to macke divers thinges for the playe of the spencers the some of	xv *li*

Lent vnto harey cheattell & mr dickers in parte of
payment of ther boocke called Troyelles & cresseda
the 16 of Aprell 1599   xx s

Delyuered vnto Thomas downton boye Thomas par-
sones to bye dyvers thinges for the playe of the spencers the 16 of aprell 1599 the some of   v li

    Layde owt for the company of mr lord of no-
    tingame men frome the 26 of maye 1599 as
    ffoloweth   1599

Lent vnto mr dickers & mr chettell the 26 of maye
1599 in earneste of A Boocke called [troylles & cre-
seda] the tragede of Agamemnon the some of   xxx s

Lent vnto Robart shawe the 30 of maye 1599 in fulle
payment of ther Boocke called the tragedie of Aga-
memnone the some of   iij li v s
to mr dickers & hary chettell

pd vnto the mr of Revelles man for lycensynge of A
Boocke called the tragedie of agamemnon the 3 of
June 1599   vij s

Lent vnto Robarte shawe the 2 of June 1599 to paye
vnto mr chapman for his Boocke called the worlde
Runes a whelles some of   xx s

pd vnto the lace man the 8 of June 1599 at the
apoyntment of the company in part of payment to
hime for copper lace some of   v li
          li s d
ttottales   586-12-7
Reste dewe   262-12-7

82. 21 June–13 October 1599. Loan Account (extracts).

Playing may have been inhibited over the summer as a precaution against
plague. Henslowe recorded his last 'wholle galleryes' receipt from
Nottingham's Men on 3 June and cast up his loan accounts on 8 June.
Thereafter he did not record further receipts until October, 'begynynge at
myhellmas week', the usual date for the lifting of plague restraints. The

loan account, however, carried on, and this makes it difficult to argue dogmatically from the lapse in receipts that the playhouse was closed (see no. 83). Plague deaths this summer never rose above four in any week, but dogmatic arguments cannot be based on that fact either, for in July 1596 a restraint against plays had been ordered when no other evidence of plague was produced except the Privy Council's fear articulated in the inhibition itself (see no. 47). If the Rose was not open until October, plays were being performed at the Globe in September, for on the 21st a foreign visitor, Thomas Platter, saw *Julius Caesar* there. He commented: 'every day around two o'clock in the afternoon in the City of London two and sometimes even three plays are performed at different places ...; those that acquit themselves best have also the largest audiences'. Nottingham's Men knew this strict equation from experience. Although they may not have been performing over the summer, they continued to spend money, most conspicuously on new plays. Henslowe entered twenty-two payments on the Company's account: £31 for nine plays, £13 for costumes, and £1 10s for properties. Ben Jonson later disowned his contributions to *Page of Plymouth* and *The Scots Tragedy*. Chapman's *World Runs on Wheels* acquired at the last minute the title by which it survives, *All Fools*; Dekker's *Gentle Craft* eventually came to be known as *The Shoemaker's Holiday*. 'The new poete mr mastone' was probably John Marston. The blank left for the title of his play was never filled in. Other plays that the Company commissioned but that have been edited from the following extracts include: *The Stepmother's Tragedy* (Chettle and Dekker, 24 July-14 October 'in full'); *Bear A Brain* (Dekker 'in fulle' 1 August); *Tristan of Lyons* (anonymous, £3 only on 13 October); and *Poor Man's Paradise* (Haughton, two payments totalling £1 on 20 and 25 August). On 13 October Henslowe cast up the Company's accounts, subtracted the receipts from the loans, and reckoned they owed him £274. A few days earlier, on 2 October, the Company had collected £20 Court money for performances before the Queen the previous Christmas. 'Robert Shaw and Thomas Downton servauntes to Therle of Nottingham' were named in the payment warrant. Over in Ireland, Essex was careering toward disaster. The Queen learned on 10 June that he had advanced the Earl of Southampton to the Generalship of the Horse against her express command. At the end of July, when Essex still had not attacked the rebel Tyrone, the Queen revoked her former licence for him to return to Court at his own discretion; she now gave him leave to return only under her personal warrant. On 23 August, again reckless of commandment to the contrary, Essex knighted fifty-nine of his army, and on 17 September he negotiated a treaty with Tyrone. That might have been the final straw to a monarch who had ordered unconditional surrender from the rebels, but headstrong Essex contrived to make matters even worse: he returned, without the Queen's warrant, to London, riding breakneck across the country to burst into the presence chamber where 'the Queen newly up' had 'her hair about her face'. His mud-spattered clothing was meant to betoken duty, but the Queen was not impressed or amused. The next morning Essex was ordered to keep his chambers while the Privy Council considered gross dereliction and, as some thought, impudence. His rash concessiveness toward Tyrone led to the rebels' issuing a series of demands for Ireland in November. The Catholic Church and spiritual sovereignty of the Pope were to be re-established; a university was to be built with Crown revenue; the Governor of Ireland, holding at least the title of an Earl, was to sit on the Privy Council and all other officers were to be Irishmen. Mr Secretary Cecil wrote on his copy of the manifesto, 'Utopia'.

———

Lent vnto wm Borne & Jewbey the 21 of June 1599 to lend vnto mr chapman vpon his Boock called the world Ronnes a whelles the some of   xxxx s

Lent vnto thomas dowton the 2 of July 1599 to paye mr chapman in full payment for his Boocke called the world Rones a whelles & now all foolles but the foolle some of   xxx s

Lent vnto Thomas dowton the 13 of July 1599 to bye enstrumentes for the company the some of   xxx s

Lent vnto Samewell Rowley & Thomas downton the 15 of July 1599 to bye A Boocke of thomas dickers Called the gentle Craft the som of   iij li

Lent vnto Thomas downton the 17 of July 1599 to lend vnto mr chapman in earneste of A pastrall tragedie the some of   xxxx s

Lent vnto wm Borne alles birde the 10 of aguste aguste 1599 to Lend vnto bengemyne Johnsone & thomas deckers in earneste of ther boocke which they be awrittenge called pagge of plemoth the some of   xxxx s

Lent vnto wm Birde Thomas dowton wm Jube the 2 of Septmber 1599 to paye in fulle payment for A Boocke called the lamentable tragedie of pagge of plemoth the some of   vj li

Lent vnto Thomas downton the 3 of Septmber 1599 to lend vnto Thomas deckers Bengemen Johnson hary Chettell & other Jentellman in earneste of A playe calle Robart the second Kinge of scottes tragedie the some of   xxxx s

Lent vnto Jewbey & thomas towne the 12 of Septmber 1599 to
bye wemen gownes for page of plemoth the some of   x *li*

Lent vnto Samwell Rowley & Robart shawe the 15 of septmber
1599 to lend in earneste of A Boocke called the scottes tragedi
vnto Thomas dickers & harey chettell the some of   xx *s*

Lent hary chettell the 16 of septmber 1599 in earneste of A Boocke
called the scottes tragedie the some of   x *s*

Lent vnto wm Borne the 27 of Setmber 1599 to lend vnto Bengemen Johnsone in earneste of A Boocke called the scottes tragedie
the some of   xx *s*

Lent vnto wm Borne the 28 of septmber 1599 to Lent vnto mr
maxton the new poete mr mastone in earneste of A Boocke called
the some of   xxxx *s*

Reckned with the company tof my lorde the earlle of notingames
men to this place & I haue layd owte for them the some of vj
hunderd & thirtie two pownds & they haue payd vnto me of this
deatte iij hunderd & fiftie & eyghte powndes to this day beinge
the 13 of [novmb] october 1599

83. 6 October–30 December 1599. Rose Playhouse Receipts.

Henslowe recorded his last 'wholle gallereyes' receipt from Nottingham's
Men on 3 June and cast up the Company's loan account on 8 June.
Thereafter he did not record another receipt until October, when he
opened the following receipt account. To judge by the lapse in receipts,
the Rose was closed throughout the summer. Henslowe's new account
heading is ambiguous enough to admit the opposite possibility though.
'I begane to Receue the gallereys agayne which theye Receued begynynge
at myhellmas wecke' might be interpreted to mean that the players, having
turned over their 'wholle gallereyes' to Henslowe for the twelve months
preceding, collected the galleries themselves during the summer, then, in
the autumn, resumed the old arrangement of paying off their loans by
handing Henslowe their gallery money. This reading finds some support
in the fact that the Company continued to borrow money over the
summer; production, then, was carrying on, and this may mean that the
Rose was open all summer. The possibility that the Company could not
afford to pay Henslowe any of its gallery money for four months might
indicate that they were facing a crisis. This was the first full season that
the Rose tenants were competing with their rivals at the newly erected
Globe. Financially, that competition may have spelled ruin. The autumn

receipts, intermittently robust, slumped dismally in some weeks. Christmas was bleak: just how bleak can best be gauged by comparing this account with no. 80 – the high season after Easter – and to nos. 72 and 76, Christmas 1598. The Admiral's Men did perform at Court twice this year, on 27 December and 1 January, while the Chamberlain's Men gave three performances. They were paid for these performances on 18 February.

———

Heare I begane to Receue the gallereys agayne which theye Receued begynynge at myhellmas wecke beinge the 6 of october 1599 as foloweth

[Rd the 6 of october 1599	v *li* iij *s*]
Rd the 20 of october 1599	iiij *li* iij *s*
Rd the 27 of october 1599	iij *li* xiiij *s*
Rd the 3 of novmber 1599	viij *li* xvj *s*
Rd the 10 of novmber 1599	vj *li* ix *s*
Rd the 18 of novmber 1599	ij *li* xvij *s*
Rd the 25 of novmber 1599	vij *li* iiij *s*
Rd the 1 of desember 1599	v *li* xiij *s*
Rd the 8 of desember 1599	iiij *li*
Rd the 16 of desember 1599	ij *li* xvij *s*
Rd the 23 of desember 1599	iij *li* iij *s*
Rd the 30 of desember 1599	x *li* viij *s*

84. 8 November 1599. Letter.

Robert Shaa's letter authorising Henslowe to pay Robert Wilson for *II Henry Richmond* on the Company's account must have been fairly typical of the way company business was transacted. The unfortunate detail of Shaa's being 'trobled with a scytation' for debt is not typical. Players were sometimes financially embarrassed. The precarious nature of their job made embarrassment inevitable. But they were not, as was so frequently true of playwrights mentioned in Henslowe's Diary, improvident. On the back of the letter is what appears to be an outline of several scenes of *Henry Richmond*. The date of the letter is fixed by an acquittance, in Wilson's hand, acknowledging receipt of the payment from Henslowe, which was duly entered in the Company's loan account (see no. 85).

———

Mr Henshlowe we haue heard their booke and lyke yt their pryce is eight poundes, which I pray pay now to mr wilson, according to our promysse, I would haue Come my selfe, but that I ame trobled with a scytation

yors Robt Shaa

[on the back]

Enter Richard

1. Sce Wm Wor: & Ansell & to them *th*e plowghmen
2. Sce: Richard Q. & Eliza: Catesbie, Louell, Rice ap Tho: Blunt, Banester
3. Sce: Ansell Dauye Denys Hen: Oxf: Courtney Bourchier & Grace/to them Rice ap Tho: & his Soldiors
4. Sce: Mitton Ban: his Wyfe & children
[6. Sce:]
5. Sce: K Rich: Catesb: Louell. Norf. Northumb: Percye

85. 16 October–29 December 1599. Loan Account (extracts).

Over these months Henslowe made thirty-one payments for Nottingham's Men: £57 5s toward nine plays, £20 15s on costumes, 14s on licences, and 10s on miscellaneous purchases. The flurry of negotiations that attended *Sir John Oldcastle* was quite unlike the Company's standard procedure in commissioning new plays. They paid over the odds for the original script (although it should be noticed that, increasingly, new plays were fetching much more than the standard £6; see *Patient Grissell* for example or *II Henry Richmond* on 8 November). A sequel was commissioned on the spot, and, 'at the playnge of *Sir* John oldcastell the firste tyme', the Company gave the playwrights a 10s bonus 'as A gefte'. Henslowe wrote this note in the margin of his Diary as if deliberately careful to supply some explanation for aberrant behaviour. But the players had not run mad. Rather, they were conducting themselves with the nervy calculation of soldiers in a trench who finally see the enemy make a tactical blunder they can pounce upon. Since the previous spring, when the Chamberlain's Men opened at the Globe, Henslowe's receipts seem to show that Nottingham's Men had been battling for audiences, and steadily losing ground. But now the rival company may have made a mistake. They put upon their stage a villainous fat knight they originally called Oldcastle but later, under pressure, rechristened Falstaff. Umbrage was taken at the characterisation, and Nottingham's Men, perhaps smelling revenge, went on the offensive with their own *Oldcastle* play whose Prologue informed Rose audiences that 'It is no pamper'd glutton we present,/Nor aged Councellor to youthful sinne,/But one, whose vertue shone above the rest,/A valiant Martyr and a vertuous Peere'. Certainly, that was *one* version of the historical Sir John, Lord Cobham, a Wycliffite who was burned at the stake for his anti-papist views and so earned a place in Fox's *Book of Martyrs*. Catholics, of course, saw him differently, as 'a Ruffian-Knight as all England knoweth, & commonly brought in by comediants on their stages: he was put to death for robberyes and rebellion under ... K. Henry the fifth'. Understandably, the present Lord Cobham had been angered at having his title paraded so unflatteringly across the public stage at the Globe, and he took measures to force changes in Shakespeare's *dramatis personae*. For their part, the Chamberlain's Men perhaps considered Cobham fair game. The seventh Lord, who died in 1597, preceded the current Lord Chamberlain in office. He had not patronised a cry of players since his youth, even after his office placed him near the top of the pyramid that reached from the Queen through the Revels Office to the professional players. It was hardly likely, then, that the Chamberlain's Men, who re-acquired their name when their own patron, George Carey, took office at Cobham's demise, owed him much allegiance or even respect. They reckoned, however, without the present Lord Cobham, a brother-in-law of Robert Cecil and a courtier who ranged among the faction that opposed Essex. Insofar as the Chamberlain's Men could be identified with the smart young gentlemen who buzzed around Essex, Nottingham's Men could be said to have supported the Establishment. And Essex was in disgrace, his mismanagement of Ireland and his consequent imprisonment finally declared in open court at Star Chamber on 1 December but certainly bruited from his spectacularly miscalculated return to Court in September. Thus, by circuitous and muddy paths, politics walked hand-in-hand with the patronage through the doors of the public playhouse. *Oldcastle* opened at the Rose some time between 16 October and 8 November. The play may have been responsible for boosting receipts the week of 3 November (see no. 83) and, if it were seen as a thrust at Essex, the weeks of 25 November and 1 December. Other plays the Company commissioned this autumn that have been edited from the following extracts include two Haughton- Day collaborations, *John Cox* (completed 14 November) and *The Tragedy of Thomas Merry*, i.e., *Beech's Tragedy* (completed 6 December, licensed between 10 and 18 January). This second play was no doubt inspired by events recounted in the 1594 ballad titled 'the pitifull lamentacon of Rachell Marrye whoo suffred in Smithfield with her brother Thomas Merrye the vjth of September 1594'. Their crime must have been sensational, for the ballad was entered in the Stationers' Register the day after the Merrys were executed. Two other plays this autumn – *The Orphan's Tragedy* (Chettle, 27 November) and *The Arcadian Virgin* (Chettle-Haughton, 13 and 17 December) – were evidently abandoned, although two years later, on 24 September 1601, Chettle submitted another 10s instalment of *The Orphan's Tragedy*, probably hoping nobody would recognise the title. The Company seems to have made an overnight decision to rehearse Dekker's *Old Fortunatus* for their Christmas appearance at Court. Dekker handed in the final instalment on 30 November and the next day was paid £1 for 'altrenge of the boocke'. The second payment for revisions, on 12 December, refers to the new 'eande of fortewnatus for the corte'. In all, Dekker collected £3 for his revisions, half as much again as he earned for the original script. The Company appeared at Court on 27 December and 1 January, while the Chamberlain's Men appeared on 26 December, 6 January and 3 February. They were paid for these performances on 18 February. Already, Nottingham's Men were casting about for new premises. On 24 December Edward Alleyn acquired the lease to a site on which a playhouse could be built far away from the Globe and the Chamberlain's Men. Perhaps relocating seemed the easiest solution, but the new playhouse embattled the Company even further (see nos. 87, 88, 91 and 93). In the following accounts the signed or authorised entries ('Receued by me . . .') are all autograph.

———

this 16th of october 99

Receued by me Thomas downton of *p*hillipp Henchlow to pay mr *m*onday mr drayton & mr wilsson & haythway for the first *p*arte of the lyfe of Sr Jhon Ouldcasstell & in earnest of the Second *p*arte for the vse of the compayny ten pownd I say receued   10 *li*

Receved by me Samuell Rowlye of phyllyp henchloe for harrye chettell in Earneste of the playe of patient Gryssell for the Vse of the Comepanye   xx *s*

as A   Receved of Mr hincheloe for Mr Mundaye & the Reste of
ge*f*te   the poets at the playnge of Sr John oldcastell the ferste
        tyme   x *s*

Receau*e*d of mr Ph: Hinchlow by a note vnder the hand of mr Rob: Shaw in full payment for the second *p*art of Henrye Richmond sold to him & his Companye the some of eight pownd*es* Current money*e* the viijt daye of November 1599   viij *li*
By me R Wilson
the ix*th* of november
Receued of phillipp Hinchlow to pay Thomas Deckker in earnest of abooke cald the hole hystory of ffortunatus xxxx *s* by me Thomas downton   xxxx *s*

Lent vnto Thomas dickers the 24 of novmb*er* 1599 in earneste of his Boock*e* called the wholl*e* history of fortewnatus the some of wittnes John: Shaa   iij *li*

Receaued of Mr Henshlowe this xxxth of novembr 1599 to pay Mr deckers in full payment of his booke of fortunatu*es*
By me Robt Shaa   xx *s*

Receaued of mr Henshlow this xxxith of novem 1599 ffor
the vse of the Com ten pownd ffor wemenes gowns
            By me Thomas Downton   x *li*

Lent vnto Thomas dickers at the A poynt ment of Robart
shawe the 31 of novmb*er* 1599 w*h*i*c*h I borowed of mr
greffen for the altrenge of the boocke of the wholl history
of fortewnatus the some of   xx *s*

Receued of Mr Hinchlow for the vse of the Company x *li*
ffor to by thing*es* for ffortunatus
            By me Thomas Downton   x *li*

pd vnto mr deckers the 12 of desemb*er* 1599 for the eande
of fortewnatus for the corte at the a poyntment of Robarte
shawe the some of   xxxx *s*

Lent vnto thomas dickkers harey chettell wm harton in
earneste of A Boock*e* called patient grissell at the a poyntment of Robart shawe by his letter the some of three
pownd*es* the 19 of desemb*er* 1599   iij *li*

Receaued of mr Henshlowe to pay to the taylor xxv *s* & to
the mr of the Revells man xiiij *s* for the lycensinge of 2
book*es*
          by me RobtShaa   xxxix *s*

Receued of mr Henchlow for the vse of the Compa*n*y to
pay mr drayton for the second p*ar*te of Sr Jhon ould Casell
foure pownd I say receud
           p*er* me Thomas Downton   iiij *li*

Receaued of mr Henslowe the 26th of decembr 1599 to pay
Tho: Deckers: H. Chettle: & Will: Hawton for pacient
Grissil vj *li* I say Receaued
          by me RobtShaa   vj *li*

Lent vnto thomas deckers the 28 of desemb*er* 1599 in
earneste of a play*e* called pacyent gresell the some of   v *s*

Lent vnto wm harton the 29 of desemb*er* 1599 in earnest of
patient gresell some of   v *s*

86. October 1599–January 1600. Rose Licensing Fees.

Henslowe's payment to the Master of the Revels to license his playhouse had doubled between 1592 and 1596, from 5s per week to £2 per month. Now the fee rose again, to £3 per month.

——

xxvth daie of October 1599.

Rec the daie aforesaid for the vse of my mr Edmond Tylney Esquier of mr Henslowe the some of   iij *li*

per me Rich: veale:/

xx die Novembr 1599

Rec *the* daie aforesaid for *the* vse of my mr Edmond Tylney Esquier of mr Henslowe the some of   iij *li*

per me Rich: veale:

the ixth daye Januarye 1600

Rec *the* daye aforesayde for *the* vse of my mr Edmond Tyllney Esquire mr of the reuells of mr Henslowe the Som   iij *li*

per m*ei* Willi*a*m Playstowe

87. 8 January 1600. Building Contract for the Fortune Play-house (extracts).

The Globe had been open for nearly a year. Henslowe, whose house stood 'right over against the clink' prison, had to walk past the rival theatre *en route* to the Rose, where receipts still had not recovered from the competition of the Chamberlain's Men. Perhaps despairing of winning their audiences back, Nottingham's Men decided to vacate their home on the Bankside. Their new playhouse was to be built north of the City on Golding Lane on the parish of St Giles-without-Cripplegate, and it was to be paid for with Philip Henslowe's money, backed by Edward Alleyn's yet undiminished prestige, and made good with Peter Street's carpentry. Details of the agreement are contained in the following contract between Street and the Henslowe–Alleyn partnership, dated 'the Eighte daie of Januarye 1599', i.e., 1600. The contract deals exclusively with construction: no future tenants are named or provided for; not even the partnership between Henslowe and Alleyn is illuminated. But it is quite clear from future developments that the project relied upon the mutual dependency of the Henslowe–Alleyn–Nottingham's Men collaboration. The Company was not rich enough to build a playhouse; Henslowe was neither famous enough to outweigh the objections that would be raised against the erecting of yet another playhouse, nor speculative enough to build without tenants in mind. He had grown greyer in theatrical enterprise since he struck that first bargain over the Rose in 1587. The new playhouse was to be called the Fortune, hopefully, no doubt. Its blueprints – the 'Plott thereof drawen' that has not survived – were carbon copies of the Globe except in minor details, and by employing Peter Street, Henslowe made sure the blueprints would be read exactly: Street had recently erected the Globe. Work began on the new playhouse almost immediately. By 17 January the bricklayers had already collected a payment from Henslowe. But for the Little Rose, such developments could only spell the end to an illustrious decade. Her story from this date is one of decline.

———

The frame of the saide howse to be sett square and to conteine ffowerscore foote of lawfull assize everye waie square withoute, and fiftie fiue foote of like assize square everye waie within, with a good suer and stronge foundacion of pyles brick lyme and sand, both withoute & within, to be wroughte one foote of assize att the leiste aboue the grounde And the saide fframe to conteine Three Stories in heighth The first or lower Storie to Conteine Twelue foote of lawfull assize in heighth The second Storie Eleauen foote of lawfull assize in heighth And the Third or vpper Storie to conteine Nyne foote of lawfull assize in height/All which Stories shall conteine Twelue foote and a half of lawfull assize in breadth througheoute besides a Juttey forwardes in eyther of the saide Two vpper Stories of Tenne ynches of lawfull assize, with ffower convenient divisions for gentlemens roomes and other sufficient and convenient divisions for Twoe pennie roomes with necessarie Seates to be placed and sett Aswell in those roomes as througheoute all the rest of the galleries of the saide howse and with suche like steares Conveyances & divisions withoute & within as are made & Contryved in and to the late erected Plaiehowse On the Banck in the saide parishe of Ste Saviors Called the Globe With a Stadge and Tyreinge howse to be made erected & settupp within the saide fframe, with a shadowe or cover over the saide Stadge, which Stadge shalbe placed & sett As alsoe the stearecases of the saide fframe in suche sorte as is prefigured in a Plott thereof drawen And which Stadge shall conteine in length ffortie and Three foote of lawfull assize and in breadth to extende to the middle of the yarde of the saide howse. The same Stadge to be paled in belowe with good stronge and sufficyent newe oken bourdes And likewise the lower Storie of the saide fframe withinside, and the same lower storie to be alsoe laide over and fenced with stronge yron pykes And the saide Stadge to be in all other proporcions Contryved and fashioned like vnto the Stadge of the saide Plaiehowse Called the Globe, With convenient windowes and lightes glazed to the saide Tyreinge howse And the saide fframe Stage and Stearecases to be covered with Tyle, and to haue a sufficient gutter of lead to Carrie & convey the water frome the Coveringe of the saide Stadge to fall backwardes And alsoe all the saide fframe and the Stairecases thereof to be sufficyently enclosed withoute with lathe lyme & haire and the gentlemens roomes and Twoe pennie roomes to be seeled with lathe lyme & haire and all the fflowers of the saide Galleries Stories and Stadge to be bourded with good & sufficyent newe deale bourdes of the whole thickness wheare neede shalbe And the saide howse and other thinges beforemencioned to be made & doen To be in all other Contrivitions Conveyances fashions thinge and thinges effected finished and doen accordinge to the manner and fashion of the saide howse Called the Globe Saveinge only that all the princypall and maine postes of the saide fframe and Stadge forwarde shalbe square and wroughte pallasterwise with carved proporcions Called Satiers to be placed & sett on the Topp of every of the same postes And saveinge alsoe that the saide Peeter Streete shall not be chardged with anie manner of payntinge in or aboute the saide fframe howse or Stadge or anie parte thereof nor Rendringe the walls within Nor seelinge anie more or other roomes then the gentlemens roomes Twoe pennie roomes and Stadge before remembred/nowe theiruppon the saide Peeter Streete dothe covenante ... to and with the saide Phillipp Henslowe and Edward Allen ... That he ... will att his ... owne propper costes & Chardges Well woorkmanlike & substancyallie make erect, sett upp and fully finishe ... with good stronge and substancyall newe Tymber and other necessarie stuff All the saide fframe and other woorkes ... (beinge not by anie aucthoretie Restrayned, and haveinge ingres egres & regres to doe the same) before the ffyue & Twentith daie of Julie next Commeinge after the date hereof ... And shall alsoe make all the saide fframe in every poynte for Scantlinges lardger and bigger in assize Then the Scantlinges of the Timber of the saide newe erected howse, Called the Globe .../In consideracion of all which ... The saide Phillipp Henslowe & Edward Allen ... Shall & will well & truelie paie or Cawse to be paide vnto the saide Peeter Streete his executors or assignes Att the place aforesaid appoynted for the erectinge of the saide fframe The full somme of ffower hundred & ffortie Poundes of lawfull money of Englande in manner & forme followeinge, that is to saie, Att suche tyme And when as the Tymberwoork of the saide fframe shalbe rayzed & sett upp ... Twoe hundred & Twentie poundes And att suche time and when as the saide fframe & woorkes shalbe fullie effected & ffynished as is aforesaide Or within Seaven daies then next followeinge, thother Twoe hundred and Twentie poundes withoute fraude or Coven .../In witnes whereof the parties abouesaid to theis presente Indentures Interchaungeably haue sett theire handes and Seales/Yeoven the daie and yeare ffirste abouewritten

P S

Sealed and deliured by the saide Peter Streete
in the presence of me william Harris Public Scrivener

And me frauncis Smyth appr*entice* to the said Scri*vener*
[endorsed:]
Peater Streat ffor The Building of the ffortune

88. 12 January 1599/1600. Warrant.

Charles Howard, Earl of Nottingham, threw his considerable weight
behind the company that bore his name by defending their proposed new
playhouse. He directed this warrant 'To all & euery her ma*jesties* Justices
& other Ministers and Officers within the Countye of Midd*lesex* ... And
to all others whome it shall Concerne'. The magic word was 'Alleyn', for
although the thundering tragedian had not acted with the Company for
nearly two and a half years, his name was still one to conjure with.
Henslowe the money-man did not merit even a mention, but that is not
surprising: the silencing of public indignation is not to be achieved by
reference to grubby financial matters. Nottingham's defence rested upon
high-minded allusions to Her Majesty's 'greate lykeinge and Contentme*nt*' in the 'acceptable Service, w*hi*ch my saide Servant and his Companie
haue doen and presented before her Highenes'. His description of the
Rose, 'that Howse ... on the Banck', as dangerously decayed and 'verie
noysome for resorte of people in the wynter tyme' was patently untrue.
Audiences had been 'resorting' to the Bankside for years, and the
Chamberlain's Men, newly installed there, were certainly making no
objections about the locale. As for the condition of the building itself: the
Rose continued to be used as a playhouse for the next three years, and
when it finally fell it was because Henslowe, not the fabric, had cracked
(see no. 112). Nottingham ended his directive 'not doubtinge of yor
observac*i*on in this behalf'. He took too much for granted, though, and
was probably unprepared to have the ground cut out from under him by
the Privy Council's instruction of 9 March (see no. 91).

—

Wheareas my Servant Edward Allen (in respect of the dangerous decaye
of that Howse w*hi*ch he and his Companye haue nowe, on the Banck,
And for that the same standeth verie noysome for resorte of people in the
wynter tyme) Hath/thearfore nowe of late, taken a plott of grounde neere
Redcrossestreete london (verie fitt and convenient) for the buildinge, of a
new Howse theare, and hath prouided Tymber and other necessaries for
theffectinge theareof to his great chardge: fforasmuche as the place
standeth verie convenient, for the ease of People, And that her Ma*jestie*
(in respect of the acceptable Service, w*hi*ch my saide Servant and his
Companie haue doen and presented before her Highenes to her greate
lykeinge and Contentme*nt*; aswell this last Christmas as att sondrie other

tymes) ys gratiouslie moued toward*es* them w*i*th a speciall regarde of
fauor in their proceeding*es*: Theis shalbe thearefore to praie and requier
yow and euerie of yow To permitt and suffer my saide Servant to proceede
in theffecting and finishinge of the saide Newhowse, w*i*thout anie yor lett
or molestac*i*on toward*es* him or any of his woorkmen And soe not
doubtinge of yor observac*i*on in this behalf I bidd yow right hartelie
farewell att the Courte at Richmond the xijth of Januarye 1599

Notingham

To all & euery her ma*j*esti*es* Justices &
other Ministers and Officers w*i*thin
the Countye of Midds & to euery
of them And to all others whome
it shall Concerne:

89. 6 January–30 March 1599/1600. Rose Playhouse Receipts.

While construction of the new playhouse began, business at the Rose
continued as usual. Nottingham's Men went on paying Henslowe all of
their gallery money to balance against their loans, but in some weeks
Henslowe collected precious little. The Company's current borrowing
was keeping pace with repayments (£17 12s on the loan account against
£22 3s repayments by 27 January), but they were not managing to strike
off much of their former debt. A month-long interruption stopped playing
between mid-February and March. The Company might have had sufficient funds to tide themselves over a short interruption, for on 18 February
they had been paid their Court money, £20, for performances the previous
Christmas. Evidently, though, they went on tour, for on 6 February they
bought 'a drome to go into the contry' (see no. 90). Henslowe noted in the
margin of the Company's loan account that payments after 10 February
were made 'sence we left playing'.

Rd the 6 of Janewary 1599	ix *li* ix s
Rd the 13 of Janewary 1599	vj *li* xvj s
Rd the 20 of Janeway 1599	iij *li* ij s
Rd the 27 of Janeway 1599	j *li* xvj s
Rd the 3 of febreary 1599	vij *li* xiiij s
Rd th 10 of febreary 1599	vij *li* xiij s
Rd the 9 of march 1599	iij *li* xiij s
Rd the 16 of march 1599	vj *li*
Rd the 23 of march 1599	iiij *li* xvij s
Rd the 30 of march 1599	xj *li* xiiij s

90. 9 January–18 March 1599/1600. Loan Account (extracts).

Of twenty-eight payments Henslowe made for Nottingham's Men during this period, £22 1s went toward nine playbooks, £50 10s was spent on costumes, 7s on a single play licence, £2 3s 6d on properties and £5 10s on miscellaneous expenses. The Company valued *Patient Grissell* sufficiently – they had paid over £9 for the playbook in December – to want to prevent its publication. They gave 'the printer' £2 on 18 March 'to staye the printinge of patient gresell'; ten days later it was entered in the Stationers' Register. Of course, entry in the Register served only to establish a printer's right to the material. Whether or not he actually printed it or not was another matter, but since the entry prevented anyone else from printing the material, it was a form of insurance. The Company's £2 seems not to have been wasted on this occasion: no edition of *Patient Grissell* is known before 1603. Another Dekker play, *Old Fortunatus*, was entered for printing on 20 February. Payments for *The Seven Wise Masters* give a clear indication of the relative financial weight placed on script *v.* wardrobe in a new production, for while the playwrights collected £5 for that play, the Company spent £38 to costume it. Scripts undoubtedly represented more of a gamble than costumes did; one was less likely to be completed than the other and sometimes assurances had to be given: see, for example, William Bird's guarantee of Boyle's new play. In the second week of February the Company evidently went on tour. Henslowe's receipts are interrupted by a month-long break (see no. 89) and payments in the loan accounts for '2 trumpettes' and 'a drome to go into the contry' are sure enough signs of travel. Coachman Sims may have been hired to haul the touring gear. Henslowe continued to make disbursements for the absent players, marking them 'sence we left playing'. The payment to 'Father ogell' may have been for beards. He and his father appear as beardmakers in the Master of the Revels' account book; and in *Sir Thomas More*, a play by Rose dramatists, the travelling comedians who entertain More send to 'Oagle' for a missing beard. By the beginning of March some of Nottingham's Men were in London – having returned, or, if a reduced company was touring, never having left – for the signatures of William Bird on 1 March and of Samuel Rowley on 8 March are autograph. Shaa's signatures after 18 March are likewise autograph. Other plays the Company commissioned this season include *Owen Tudor* (Drayton, Munday, Hathaway, Wilson; n.d. 10–18 January), *The Spanish Moor's Tragedy* (Haughton, Day, Dekker; 13 February) and *Ferrex and Porrex* (Haughton; 18 March–13 April). Only the last was completed. It was licensed around 6 May. Another tragedy by Day was left unfinished and apparently incompletely titled, it being entered by Henslowe on 10 January as 'the etalyan tragedie of [blank]'. For this single instalment Day was paid £2. Nothing more is heard of his tragedy. Three years later, however, Wentworth Smith, writing for Worcester's Men at the Rose, submitted a play titled 'the etallyan tragedie'. If Smith took over Day's abandoned tragedy after three years, this is the single instance of such an occurrence in the Diary. It seems improbable, though, that a fragment would survive so long in the tiring house or wherever playbooks were stored at the Rose, would avoid being moved or destroyed when Nottingham's Men vacated the playhouse, and would fall into the hands of a dramatist employed by the next Rose tenants. The greater likelihood would appear to be that two Italian tragedies were written. 'Italy' was practically synonymous with 'tragedy' by 1603 anyway, so neither dramatist would get marks for originality in titling their plays so obviously. Since Smith was eventually paid the full £6 rate for his tragedy, if he knew Day's play, he was probably relying on it for only the plot or was reworking the material completely.

———

Receaued this ixth of January 1599 in behalfe of the
Company to pay the laceman v *li* I say Receaued
       Robt Shaa   v *li*

pd vnto the mr of the Revelles man for lycensynge of
A Boock*e* called Beches tragedie the some of   vij *s*

Lent vnto Thomas towne the 18 of Janewary 1599 to
lend thomas dickers in earneste of A playe Boock*e*
called trewght*es* suplication to candelighte some of   xx *s*
          as may a pere

Receaued of Mr Henshlowe this 26th of January 1599
xx *s* to geue vnto the tayler to buy a grey gowne for
gryssell I say Receaued   xx *s*
       by me RobtShaa

Lent vnto Thomas dickers at the apoyntment of the
company the 30 of Janewary 1599 in erneste of A
Boock*e* called trewth suplicaton to candelithe Rd by
wm harton for hime   xx *s*

Lent vnto the company the 6 of febrea*r*y 1599 for to by
a drome [when] to go into the contry   xj *s* vj *d*

Receaued of Mr Henshlowe this 7th of february 1599
the some of xxij *s* to buy 2 trumpett*es*   xxij *s*
       RobtShaa

Lent vnto the company the 9 of febreary 1599 to paye
the cootch man symes the some of   iij *li*

lent vnto me Wbirde the 9 of februarye to paye for a
new booke to will: Boyle cald Jugurth xxx *s* w*hich* if
you dislike Ile repaye it back   xxx *s*

Lent vnto Thomas dowton 10 of febreary 1599 for the
company to geue vnto father ogell & other thinges   x *s*

sence we
left play
ing

Layd owt for the company the 16 of febreary 1599 in
earnest of A Boocke called damon & pethy*a*s as maye
a peare some is   xx *s*
to hary chettell

Receavd of mr hinchlow the 1 of march to paye to
harry chettell Thomas decker william hawton & Jhon
daye for a boocke calld the 7 wise m*aste*rs the some of xl *s*
Wbirde

Lent vnto Samewell Rowly the 8 of marche 1599 to
paye vnto harey chettell & John daye in fulle payment
for A boocke called the vij wisse masters the some of l *s*
Samuell Rowlye

Lent vnto hary chettell the 2 of march*e* 1599 in earnest
of A Boocke called the 7 wisse masters the some of   xxx *s*

Lent vnto wm Birde the 10 of marche 1599 to geue
harey chettell in earneste of his Boocke called damon
& pethias the some of   xxvj *s*

Lent vnto Robarte shaw the 10 of march*e* 1599 to Lend
wm harton to Releace hime owt of the clyncke the
some of   x *s*

Dd vnto the littell tayller at the apoyntment of Robart
shawe the 12 of march*e* 1599 to mack*e* thinges for the
2 p*ar*te of owld castell some of   xxx *s*

Lent vnto Robarte shawe the 18 of march 1599 to geue
vnto the printer to staye the printing of patient gresell
the some of   xxxx *s*
by me Robt Shaa

Receaued of Mr Henslowe to lay out for the play of
the 7 wise Mrs in taffataes & sattyns the some of   xx *li*
in behalfe of the   by me Robt Shaa
Company

Receaued more of mr Henshlowe to lay out for the
play for the 7 wise Maisters in behalfe of the Company   x *li*

Receaued more of Mr Henshlowe to lay out for the
play of the 7 wyse maisters in behalf of the Company   viij *li*
            by me Robt Shaa

91. 9 March 1600. Privy Council Minute.

In January, the Earl of Nottingham had issued his personal warrant
authorising Edward Alleyn's Fortune playhouse (see no. 88). Two months
later, the Privy Council, convened on 'Sunday. At the Court of Riche-
mond', listened sympathetically to complaints submitted by 'Lord Willoughby, and other gentlemen and Inhabitauntes in the parishe of St. Giles
without Creplegate' that there was 'Intent in some persons to erect a
Theatre in white crosstreete'. The Council upheld Willoughby's grievances. They issued the following injunction against the new playhouse on
which Henslowe had already spent £155. The Fortune, it seemed, would
not be permitted after all, in spite of Nottingham's defence. So far, the
warrant and counter-warrant seem merely another example of the Privy
Council's characteristically uncoordinated handling of the public playhouses: the right hand, Nottingham, had probably not bothered to inform
the left hand what it was doing. As it turns out, however, the Richmond
injunction is even more curiously devious than simple muddle suggests,
for Nottingham himself was present at the Sunday meeting. He evidently
concurred with the decision. Yet within a month he must have thrown his
considerable influence behind an initiative to reverse the policy, for the
Privy Council rescinded the injunction against the Fortune in April (see
no. 98), by which time Philip Henslowe may have turned white with
worry. One wonders at Nottingham's methods. It is certainly true that
his warrant carried more weight than Willoughby's complaints, so why
did he not enter any counter-argument in the Richmond debate, particularly if he intended to override Willoughby's petition within weeks? As
ever, there is no answer to such questions. Individual members remain as
inscrutable as the entire Privy Council on the issue of the playhouses. But
in this instance there is possibly additional evidence, amounting to little
more than surmise, to consider. Nottingham may have kept diplomatic
silence on 9 March. The Privy Council had assembled to discuss matters

of the utmost urgency, all to do with the wars in Ireland. They spent the entire day issuing orders on coat and conduct money, officers' pay, the musters, ship money, subsidies and complaints from local citizens about taxes raised to support the wars. The single unrelated item of business was Willoughby's petition, slipped in, it appears from the minutes, about mid-day. Perhaps Nottingham, judging the political temperature of the day, decided to save the Fortune battle for another time when bigger battles were not clamouring. Then again, Nottingham may not have been present when the decision to issue the injunction was made. His name does appear at the head of the day's business as among those in attendance, but since the specific injunction was not entered in the Act Book as signed by any Privy Councillor, it is just possible that certain members of the Council had contrived to consider Willoughby's petition when Nottingham was absent from the table. The debate can only have taken fifteen or so minutes. If it is right to describe the petition as 'slipped in', then perhaps it was slipped in before protesting Nottingham returned from dinner. No wonder, then, that Nottingham would react so vigorously within a month. Either scenario invites the observation that London's halls of government have always been crowded with the red faces of the angry and the embarrassed. One likewise sees from the injunction and the reversal how deeply divided Elizabeth's Privy Council might be – permanently or expediently – on this issue of the public playhouse.

———

A lettre to Sir Drew Drewry knight William waad Esquier, Clerke of the Councell, Thomas ffowler, Edward Vaughan and Nicholas Collyns, Esquires, Justices of the peace in the countie of Middlesex. Wee are given to vnderstand by our very good Lord the Lord Willoughby, and other gentlemen and Inhabitauntes in the parishe of St. Giles without Creplegate that there is a purpose, and Intent in some persons to erect a Theatre in white crosstreete neere unto the Barres in that parte that ys in the countie of Middlesex, wherof ther are to manie allreadie not farr from that place, And as you knowe not longe sithence you receaued speciall direction to pluck downe those, and to see them defaced, Therefore yf this newe erection should be suffered, yt would not onlie be an offence, and scandall to divers, but a thinge that would greatly dysplease her Majestie. These are therefore to will and Require you in any case, to take order that no soche Theatre or plaie howse be built there, or other howse to serve for soche use, both to avoide the many Inconveniences that therby are lyklie to ensue, to all the Inhabitantes, and the offence yt would be to her Majestie, havinge heretofore given sufficient notice unto you of the great myslyke her highnes hath of those publicke and vayne buildinge for soche occacions that breed Increase of Base, and Lewde people, and divers other disorders. Therefore wee require you not to faile forthwith to take order that the foresaid intended Buildinge maie be staied, and yf any be begone, to see the same quite defaced. So, &c.

92. 28 March 1600. Vestry Minute.

The Vestry of St Saviour's, Southwark, faced with the reality of two playhouses in their parish, took up a suggestion made as long ago as 1587 (see no. 2) and decided to encourage the players to contribute to parish tithes and poor relief. This Vestry minute indicates that they were acting upon instructions from the Archbishop of Canterbury and the Bishop of Winchester, both of whom stood at the heads of vast financial empires. Indeed, the Bishop of Winchester held manorial title to the Liberty of the Clink, in which the Rose and Henslowe's own house stood, as well as wielding diocesan jurisdiction over all of Southwark and its environs, including the brothel district – hence the cant term for whores, 'Winchester geese' – as part of a tract that remained in Church hands after the dissolution of the monasteries in the mid-1530s. Being realistic, the Bishops knew it was unlikely that the playhouses would be suppressed, and if a shrug of the shoulders could turn profane pastime into parish poor relief, they were probably ready to shrug accommodatingly.

———

It is ordered that the churchwardens shall talk with the players for tithes for their playhouses within the liberty of the Clinke, and for money for the poore, according to the order taken before my lords of Canterbury and London and the Master of the Revels.

93. 8 April 1600. Warrant.

Some time in March the inhabitants of Finsbury, in whose district the Fortune was to be built, petitioned the Privy Council to overturn their injunction of 9 March and to tolerate the new playhouse. They enumerated three reasons in defence: the site was so 'remote frome any person or Place of accompt As that none cann be Annoyed thearbie'; the builders 'are contented to give a very liberall porcion of money weekelie, towardes the releef of our Poore'; and 'wee are the rather Contented to accept this meanes of releif of our Poore, because our Parrishe is not able to releeue them'. The petition carried twenty-seven signatures, among them the local constable's and the warden's along with the names of two overseers of the poor. It is interesting to speculate upon how this document came to be written, for local petitions are rarely the work of spontaneous co-opera-tion. Somebody must have organised the petitioners. Somebody must have canvassed the community. And somebody must have paid the scrivener. Perhaps one of Finsbury's worthies, seeing that a playhouse would enrich his district and relieve his burden of taxation, did all three. But to look back to the Waterman's Petition of 1592 (no. 20) and to consider who stood to gain most from a new Council decision is perhaps to suspect that Philip Henslowe was the ghost writer shadowing the petition. Be that as it may, on 8 April the Privy Council did reverse the injunction by issuing the following warrant. Two of the points they raise are significant: first, that the Queen 'Hath sondrye tymes signified her pleasuer' to see Alleyn act once more; second, that the Fortune would not increase the number of London playhouses 'because an other howse is pulled downe, in steade of yt'. The lords were partly right. Alleyn did emerge from retirement and did play before his monarch. But the promised demolition did not occur. Only three Privy Councillors signed this warrant – the Earl of Nottingham, the Lord Chamberlain, and Mr Secretary Cecil – which, since two of them patronised companies of players, might lead suspicious minds to accusations of collusion, particularly in view of the fact that this warrant survives only in Henslowe's copy and not in a Privy Council copy. The warrant was not entered in the Privy Council Act book although the full Council did sit this day. They did not discuss the playhouses. Thus, it seems the warrant was a private initiative. As it turned out, even the authority of Nottingham, Cecil and Hunsdon did not end the Fortune controversy (see no. 98).

––––

After our hartie comendacions. Whereas her Majestie (haveinge been well pleased heeretofore at tymes of recreacion with the services of Edward Allen and his Companie. Servantes to me the Earle of Nottingham whearof, of late he hath made discontynuance:) Hath sondrye tymes signified her pleasuer, that he should revive the same agayne: fforasmuche as he hath bestowed a greate some of money, not onelie for the Title of a plott of grounde, scituat in averie remote and exempt place neere Goulding lane, theare to Erect a newe house/but alsoe is in good forwardnes aboute the frame and woorkmanshipp theareof The conveniencie of which place for that purpose ys testified vnto us; vnder the handes of manie of the Inhabitantes of the Libertie of fynisbury wheare it is and recomended by some of the Justices them selves. Wee thearfore haveinge informed her Majestie lykewise of the decaye of the howse, wherein this Companye latelie plaied scituate vppon the Bancke verie noysome, for the resorte of people in the wynter tyme haue receaued order to requier you to Tollerate the proceedinge of the saide Newhowse neere Goulding lane And doe heerbye requier you and everie of you To permitt and suffer the said Edward Allen to proceede in theffecting and finishinge of the same Newehowse, without anie yor lett or interrupcion, towardes him, or anye of his woorkmen the rather because an other howse is pulled downe, in steade of yt. And soe not doubtinge of yor conformitye heerein. Wee committ you to God, frome the Courte at Richmond the viijth of April 1600. Yor loveinge freindes

Notingham

G Hunsdon

Ro: Cecyll

To *the* Justices of Peace of *the* Countye of Midd*lesex*
especially of St Gyles wi*thout* Creplegate
And to all others whome it shall
Concerne.

94. 6 April–13 July 1600. Rose Playhouse Receipts.

These receipts document the Company's final, rather disappointing, season at the Rose; in November, Nottingham's Men opened at the Fortune. One wonders what huge success the Company performed the week of 18 May to treble their receipts.

———

Rd the 6 of Aprell 1600	vj *li* ij *s*
Rd the 14 of aprell 1600	v *li* x *s*
Rd the 21 of aprell 1600	vj *li* xiiij *s*
Rd the 29 of aprell 1600	iiij *li* x *s*
Rd the 4 of maye 1600	iiij *li* vij *s*
Rd the 11 of maye 1600	iiij *li* xv *s*
Rd th 18 of maye 1600	xij *li* iiij *s*
Rd the 25 of maye 1600	iiij *li* vij *s*
Rd the 1 of June 1600	iiij *li* xvij *s*
Rd the 8 of June 1600	vj *li* xj *s*
Rd th 15 of June 1600	iij *li* xiij *s*
Rd th 22 of June 1600	vij *li* ij *s*
Rd the 1 of Julye 1600	v *li* viij *s*
Rd th 6 of Julye 1600	iiij *li* xij *s*
Rd th 13 of July 1600	iiij *li* xij *s*

95. 2 April–10 July 1600. Loan Account (extracts).

Of the twenty-nine payments Henslowe made for Nottingham's Men during this period, £34 13s went toward eleven plays, £11 8s was spent on costumes, 14s on licences, and £2 15s on miscellaneous expenses. *The Wooing of Death* by Chettle in April and three plays by Haughton – *The English Fugitives* (16–24 April), *The Devil and his Dam* (6 May) and *Judas* (27 May) – were also commissioned this season. None was finished, though two members of the Company, Bird and Rowley, were enough struck with Haughton's 10s instalment of *Judas* to write their own Judas play as a first venture into playwriting in December 1601. The following November Bird and Rowley would revise Marlowe's *Faustus*. Henslowe's loan 'vnto the company to goo to winswarth to the installinge' on 27 April cannot be explained. Knights of the Garter were installed at Windsor so it is likely that Nottingham's Men had been summoned for a performance there. Over these months the Company's new playhouse, the Fortune, rose steadily in Golding Lane (a neighbourhood Henslowe habitually described as being 'in the contrey'). Henslowe paid Peter Street's 'labereres' £3 8s 'at the eand of the fowndations' on 8 May and three weeks later spent £4 10s for 'ix thowsand of brickes'. Throughout June Henslowe dined with Street nearly every day, probably at the building site where delays seem to have been hindering work. Henslowe had to give the carpenter 4s on 10 June 'to pasify hym'. The Fortune contract stipulated that work was to be completed by 25 July. On 10 July, to reckon accounts before vacating the Rose, Nottingham's Men set their hands to a debt of £300. Their signatures at the end of this loan account are autograph.

———

Lent vnto Robarte shaw the 2 of aprell 1600 for to by a Robe
for tyme some of

              xxxx s

Lent vnto harey chettell the 26 of aprell 1600 in parte of
payment of A Boocke called damon & pethias at the a poyntment of Robart shawe the some of

              xxx s

Lent vnto the company to goo to winswarth to the installinge
the 27 of aprell 1600

              l s

Receaued of mr Henshlowe in behalfe of the Company to geue
Tho: Deckers & Jhon Day in earnest of a booke Called The
golden Ass & Cupid & Psiches
        by me RobtShaa

              xxx s

Payd to Harry Chettle in full payment of vj^{li} for his booke of
Damon & Pithias xxxxiiij s

              xxxxiiij s

Lent at the apoyntment of Robart shawe to Thomas deckers
& John daye & harye chetell the 10 of maye 1600 in parte of
payment of A Bocke called the gowlden asse cuped & siches
some of

              iij *li*
        by John day to the vse of Th Dekker Harry
        Chettle and himselfe

pd at the apoyntment of Robert shawe the 14 daye of maye
1600 in fulle payment of a Boocke called the gowlden asse
cuped & siches to thomas deckers & hary chettell John daye
some of — xxx s

pd vnto the mr of the Revelles man for licensynge of A Boocke
called damon & pethias the 16 of maye 1600 some of — vij s

Receaued of Mr Henshlowe the 17th of May 1600 in behalfe
of the Company to pay Will: Haulton & mr pett in full
payment of a play Called straunge newes out of poland — vj li

Receaued of Mr Henshlowe the 26th of May 1600 in behalfe
of the Company to pay H. Chettle & Jhon Day in full payment
of a booke Called the blynd begger of bednall greene the some
of — v li x s

Dd vnto the littell tayller at the apoyntement of Robart shaw
the 25 of maye 1600 for to macke sewtes for the playe called
strange newes owt of powland — iij li

Receaued of Mr Henshlowe the 3th of June 1600 in behalfe of
the Company to An: Munday & the rest in parte of payment
for a booke Called the fayre Constance of Roome the some of — iij li v s

Lent vnto Thomas dowton the 5 of June 1600 to bye a sewt
for his boye in the playe of cvped & siches the some of — xxxx s

pd vnto drayton hathway monday & deckers at the a poyntment of Robart shawe in full payment of A Boocke called the
fayer constance of of Rome the 14 of June 1600 some of — xxxxiiij s

Lent vnto Robart shawe the 20 of June 1600 to lend them
hathway in earneste of ther second parte of constance of Rome
the some of — xx s

[The full some of our debt]
payd to Mr Allen by mr Henshlowe in behalfe of the Company
the some of xj li which is the remainder of a debt of l li for the
payment of which we stood bound in a C li — xj li

So that the full some of all the debtes which we owe Mr
Henshlowe this xth of July 1600 comethe to Just the some of
three hundred poundes — CCC li

Whiche some of three hundred pound*es* we whose names are
here vnder written, doe acknowledge our dewe debt & doe
promyse payment: [out of our p*art*]

JSingger

Thomas Downton

Humfry Jeffes

Anthony Jeffes

Charles Massye

Samuell Rowlye

Robt Shaa

Thomas towne

Wbirde

Edward Jubye

Richard Jones

96. 14 June 1600. Letter.

Without this note, which can be dated by cross-referencing it to an entry
in Henslowe's Diary, Robert Wilson's participation in *Fair Constance of
Rome* would remain unknown, for neither the entry of 3 June or 14 June
mentions him among the collaborators (see no. 95).

———

I praye you mr Henshlowe deliuer vnto the bringer hereof the some of
fyue & fifty shillinges to make the 3 *li*-fyue shilling*es* w*hi*ch they receaued
before, full six pound*es* in full payment of their booke called the fayre
Constance of Roome. whereof I pray you reserue for me Mr Willsons
whole share w*hi*ch is xj *s*. w*hi*ch I to supply his neede deliuered hime
yesternight.

yor Lovinge ffrend   Robt Shaa

97. Undated (Fiscal Year 1599). Warrant.

Playing at the Rose may have been inhibited over part of the summer, for
while Henslowe recorded receipts and loans through July and loans again
after 14 August, he made no entries in the Company's account for some
four weeks between those dates. If Nottingham's Men went 'into the
contrey' to play, they probably visited Canterbury. The following payment warrant documents an appearance by the Company in that city
some time during the fiscal year 29 September 1599 to 28 September 1600.
A summer visit fits, though the Company may have been there the previous
February when they likewise faced a month-long interruption at the Rose
(see no. 89). The Company continued to be styled 'Admiral's Men' since
their patron remained Lord Admiral.

———

To the lorde Admiralls Players, in rewarde for a Playe w*hi*ch they played
before Mr Maior and manye of his frend*s* in the Courte halle, and so

ordered bye Mr Maior and the Aldermen vnder there hands, whose names
ar here written, viz. – Robart Wynne maior. Richard Gaunte. Marcks
Berrye. Edward nethersole. Thomas Longe. Jeames ffrench-
man. Charles wetenhull Aldermen .... xl s

98. 22 June 1600. Privy Council Order.

The Fortune playhouse was scheduled for completion in just over a
month, but the bureaucratic controversy surrounding its construction
dragged on. The Privy Council had shifted positions twice before issuing
the following, carefully worded statement 'At the Courte at Grenwich
... for the restrainte of the imoderate vse and Companye of Playhowses
and Players'. They were finding it difficult to agree among themselves.
Nottingham, Hunsdon and Cecil had stated their position clearly (see no.
93) but may have been challenged or may have found it expedient to
compromise. In any case, the clerk responsible for copying this order into
the Privy Council Act Book noted that it had been much debated and
revised: 'Memorandum, that the alteracion and interlyninges of this order
was by reason that the said order after the same was entred in the Book
came againe in question and debate, and the said interlyninge & amend-
mentes were sett down accordinge to the laste determinacion of their
lordshippes'. (In the following transcription, the interlinings appear in
square brackets.) Over the years, the Privy Council had sent out what
amounted to *ad hoc* and sometimes inconsistent orders about the playhouses. Here they were trying to assemble a comprehensive policy statement. The statement did not materially alter the Council's stance over the
past two decades; indeed, all the rusty arguments were made to serve once
more: abuses were admitted, the Queen's pleasure was entered, conces-
sions were promised to the enemies of the playhouse. The single difference
was that the issue was finally being dealt with in a seemingly coherent
way. Antagonists might have gained a measure of comfort from that. And
yet, nothing much came of even this exhaustively deliberated Privy Council order, for the two reforms it proposed simply were not enforced. Faced
yet again with this same stalemate between proclamation and performance, one concludes either that the lords were inept or that their policy
was based on studied subterfuge – the Queen might have called it compromise, this nice balance between playhouses that were the 'daylie occasion of the ydle ryotous and dissolute living of great nombers of people'
and playgoing that was 'not ... euill in yt self'. Of course, it is possible
that the Council's decision was misinformed: they were depending on
information supplied by Edmund Tilney to declare that the Fortune 'now
in hand to be builte ... is not intended to encrease the number of the
playhowses, but to be insteede of an other (namely the Curtayne) which

is either to be ruyned and plucked downe or to be putt to some other good vse'. On this account Tilney himself may have been misinformed. (Henslowe entered among his Fortune payments one on 13 June 'for goinge by water with the master of the Revelles'. Perhaps Tilney had been invited to inspect the new playhouse and had taken the opportunity to voice his concern over the number of playhouses that seemed to be springing up like mushrooms in a ring around the City. Henslowe might obligingly have suggested that the oldest of these playhouses, the Curtain – oldest now that the Theatre had been pulled down to be used as timber for the Globe – could well be demolished.) It is possible, too, that Tilney prevaricated: it was to his advantage to have as many playhouses open and paying him fees as possible. Either way the Council's policy was frustrated. The Curtain was still standing in 1604, neither 'ruyned' nor converted but occupied by 'players that use to recyte their playes' there. The second reform the Privy Council announced – confining playing to two days a week – was no doubt frankly ignored, for although by this time Henslowe was no longer recording weekly receipts that would indicate a sudden drop in revenue if the limitation were enforced, he was still making payments for Nottingham's Men in their loan account. The Company's rate of spending continued unabated, which would hardly have been necessary had the Company been playing so restricted a schedule. At the same time the Privy Council issued the following order, they addressed letters of conveyance to the Lord Mayor and Justices of the Peace. The tone of these letters is hard to gauge, particularly in the final comment: 'as wee have donne our partes in prescribinge the orders, so unlesse you perfourme yours in lookinge to the due execution of them we shall loose our labor and the wante of redresse must be imputed unto you'. If the Lord Mayor heard a vague threat, or a veiled irony, or the sound of Pilate washing his hands, he was perhaps not much wrong. The order was signed by Nottingham as Lord Admiral, by the Lord Treasurer, by Robert Cecil, the Queen's Secretary, and by the Lord Keeper of the Seal, the Comptroller, and Lord North.

———

Whereas diuers Complaintes haue bin heretofore made vnto the Lordes & others of hir Maiesties privy Counsell, of the manyfolde abuses and disorders that haue growen and doe contynew by occasion of many houses erected & employed in and about the Cittie of London for common stage playes: And now verie latelie by reason of some Complainte exhibited by sondry persons against the buyldinge of the like house in or nere Golding Lane by one Edward Allen a seruant of the right honorable the Lord Admirall the matter aswell in generalitie touchinge all the said houses for stage plaies and the vse of playenge as in particuler concerninge the said house now in hand to be builte in or neere Goldinge Lane hath bin brought into question & consultacion amonge their Lordshippes fforasmuch as yt is manifestly knowne and graunted that the multitude of the said houses and the misgouerment of them hath bin made and is daylie occasion of the ydle ryotous and dissolute livinge of great nombers of people that leavinge all such honest and painefull course of life as they should followe doe meete and assemble there and of many particuler abuses and disorders that doe there vpon ensue And yet neuertheles it is Considered that the vse and exercise of suche playes (not beinge euill in yt self) may with a good order and moderacion be suffered in a well gouerned state and that hir Maiestie beinge pleased at some tymes to take delight and recreation in the sight and hearinge of them; some order is fitt to bee taken for the allowance and maynetenance of suche persons as are thoughte meetest in that kinde to yeald hir Maiestie recreation and delighte and consequently of the howses that must serue for publike playinge to keepe them in exercise; To the end therefore that bothe the greatest abuses of the playes and playinge houses maye be redressed, and yet the aforesaide vse and moderation of them retayned. The Lordes and the reste of hir Maiesties privie Councell with one and full consent haue ordered in manner and forme as followeth.

ffirst that there shall bee about the Cittie two houses and no more allowed to serue for the vse of the Common Stage playes; of the which houses one shalbe in Surrey, in that place which is Commonly called the Banckeside or there aboutes and the other in Middlesex. And forasmuche as their Lordshippes haue bin enformed by Edmund Tylney esquire hir Maiesties servante and Master of the Reuelles that the howse now in hand to be builte by the saide Edward Allen is not intended to encrease the nomber of the playhowses, but to be insteede of an other (namely the Curtayne) which is either to be ruyned and plucked downe or to be putt to some other good vse as also that the scytuation thereof is meete and convenient for that purpose; it is like wise ordered that the said howse of Allen shall be allowed to be one of the two houses, and namely for the house to be allowed in Middlesex [for the company of players belongine to the Lord Admyrall] so as the house called the Curtaine be (as yt is pretended) either ruynated or applyed to some other good vse. And for the other house allowed to be on Surrey side, Whereas [their lordshippes are pleased to permitt] to the Company of players that shall play there to make there owne Choice which they will haue [of diuers houses that are there] Choosinge one of them and noe more [And the said company of plaiers being the Seruantes of the Lord Chamberlen that are to play there haue made choise of the house called the Globe, yt is ordered that the said house & none other shall be there allowed] And especially it is forbidden that any stage playes shalbe played (as some tymes they haue bin) in any Common Inn for publique assembly in or neare aboute the Cittie.

Secondly forasmuch as these stage plaies by the multitude of houses and company of players haue bin too frequent not serving for recreation but invitinge and callinge the people dayly from their trade and worke to myspend there tyme it is likewise ordered that the two seuerall Companies of players assigned vnto the two howses allowed may play each of them in there seuerall howse twice a weeke and no oftener and especially that they shall refraine to play on the Sabbath day vpon paine of imprysonment and further penaltie and that they shall forbeare altogether in the tyme of Lent and likewise at such tyme and tymes as any extraordinary sicknes or infection of disease shall appeare to be in or about the Cittie.

Thirdly because these orders wilbe of little force and effecte vnlesse they be duely putt in execution by those vnto whom yt appertayneth to see them executed; It is ordered that seuerall Copies of these orders shalbe sent to the Lord Maior of London and to the Justices of the peace of the Counties of Middlesex and Surrey and that lettres shalbe written vnto them from their Lordshippes straightly charginge them to see to the execucion of the same aswell by comyttinge to prison the owners of playhouses and players as shall disobey and resist these orders as by any other good and lawfull meanes that in there discretion they shall finde expedient, And to certifie their Lordshippes from tyme to tyme, as they shall see cause of there proceedinges therein.

Examinatum per Tho: Smithe.

99. 14 August–11 November 1600. Loan Account (extracts).

Over the summer Henslowe entered only seven payments for Nottingham's Men. Their new playhouse was scheduled for completion according to contract on 25 July, but delays interfered. On 2 August Henslowe paid for another 'lode' of timber, and he kept in daily contact with Peter Street until the 8th. They dined together every day. By mid-August the structure may have been fully erected and yet the playhouse would not have been ready, for the contract mentioned 'payntinge in or aboute the said fframe howse or stage' from which Street was exempt. This work would have remained once the joiners left the site. It was not until the autumn that Nottingham's Men opened at the Fortune. A Diary payment on 11 November to Alleyn from the Company 'A bowt ther composicion' refers to the new articles of agreement binding the players, while the payment following, 'vnto my sonne alleyn for the firste weckes playe', would seem to document the opening performances. The first week was triumphant. The players shared £17 9s. If that sum represents their gallery money, they had quadrupled their last week's earnings at the Rose. Each of them collected £1 12s, more than six times the amount set by statute as the maximum weekly wage for a skilled craftsman. The move to the Fortune looked to be a success, but the move meant an end to the Company's six-year-old partnership with the Rose. Nottingham's Men continued to collaborate with Henslowe, who entered their accounts for two more years, but as their affairs are no longer relevant to the Rose, they cease to be entered here. The records should, however, be consulted in the Diary, for they refer to matters of great interest to the history of the playing company. They include Ben Jonson's 'new adicyons' to *The Spanish Tragedy* (f. 106v); Bird and Rowley's revision of *Faustus* (f. 108v); and Alleyn's sale to the Company of several privately owned playbooks (ff. 93, 96, 108). On f. 104 the Company pay off two retiring players; on f. 86v they 'geatte the boye into the ospetalle which was hurt at the fortewne'. They revive several plays, probably showcases for Alleyn who emerges from retirement to inaugurate the new playhouse: *The Jew of Malta, Faustus, The Massacre at Paris, Friar Bacon, Mahomet, Crack Me This Nut, The Blind Beggar of Alexandria*. Several among the Company turn their hands to playwriting: Bird, Rowley, Massey. Novice playwrights are given support, and wayward veterans continue to be tolerated. The continuing saga of Henry Chettle – who for ready cash at one point pawns a playbook that the Company rushes to redeem and who later secures his debts to them by binding himself to write solely for Nottingham's Men – is possibly more dramatic than anything he wrote.

———

Lent vnto Robart shawe iij *li* the 14 of aguste 1600 to bye A dublet & hosse of sewater grene satten some of   iij *li*

pd at the apoyntmente of the company the 16 of aguste 1600 for viij yard*es* of mvry satten the some of   iij *li* xij *s*

Lent vnto Robart shawe the 29 of aguste 1600 the some of fower pownd*es* I saye   iiij *li*

pd vnto Robart shawe the 2 of aguste 1600 the some of   viij *s*

Lent vnto Robarte shawe the 6 of septmb*er* 1600 to paye vnto Thomas deckers for his boock*e* called the fortewn ten*es* some of   xx *s*

Lent vnto Robart shawe the 12 of septmb*er* 1600 the some of three pownd*es* I saye   iij *li*

Lent vnto the company the 11 of novmb*er* 1600 to paye vnto my sonne EAlleyn A bowt ther composicion the some of fower pownd*es* I saye lent   iiij *li*

pd vnto my sonne alleyn for the firste weckes playe the xj
parte of xvij *li* ix *s* *which* came to therti & ij shelleng*es* I saye
pd   xxxij *s*

100. 28 October 1600. Rose Playhouse Receipts.

Undeterred by the Privy Council's order of 22 June, Henslowe moved
swiftly to find new tenants for the Rose when Nottingham's Men left.
Pembroke's Men opened on 28 October but lasted only two performances;
nothing more is ever heard of this company. Thereafter the Rose seems to
have stood empty until August 1602, but whether this was due to official
intervention, or to instability inside the playing companies, or to the
daunting competition any Rose company would have to withstand from
neighbours at the Globe, is impossible to determine. Over these months
the political tragedy that would bring Queen Elizabeth's favourite, most
ambitious courtier to the scaffold, reached its climax. Since his rash return
from Ireland in September 1599 the Earl of Essex had been living in
disgrace, confined to his own house from March 1600 and condemned by
the Privy Council of contempt in June. Abject penitence was working
Essex's slow reconciliation with the Queen, but, master of political gesture
that she was, Elizabeth put the upstart to one more test of his submission
to her authority. On 30 October she denied him his patent on the farm of
sweet wines – that is, the renewal of his monopoly to collect duty upon
the importation of wine. The denial was more than a humiliation. It
effectively withdrew the young Earl's major source of income. Essex
brooded upon his sick fortunes over the winter while at Court Elizabeth
kept Christmas with accustomed revelry. The Chamberlain's Men
appeared before her on 26 December and 6 January; Nottingham's Men
played on the 28th, the 6th and on 2 February. The Children of St Paul's,
the Children of the Chapel, and a company described as 'Robert Browne's
men' also appeared. At Essex House discontent festered. The Earl collected around himself a group of young nobles – among them Roger
Manners, Earl of Rutland, and Henry Wriothesley, Earl of Southampton
– who encouraged his dangerous mood and seconded him when he declared that the old Queen was as crooked in mind as she was in body. On
7 February the Privy Council, having intelligence of the traffic at Essex
House, sent for the Earl. He refused attendance, declaring later that he
feared enemies at Court had turned his monarch's ear deaf to his petitions
for pardon. That same day Sir Charles Percy, Sir Josceline Percy and the
Lord Mounteagle paid the Chamberlain's Men £2 by way of persuasion
to play *Richard II*, an 'old play'. When Elizabeth eventually heard of it
she is reputed to have declared, 'By Richard they mean me'. The next
morning four of the Privy Council – the Lord Keeper, the Earl of Worces-

ter, Sir William Knollys and the Lord Chief Justice – went to Essex House. Upon gaining admittance they discovered they were prisoners. Essex left his house. He testified later that his intent was to prostrate himself before the Queen. Others believed he intended to depose her. His march through the City grew more desperate by the mile. The crowds of supporters did not materialise; the Lord Mayor locked himself in his residence. By late afternoon the 'rebellion' had collapsed, and Essex was arrested the next day, 9 February. The Queen remained unperturbed. When a false report brought news that the City had revolted, the Queen 'never was more amazed than she would have been to hear of a fray in Fleet Street.' On 19 February Essex was brought to trial at Westminster. The day before, Augustine Phillips was examined by Lord Chief Justice Popham to ascertain how deeply the Chamberlain's Men were implicated in the rebellion. His answers satisfied; the playhouses were not closed; but on the eve of Essex's execution, 24 February, the Chamberlain's Men were summoned to Court to perform for Elizabeth. A letter was sent on 11 March 'to the lord mayor requiring him not to faile to take order the playes within the Cyttie and the liberties especyaly at Powles and in the Blackfriers, may be suppressed during this time of lente'. No closer links between the playhouses and Essex's disgrace were made than these subtle, perhaps unrelated, moves. But one wonders whether the political events of the previous months had not impelled a general tightening of scrutiny of the playhouses, those potential *loci* of social ferment, and whether that scrutiny was responsible for Henslowe's Rose remaining tenantless. It was perhaps for such crises as this that the Privy Council had put sleeping statutes – like the one limiting the authorised playing companies to two – on the books (see no. 64).

	My Lordes of penbrockes men begane to playe	
	at the Rosse the 28 of october 1600 as foloweth	
Rd at	Rd at the [devell] licke vnto licke	xj s 6 d
october 28	Rd at RadeRicke	v s
29		

101. 10 May 1601. Privy Council Minute.

The Council was sensitive to the representation of living persons upon the stage particularly when, 'under obscure manner', they were made stalking horses for political commentary. Essex's memory was still green; the men who had survived the affair, and, worse, the men who had built advancement upon it as Francis Bacon did, perhaps became targets for the satirists' barbs. 'Rashe and indiscreete dealing' was perhaps inevitable.

But since the Council's directive would have affected plays and players everywhere, playwrights may have judged the climate too dangerous for hunting such big game, turning instead to domestic fowl on home territory and training their guns on each other. In the autumn the skirmish that has come to be known as the 'poetomachia' broke out. The main antagonists were John Marston and Ben Jonson, the latter claiming in the 'Apologetical Dialogue' to *Poetaster* (late 1601) to have been baited by rival playwrights these 'three years': 'They did provoke me with their petulant stiles On every stage'. It seems that Jonson took as satire a portrait of himself – Chrisogonus in *Histriomastix* (1599) – Marston intended as a compliment. Thereafter Jonson made fun of Marston's universally recognised turgidness in *Every Man Out* (1599) and Marston responded with lampoons in *Jack Drum's Entertainment* (1600) and *What You Will*. By then Dekker had taken sides with Marston so Jonson attacked them both in *Poetaster*, performed at the Blackfriars probably in September 1601. Dekker's *Satiromastix* followed in November. This 'vntrussinge of the humorous poetes', performed by the Chamberlain's Men at the Globe, caricatured Jonson as Horace but entered many other dramatists as disputants. It must have seemed that the entire playwriting fraternity was on stage, hurling abuse at each other in plays of their own devising. While this internecine warfare carried on, the public playhouses were attacked on the flank. Their assailants were the boy companies at the private playhouses who this winter emerged in such strength that they 'be-rattled the common stages' and were 'most tyrannically clapp'd for it', as Rosencrantz exclaims to Hamlet. 'These are now the fashion.' The 'fashion' was upheld at Court this Christmas: Nottingham's and Worcester's gave only one performance each, while the Chamberlain's Men were matched equally with the Children of the Chapel at three performances each.

———

A *lett*re to certaine Justices of the peace in the county of Middlesex. Wee do understand that certaine players that use to recyte their playes at the Curtaine in Moorefeildes do represent upon the stage in their interludes the persons of some gent*lemen* of good desert and quallity, that are yet alive, under obscure manner, but yet in such sorte, as all the hearers may take notice both of the matter and the persons that are meant thereby. This beinge a thinge very unfitte, offensive and contrary to such direc*c*ion as have bin heretofore taken that no plaies should be openly shewed but suchas were first perused and allowed, and that might minister no occasion of offence or scandall; Wee do hereby require you that you do forthw*it*h forbidd those Players, to whomsoever they appertaine, that do play at the Courtaine in Moorefeildes, to represent any such play, and that you will examine them who made that play, and to shew the same unto you, and as you in y*our* discrec*c*ions shall thincke the same vnfitte to

be publiquely shewed, to forbidd them from henceforth to play the same
eyther priuately or publiquely, And yf upon veiwe of the said play, you
shall finde the subject so odious and inconvenient as is informed, Wee
require you to take bond of the cheifest of them to aunswere their rashe
and indiscreete dealing before us.

102. 31 December 1601. Privy Council Minute.

Some days earlier the Lord Mayor and Aldermen had sent the Privy
Council another of their complaining letters whose familiar topic was the
public playhouse. This is apparent, although the Mayor's letter itself has
not survived, from the following reply, the terseness of which the Aldermen may not have anticipated. They were thanked for their 'care and
desire to reform the disorders of the Cittie' but were otherwise answered
ironically: 'wee did much rather expect to understand that our order (sett
downe and prescribed about a yeare and a half since for the reformation
of the said disorders vpon the like Complaint at that tyme) had bin duelie
executed, then to finde the same disorders and abuses so much encreased
as they are'. How seriously the Privy Council could have intended that
order not to have inquired about its enforcement for eighteen months is
omitted from consideration; instead, the lords asked the new Lord Mayor
whether 'any thinge hath bin endeavoured by the Predecessours of you'.
What possible answer could there be to that but silence? Yet if the
Aldermen had to endure such polished verbal browbeating, they at least
learned that their complaints had been respected so far: the Privy Council
sent the following letter to the Justices of the Peace in Middlesex and
Surrey. This probably means that illicit playing was happening at the
Rose since the Swan, the only other Bankside playhouse besides the
authorised Globe, was no longer used by players. The Justices, in turn,
may have spared themselves time for ironical reflection: the Privy Council
order was unequivocal. But where was the legal power to enforce it?

———

Two *lettres* of one tenour to the Justices of Middlesex and Surrey. It is in
vaine for us to take knowledg of great abuses & disorders complayned of
and to give order for redresse, if our directions finde no better execution
and observation then it seemeth they do: and wee must needes impute the
fault and blame thereof to you or some of you the Justices of the peace
that are put in trust to see them executed and perfourmed; whereof wee
may give you a plaine instance in the great abuse contynued or rather
encreased in the multitude of Plaie howses and Stage Plaies in and about
the Cittie of London ffor Whereas about a yeare & a half since (upon
knowledge taken of the great enormities and disorders by the overmuch

frequentinge of Plaies) wee did carefullie sett downe and prescribe an order to be observed concerninge the number of Playhowses, and the use and exercise of stage plaies with lymytacion of tymes and places for the same, (namely that there should be but two howses allowed for that use, one in Middlesex called the Fortune, and the other in Surrey called the Globe; and the same with observacion of certaine daies and times as in the said order is particularly expressed), in such sorte as a moderate practice of them for honest recreation might be contynued, and yet the inordinate concourse of dissolute and idle people be restrayned; wee do now vnderstande that our said order hath bin so farr from taking dew effect, as in steede of restrainte and redresse of the former disorders the multitude of play howses is much encreased, and that no daie passeth over without many Stage plaies in one place or other within and about the Cittie publiquelie made; The default of perfourmance of which our said order we must in greate parte the rather impute to the Justices of the Peace, because at the same tyme wee gave earnest direction vnto you to see it streightly executed; and to certifie vs of the execution; and yet we have neither vnderstoode of any redresse made by you, nor receaved any certificate at all of your proceedinges therein; which default, or omission, wee do now pray and require you foorthwith to amende; and to cause our said former order to be putt duely in execution; and especiallie to call before you the owners of all the other Play howses (excepting the two howses in Middlesex and Surrey aforementioned); and to take good and sufficient bondes of them, not to exercise, use or practise, nor to suffer from henceforth to be exercised, used or practized any Stage playinge in their howses, and if they shall refuse to enter into such Bondes, then to comitt them to prison vntill they shall conforme themselues.

103. 31 March 1602. Letter.

Within three months the Privy Council was backpedalling once again. Their 'lettre to the lord Maior for the Bores head to be licensed for the plaiers' altered the policy announced on 31 December (see no. 102) and shows why the Lord Mayor's hands were tied so that, even when ordered to, he could take no effective action to repress the playhouses. Nine months later, the amalgamated company named herein moved to the Rose as Worcester's Men. Worcester's signature is attached to the following authorisation.

——

After our verey hartie Commendacions to your Lordship we receaued your lettre signifieinge some amendment of the abuses or disorders by the immoderate exercise of Stage plays in and about the Cittie by meanes of our late order renued for the restraint of them and withall shewinge a speciall inconvenience, yet remayneinge by reason that the seruants of our verey good Lord the Earle of Oxford, and of me the Earle of Worcester beinge joyned by agrement togeather in on Companie (to whom vpon noteice of her Maiesties pleasure at the suit of the Earle of Oxford, tolleracion hath ben thaught meete to be graunted notwithstandinge the restraint of our said former Orders) doe not tye them selfs to one certaine place and howse but do chainge there place at there owne disposition which is as disorderly and offensiue as the former offence of many howses And as the other Companies that are alowed, namely of me the Lord Admirall and the Lord Chamberlaine, be appointed there certaine howses and one and noe more to each Companie. Soe we doe straightly require that this third Companie be likewise to one place. And because we are informed the house called the Bores head is the place they haue especially vsed and doe best like of, we doe pray and require yow that that said howse namely the Bores head may be assigned onto them and that they be verey straightlie Charged to vse and exercise there plaies in noe other but that howse, as they will looke to haue that tolleracion continued and avoid farther displeasure. And soe we bid your lordship hartely farewell, from the Court at Ritchmond the last of March, 1602.

Your lordshippes verey lovinge friendes

T Buckurst	Notingham
E Worcester	William Knowlis
Jhon Stannope	Robert Cecyll.
John fortescu.	John Herbert.

104. 17 August–20 December 1602. Loan Account (extracts).

The Rose may have been unoccupied for two years when Worcester's Men began playing there in August. A newly amalgamated company that had absorbed the old Oxford's Men, Worcester's Men had won an important concession from the Privy Council five months earlier in being permitted to use the Boar's Head (see n. 103). That venture collapsed, possibly because the fledgling company did not have the financial backing to compete for London audiences with the powerful twin rivals at the Fortune and the Globe. If this were the case, Henslowe may have offered an attractive proposition: an invitation to move into the Rose – not in itself attractive since it meant setting up next door to the Chamberlain's Men – and – this was the incentive – an opportunity to take advantage of Henslowe's generous loan system which allowed a company capital in advance of production. Henslowe's motivation in offering such an arrangement would have been to fill his playhouse; the Company's, in accepting his terms, would have been to enable themselves, overnight, to offer the commissions and to order the costumes that would transform their fledgling pin feathers to full plumage. From the records Henslowe kept of their loan accounts, the Company's personnel, their repertoire and their playwrights can be identified. Foremost among the Company was Will Kemp, the famous, even infamous, clown who played several of Shakespeare's motley-brains before – so the story goes – falling out with him and leaving the Chamberlain's Men in 1599. Kemp was more recently notorious for accepting a wager to morris dance from London to Norwich. He won – and hung his buskins in the Guildhall as proof. (In the account Kemp wrote of his dance, *Nine Daies Wonder* (1600), appears a brief note on theatre practice: Kemp, being asked to identify two malefactors on the Norwich Road, recalled, 'I remembered one of them to be a noted Cut-purse, such a one as we tye to a poast on our stage, for all the people to wonder at, when at a play they are taken pilfering.') Others of Worcester's Men included Thomas Heywood, John Duke, John Thayer, Christopher Beeston (later to achieve prominence in Queen Anne's Men and to operate the Cockpit Theatre), Richard Perkins, Robert Pallant, Thomas Blackwood and John Lowin. Under the new company's patronage, the player-playwright Heywood blossomed while other playwrights who had reached maturity writing for Nottingham's Men now offered plays to both companies (as Chettle, Hathaway, Smith and Day did) or worked nearly exclusively for the younger company. Dekker transferred his energies to Worcester's Men, taking with him fellow collaborators Thomas Middleton and John Webster. A new 'poete' appeared, working with Day, Smith and Hathaway on a play whose title was first left blank, was then called 'John dayes comodye', then, that being scrubbed out, 'the blacke dogge of newgate'. This new poet remained anonymous. Plays, as playwrights, sometimes transferred from Nottingham's to Worcester's Men: *Oldcastle* was one, but *Tamar Cham*, an old playbook Edward Alleyn had for sale, was a mistake; it was meant for Nottingham's Men and found its way into their stock via Henslowe's accounts that same day (f. 108). (The same mistake happened in reverse over some costumes Alleyn sold to Worcester's Men on 22 October; they were first entered in the Nottingham account (f. 108).) *Oldcastle* was thoroughly refurbished for its revival by Worcester's Men. Dekker was paid a total of £2 10s in two entries for 'new A dicyons' and Goodman Freshwater, who made costumes for the Company, was paid some part of 10s on 24 August 'for owld castell' three days after the Company had spent £12 on new costumes for it. In their first four months of operation Worcester's Men made sixty-nine payments: £56 18s toward fifteen plays, £107 2s 1d on costumes, £6 9s 13d on properties and £1 15s on miscellaneous items. The lopsided split between play scripts and costumes is neither unusual nor disproportionate. Still – and this may simply be an accident of Henslowe's style in recording the entries – it does seem that Worcester's accounts compared to Nottingham's show a company who put their money into visual effects. They bought 'gyent*es* hosse' for Will Kemp and paid their tireman 'for mackynge of the devells sute & sperethes & for the witch' in *The Two Brothers* (a play that eventually seems to have acquired a third brother in its title). In the new year they laid out £1 2s on 'Lame skenes' for *The Black Dog of Newgate*. For *Byron* the Company built 'A scafowld & bare', no doubt to stage the climactic gallows scene of a play which took up the sensational story of the French Duke of Byron who, having visited England in December 1601, returned to Paris to be arrested for conspiracy against his king on 7 June. He was executed on 29 July and by 5 August an account of the trial had been entered in the London Stationers' Register. Worcester's Men had Byron's tragedy ready for the stage by the first week of October. His death scene, for which the scaffold and bar were built, may have provided some actor the rhetorical opportunity of a lifetime, a chance to wring tears from every eye and to rouse English blood against the perfidious French. A more abrupt death was devised for another Worcester's play. 'Poleyes & worckmanshipp for to hange absolo*me*' shows the Company using machinery to enact the gruesome end to the Biblical story in which Absalom, fleeing from David, is swept off his horse by a low branch and hanged. Spectacles of grim death cunningly devised seem to have figured prominently in this company's repertoire. They paid 'the paynter of the properties' for *The Two Brothers* £1 for his labours and spent another 12s on 'bordes & quarters & naylles' to 'macke a tabell & a coffen' for the same play. One wonders whether in making two payments totalling a considerable £2 to 'the armerer for targattes' the Company was planning to stage a scene like that which had gone so disastrously wrong for the Admiral's Men in 1587 (see no. 5). Other payments speak of the domestic rather than the sensational: 9s spent at the Mermaid for supper 'when we weare at owre a grement' shows the Company shaking hands all round the table with Henslowe. The 'flage of sylke' – which cost twice as much as the meal – was probably emblazoned with the Company's crest to be flown above the playhouse. Worcester's Men reached settlements with old players (Blackwood's 16s payment to Robart Shaa on 19 September must have had something to do with the retired Admiral's man's eventual sale to the new company of costumes worth £17 in December) and with playwrights: Dekker was paid 10s 'over & a bove his price' for *A Medicine for a Curst Wife*. This play, like 'John dayes comodye', was at first untitled; Henslowe left a blank into which he later squeezed the name. Henry Chettle eluded responsibility as ever. On 7, 8 and 9 September he was given payments of 10s for an untitled tragedy that never materialised. More surprising than his default is the fact that Chettle was writing for Worcester's Men at all, given his bond, sealed in March 1601/2, to write solely for Nottingham's Men. This lends support to the theory that such agreements were not attempts to bind successful playwrights exclusively to one company but only to bring debt-accumulating writers to a stricter appreciation of their responsibilities (see no. 77). Henry Chettle aside, Worcester's Men achieved an astonishing success rate with their playwrights: of the sixteen plays they commissioned before leaving the Rose in March 1603, thirteen were completed. Perhaps this was because they put pressure on their playwrights. A young company, they seem to have been constantly in a hurry, scarcely able to buy plays or to go into production quickly enough. Twice, they may have been organising properties and costumes for plays before the playwrights were paid for their final instalments. The lances they bought on 3 September for the 'comody of thomas hewedes & mr smythes' would appear to belong to *Albere Galles*, bought for £6 the following day, since those playwrights do not seem to have been at work on anything else. *Albere Galles* does not sound like the title of a comedy (neither, for that matter, does *The Black Dog of Newgate*, which, nevertheless, was John Day's 'comodye') but it is possible that the play for which lances were required had been completed before Henslowe opened Worcester's accounts. The second example is more telling. In February – the next series of accounts – Thomas Heywood sold the Company 'A womones gowne of black velluett' for *A Woman Killed With Kindness*. He did not deliver the final instalment of the script until March. The Company may have been taking a risk investing £6 in a costume before the play was completed, much less licensed. But Heywood was both a company sharer and a dependable playwright, unlikely to default or to run foul of the censor. He had also been a player with the Admiral's Men, which is perhaps how the costume came to be in his possession. Still, the connection between the play and the black velvet gown is riddling, unless one sees Heywood selling the Company an idea for a play for which he just happened to own the leading lady's best frock. Other plays commissioned this autumn but edited from the following extracts include *Marshal Osric* (Smith and Heywood, 20–30 September); *The Blind Eat Many a Fly* (Heywood, 24 November–7 January); and two untitled plays by Chettle and by Heywood. Perhaps the most interesting phenomenon these accounts reveal is the emerging pattern of involvement among collaborators. Heywood is a case in point. He began his playwriting career working independently. Between 1598, when his name first appears in the Diary opposite a play title, and September 1602, he managed to complete only four plays, one an old play he was revising and another not even mentioned in the Diary. In September 1602 he changed his habits, possibly because as a sharer he was allowed to devote all his energy to playwriting instead of dividing his time between writing and playing. He began collaborating with Chettle, Dekker and Webster, that year alone working on seven plays. Dekker and Chettle were occupied on twenty plays – some for Nottingham's Men – while John Webster served his apprenticeship as collaborator with

Heywood, Smith and Dekker. *The Overthrow of the Rebels* is probably
an alternate title to *Lady Jane*, which may survive in a version by Webster
and Heywood alone, *Sir Thomas Wyatt*.

———

Lent vnto my Lorde of worsters players
as foloweth begynyge the 17 daye of aguste
1602

Lent vnto the companye the 17 of aguste 1602 to paye vnto
thomas deckers for new A dicyons in owldcastelle the some of xxxx s

Layd owt for the company at the mermayd when we weare at
owre a grement the 21 of aguste 1602 toward our sup*per* the
some of ix s

Lent vnto wm kempe the 22 of aguste 1602 to bye buckram to
ma*cke* a payer of gyen*tes* hosse the some of v s

Lent vnto John ducke & John thayer the 21 of aguste 1602 to
bye A sewt for owld castell & A sewt & A dublet of satten the
some of *xij li*

Lent vnto John ducke to paye for the tvrckes head & ij wemens
gownes mackenge & fresh wat*r* for owld castell & the merser
bill & harey chettel *in* earenest*e* of a tragedie called
the 24 of aguste 1602 x s

Layd owt more for the company in p*arte* of payment for A
Boocke called medsen for a cvrst wiffe the some of vnto thomas
deckers x s

Lent vnto John ducke the 28 of aguste 1602 to paye vnto xpofer
bestone for A manes gowne of branshed velluet & A dublet for
the some of vj *li*

pd at the A poyntment of the company the 1 of septmb*er* 1602
in p*arte* of payment for A comody called medysen for A cvrste
wiffe to thomas deckers some of iiij *li*

pd at the A poyntment the comp*any* the 2 of septmb*er* 1602 in
fulle paym*ent* for A comody called A medysen for A cvrste wiffe
to thomas deckers the some of xxx s

Layd owt for the company the 3 of septmb*er* 1602 to bye iiij
Lances for the comody of thomas hewedes & mr smythes some
of viij s

Layd owt for the company the 4 of septmber 1602 to bye A flage
of sylke the some of   xxvj s 8d

pd at the A poyntment of the company the 4 of septmber 1602
vnto Thomas Hewod & mr smyth in fulle payment for A
Boocke called albere galles some of   vj li

Lente vnto John thare the 7 of septmber 1602 to geue vnto
Thomas deckers for his adicions in owld castell the some of   x s

Lent vnto thomas blackwode the 19 of septmber 1602 to paye
vnto Robarte shawe the some of   xvj s

pd vnto Thomas hewode the 20 of septmber for the new a
dicyons of cvttyng dicke some of   xx s

Lent vnto Johen thare the 21 of septmber 1602 to paye for
targates the some of   xx s

Lent vnto John ducke the 25 of septmber 1602 to bye A blacke
sewt of satten for the playe of burone the some of   v li

pd vnto thomas deckers the 27 of septmber 1602 over & a bove
his price of his boocke called A medysen for A cvrste wiffe some
of   x s

Lent vnto John thare the 30 of septmber 1602 to paye vnto the
armerer for targattes in full payment the some of   xx s

pd at the A poyntment of the company the 1 of october 1602 to
mr smythe in parte of payment for A tragedie called the ij
brothers the some of   xxxx s

[pd vnto my sonne EAlleyn at the A poyntment of the company
for his Boocke of tambercame the 2 of october 1602 the some
of   xxxx s]

Layd owt at the apoyntmente of the companye to macke A
scafowld & bare for the playe of Berowne & carpenters wages   xiij s

Lent at the a poyntment of John ducke in earneste of A playe
called   the some of   3 of october 1602
to mr mydellton   xx s

pd for poleyes & worckmanshipp for to hange absolome   x s ij d

pd at the A poyntment of John dewcke vnto mr smythe in parte
of payment of his Boocke called the ij brothers tragedie the 11
of october 1602 the some of   xxxx s

pd at the apoyntmente of John ducke to mr smyth in fulle
payment of his Boocke called the ij brothers the 15 of october
1602 the some of   xxxx s

Lent vnto John thare the 15 of october 1602 to geue vnto harey
chettell Thomas deckers thomas hewode & mr smythe & mr
webster in earneste of A playe called Ladey Jane the some of   l s

Lent at the apoyntment of the company to the tyerman to by
sowtedge to make devells sewtes for the new playe of the ij
brothers tragedie the some of   viij s

Lent at the apoyntment of the company vnto the tyerman to
bye saye for the playe of the ij brethers to macke a wiches
gowne the some of   18s

Lent vnto thomas hewode the 21 of october 1602 to paye vnto
mr deckers chettell smythe webester & hewode in fulle payment
of ther playe of ladye Jane the some of   v li x s

pd vnto EAlleyn the 22 of october 1602 at the a poyntment of
the company for a grogren clocke ij veluet gerkens ij dubletes ij
hedtyers the some of   xx li

pd for bordes & quarters & naylles for to macke a tabell & a coffen for the playe of the iij brothes the 22 of october 1602 some of   xij s iij d

Lent vnto John thare the 23 of october 1602 to paye vnto the
paynter of the properties for the playe of the iij brothers the
some of   xx s

pd vnto the tyer man for mackynge of the devells sute &
sperethes & for the witche for the playe of the iij brothers the
23 of october 1602 some of   x s ix d

Lent vnto John ducke the 27 of october 1602 to geue vnto
thomas deckers in earneste of the 2 parte of Lady Jane the some
of   v s

Lent vnto Thomas hewode & John webster the 2 of novmber
1602 in earneste of A playe called cryssmas comes but once
ayeare the some of   iij *li*

Lent vnto John dewcke the 6 of novmber 1602 for to macke a
sewt of satten of   for the playe of the overthrowe of
Rebelles the some of   v *li*

pd at the a poyntment of John lowen the 12 of novmber 1602
vnto mr smyth the some of   x *s*

Lent vnto John dewcke the 23 of novmber 1602 to paye vnto
hareye chettell & thomas deckers in parte of paymente of A
playe called crysmas comes but once A yeare the some of   xxxx *s*

pd at the A poyntment of John ducke the 24 of novmber 1602
to mr hathwaye in earneste of A playe called [John dayes
comodye] the blacke doge of newgate some of   xxxx *s*

pd at the A poyntment of Thomas hawode the 26 of novmber
1602 harey chettell in fulle paymente of A playe called cryssmas
comes but once A yeare the some of   xxxx *s*

Lent vnto xpofer beston & Robart palante the 26 of novmber
1602 to paye vnto John day mr smythe mr hathway & the other
poete in parte of payment of the playe called [John dayes
comody] the some of the blacke dogge of newgate   xxxx *s*

Bowght for the company of Robart shawe the 6 of desember
1602 iiij clothe clockes layd with copper lace for iiij *li* a clocke
& for my forberance of my mony to a lowe me v *s* vpon euery
clocke some is   xvij *li*

Sowld vnto the company the 9 of desember 1602 ij peces of
cangable taffetie to macke a womones gowne & a Robe some
of   for the play of crysmas comes but once a year iij *li* x *s*

pd at the apoyntment of the company the 20 of desember 1602
vnto mr hathway mr smythe & John daye & the other poyet in
fulle payment for A playe called the blacke dogge of newgat
some of   xxxx *s*

105. c. 10 December 1602. Memorandum.

Robert Shaa retired from Nottingham's Men in December 1601. A year later he was endeavouring to sell back to them and to Worcester's Men old stock, some that he would have accumulated over his long career, some that would have come into his possession as part of his retirement settlement. The playbook mentioned below was evidently of the former category, there being no evidence that it was ever performed by any company at the Rose. Nor does it seem to have aroused much enthusiasm in Nottingham's Men, for although they accepted *The Four Sons of Aymon* into joint stock (the relevant entry in the Company's loan account on f. 109 of the Diary dates the memorandum), they took the unusual step of requiring Shaa to guarantee that if the play 'be not playd by the company of the fortune nor noe other company' by 'Cristmas next', he would repay the £2 and reclaim his book. Presumably the 'other company' he had in mind was Worcester's Men at the Rose: Shaa had sold them four cloaks – old costumes – on 6 December. In the event, no company would have had much opportunity to perform *Aymon*, for in March the playhouses closed, not to reopen until the following year.

—

Memorandum that I Robert Shaa
haue receaued of mr Phillip Henshlowe
the some of forty shillinges vpon a booke
Called the fower sones of Aymon which booke
if it be not playd by the company of the
fortune nor noe other company
I doe then bynd my selfe by theis presentes to
repay the sayd some of forty shillinges
vpon the deliuery of my booke att Cristmas
next which shall be in the yeare of our Lord
god 1603 & in the xlvjth yeare of the
Raigne of the queene
                          per me Robt Shaa

106. 1 January–16 March 1602/3. Loan Account (extracts).

Of the thirty-eight payments Henslowe made for Worcester's Men during this period, £31 10s was spent on plays and £43 9s 4d on costumes. Henslowe reckoned the Company's account on 7 March: a debt of £220 13s 3d had accumulated in the seven months since Worcester's Men had moved into the Rose, but the Company had repaid Henslowe nearly £100, so the 'Reste dew' stood at £131 12s 4d. Thomas Blackwood signed the reckoning in acknowledgment for the Company. Evidently their credit

fell into disrepute with some of the tradesmen who supplied them: in
March, when they had not paid bills for satin totalling £8 10s, the mercer
finally arrested John Duke. There is no indication from the Revels or
Chamberlain's accounts that Worcester's Men appeared before the Queen
this holiday season, but Henslowe's payment on 1 January for two coro-
nets 'for hed tyers for the corte' belies this. The 'adicyones' to *The Black
Dog of Newgate Part II* suggest that that play was being prepared for
Elizabeth's Court. Costumes had already been bought, which presumably
means that the play had already been licensed, which in turn should mean
that the additions were not required by the censor as a condition to
licensing. This leaves a Court performance as the apparent reason 'adicyones' were required. If *The Black Dog* played before the Queen it was
among the last plays she saw. She was near death. On 6 March she
watched Nottingham's Men perform. On 19 March the playhouses
officially closed, anticipating national mourning. By this time, though,
Worcester's Men had already left London (see no. 107). They never
returned to the Rose.

———

Lent vnto John thare the 1 of Janewary 1602 to geue vnto
mrs calle for ij cvrenetes for hed tyers for the corte the some
of   x s

Lent vnto John dewcke the 10 of Janewarye 1602 to by Lame
skenes for the blacke dogge of newgate the some of   x s

pd more for the company the 16 of Janewarye 1602 vnto
goodman freshwatr for A canves sewt & skenes for the black
doge of newgate   xij s

Lent vnto John Lewen vpon John duckes noote of his hande
the 29 of Janewarye 1602 to geue in earneste of the second
part of the boocke called the black dooge of newgate vnto
mr hathwaye & John daye & mr smyth & the other poete
the some of   iij li

pd at the apoyntment of John ducke the 3 of febreary 1602
vnto mr hathwaye mr smythe John daye & the other poet in
fulle payment for the boocke called the seconde part of the
blacke dooge the some of   iiij li

pd vnto Thomas hewode the 5 of febreary 1602 for A womones gowne of black velluett for the playe of A womon kylld
with kyndnes some of   vj li 13 s

pd at the A poyntment of the company the 12 of febreary
1602 vnto thomas Hewwod in part of payment for his playe
called A womon kylled with kyndnes the some of   iij *li*

dd vnto the tyerman for the companye 1602 to bye viij yrdes
& A hallfe of blacke satten at xij *s* a yrde to macke a sewt
for the 2 parte of the blacke dogge the some of   v *li* ij *s*
15 of febrearye

Lent vnto Thomas blacke wode the 21 of febreary 1602 to
geue vnto the 4 poetes in earneste of ther adicyones for the
2 parte of the blacke dog the some of   x *s*

Lent vnto Thomas blacke wode the 24 of febreary 1602 to
geue vnto the 4 poetes in parte of paymente for ther adycyons
in the 2 parte of the blacke doge   x *s*

Lent vnto John dewcke the 26 of febreary 1602 to paye the
poetes in fulle payment for ther adycyones for the 2 parte of
the blacke doge the some of   xx *s*

pd at the apoyntment of the company the 6 of marche 1602
vnto Thomas Hewode in fulle payment for his playe called
a womon kyld with kyndnes the some of   iij *li*

pd at the apoyntment of thomas blackewod & John Lewen
the 7 of marche 1602 vnto mr smythe in earneste of &
etalleyon tragedie the some of   xxxx *s*

pd at the apoyntmente of Thomas blackwode the 7 of
marche 1602 vnto the tayller which made the blacke satten
sewt for the womon kyld with kyndnes the some of   x *s*

pd at the a poyntment of John Lowine the 12 of marche 1602
vnto mr smythe in fulle payment for his tragedie called the
etallyan tragedie the some of   iiij *li*

pd for the company the 16 of marche 1602 vnto the mercers
man wm Pvleston for his master John willett deate the some
of eighte powndes & x *s* which they owght hime for satten
& charges in the clyncke for arestynge John ducke I say as
maye apere   viij *li* x *s*

Memorandum that the fulle some of all the deatbtes which
we owe vnto mr Henslow to this xvj of mrche 1603 comethe
to Juste the some of 140^{li} - 1^s - 00^d which some of 140^{li} - 01^s
- 00^d we whosse names are here vnder wrytten do a know-
ledge ower dew deatte & promysse trewe payment
Thomas Blackwod

107. 12 March 1602/3. Private Loans.

The news at Court was that the old Queen was ill. Weary of governing,
she waved aside political discourse to take delight in old Canterbury tales.
Perhaps sensing that an inhibition was inevitable, Worcester's Men left
London several days before the restraint fell. These loans show them
underwriting their ride into the country with money from Henslowe.

———

Lent the 12 of marche 1602 vnto Thomas blackwode when
he Ride into the contrey with his company to playe in Redy
mony the some of   x s

Lent vnto John lowyn the 12 of marche 1602 when he went
into the contrey with the company to playe in Redy mony
the some of   v s

Lent vnto Rychard perckyns the 12 of marche 1602 when he
Rid with the company to playe in the con trey in Redy mony
the some of   x s

108. 19 March 1603. Privy Council Minute.

Queen Elizabeth died on 24 March.

———

Lettres to the Lord Mayor and Justices of Middlesex and Surrey for the
restraint of stage-plaies till other direction be given.

109. Undated. Forbearance Payment.

Nottingham's Men entered their last loan from Henslowe on 12 March,
the day Blackwood, Lowin and Perkins rode out of London with Worcester's Men. Like the Rose, the Fortune closed. Alleyn's company made for
Canterbury where they were paid *not* to perform. No doubt the Rose

company, wherever they were, met with similar rejections. It was, of course, no mistake for Alleyn's company to be styled 'Admiral's Men' by the Canterbury record keeper since their patron, Nottingham, continued to serve the government as Lord Admiral. The date limits on this document are 19 March to 9 May 1603, the dates on which the playhouses closed and reopened.

———

Item paid to Thomas Downton one of the Lord Admiralls Players for a gift bestowed vpon him & his company being so appointed by Mr maior & the Aldermen becaus it was thought fitt they should not play at all in regard that our late queene was then ether very sick or dead as they supposed .... xxx s

110. 7 May 1603. Royal Proclamation (extracts).

The playing companies were on tour. James Stuart left Edinburgh on 5 April, Elizabeth Tudor was buried on 28 April, and London received her new monarch on 7 May. King James wasted no time articulating his distaste for certain of the laxer aspects of English life. The day he arrived in London he issued a proclamation that included the following comments upon 'impious prophanation' of the Sabbath day and that elsewhere admonished those of his 'vulgar' subjects who desired to submit petitions to him to 'forbear all assembling and flocking together in multitudes'.

———

And for that we are informed that there hath beene heretofore great neglect in this kingdome of keeping the Sabbath-day: For better observing of the same and avoyding all impious prophanation, we do straightly charge and commaund, that no Beare-bayting, Bul-bayting, Enterludes, Common Playes, or other like disordered or unlawful Exercises, or Pastimes, be frequented, kept, or used at any time hereafter upon the Sabbath-day.

111. 9 May 1603. Loan Account.

The playhouses opened soon after King James arrived in London but almost immediately closed again as the city was struck with the most virulent outbreak of plague it had experienced since 1593. The coronation had to be postponed for nearly a year while the playhouses were empty for ten months. The following payment, which fits into the brief resumption of playing between the two inhibitions, is the last record of Worcester's Men at the Rose. Unlike Nottingham's Men at the Fortune, they did not resume accounts with Henslowe when the inhibition was lifted and he began fresh Diary entries in March 1604. 'A playe wherin shores wiffe is writen' – Jane Shore being the notorious mistress to Edward IV – was the last play to be commissioned for the Rose; after 9 May 1603 there is no evidence that plays were ever seen there again. Henslowe's memorandum of 25 June may explain why (see no. 112).

——

Begininge to playe Agayne by the kynges licence & Layd owt sence for my lord of worsters men as folowethe   1603   9 of maye

Lent at the apoyntment of Thomas hewode & John ducke
vnto harey chettell & John daye in earneste of A playe
wherin shores wiffe is writen the some of   xxxx s

112. 25 June 1603. Rose Lease Renewal.

The original lease on the Little Rose, negotiated in 1574 for a term of thirty-one years, was due to expire in 1605. Henslowe had held the lease since 1585. He was evidently eager to renew it, for he took up the matter 'with mr Pope' well in advance of the contract's expiration date. The outraged tone of the following memorandum makes it clear that Henslowe intended to negotiate the new lease on the same terms as the old. For the past eighteen years he had been paying the parish of St Mildred's, Bread Street, in the City of London, £7 a year rent for the Rose messuage, which included not just the ground on which the playhouse stood but five other properties as well. These were developed as tenements that Henslowe in turn sub-let, collecting from them nearly £30 a year. The playhouse of course earned him much more – altogether a tidy profit on £7 outgoing a year. Yet when Henslowe approached the parish about renewing the lease to learn that the property had been revalued so that his rent would be tripled and he would be required to contribute 100 marks toward parish maintenance, he declared that he 'wold Rather pulledowne the playehowse then ... do so'. Henslowe may have been bluffing. He could pluck grass to judge the wind as shrewdly as any other man: by going to the parish this June, a full year earlier than was probably necessary, when plague was ravaging the City and an inhibition was in effect, Henslowe could point to an empty playhouse and to tenants unable to pay their rent. This June his properties were worthless. The parish could hardly ignore the general state of depression when making their assessment. If this was Henslowe's strategy, the parish was not fooled. They deemed the Rose property phenomenally lucrative to judge by the rent increase, and it could only have been the playhouse that was responsible for that. For ten years, the parish may have seen itself in the galling position of having disposed cheaply of a rubbish tip – Southwark not being the most salubrious of districts – on which a gold mine was discovered. Ten years of watching Henslowe rake in profits from such a dubious risk as a playhouse might have whetted their appetite for a share in the venture. They would not be fobbed off with meagre excuses. But what if Henslowe was not bluffing? What if the parish was simply too late? They may well have seen a decade's worth of gold extracted from the Rose, may have leaped upon the first opportunity to stake a claim and yet may have arrived when the vein had dried up. After four years of competing with the Globe in a rivalry that cost the Rose her most prestigious tenants, the Little Rose may not have been worth £20 a year. It is true that Henslowe did not 'pulledowne the playehowse' as he threatened, but neither did he record any evidence of its ever having been used by players again.

Memorandom that the 25 of June 1603 I talked with mr Pope at the scryveners shope wher he lisse consernynge the tackynge of the leace A new of the Littell Roose & he showed me A wrytynge betwext the pareshe & hime seallfe which was to paye twenty pownd A yeare Rent & to bestowe A hunderd marckes vpon billdinge which I sayd I wold Rather pulledowne the playehowse then I wold do so & he beade me do & sayd he gaue me leaue & wold beare me owt for yt wasse in hime to do yt

113. 21 October 1603. Letter (extracts).

The Rose remained shut. Companies that had worn themselves to tatters on the road returned to London, probably hoping that Michaelmas would bring a resumption in playing. Edward Alleyn remained in Sussex with friends, preferring to wear his 'appayrell to Rags' in 'hauckinge' than in joining the Company on tour. His wife wrote to him, mentioning the players and in passing how Henslowe was occupying himself. Henslowe had been a Groom of Her Majesty's Chamber in Elizabeth's household; evidently he was serving the new King.

Jhesus

My Intyre & welbeloved sweete harte still it Joyes me & longe I pray god may I Joye to heare of your healthe & welfare as you of ours Allmighty god be thancked my owne self your selfe, & my mother & whole house are in good healthe & about vs the sycknes dothe Cease & likely more & more by godes healpe to Cease. All the Companyes be Come hoame & well for ought we knowe, but that Browne of the Boares Head is dead & dyed very pore. He went not into the Countrye at all. and all of your owne Company ar well at theyr owne houses. my father is at the Corte but wheare the Court ys I know not I am of your owne mynde, that it is needles to meete my father at Basynge the Incertayntye being as it ys & I Commend your discretion it were a sore Journey to loase your labour besyd expenses & Change of Ayre mighte hurte you therfore you are Resolved vpon the best Course. for your Cominge hoame I am not to advyse you neither will I, vse your owne discretion yet I longe & am very desyrous to see you & my poore & symple opinion is yf it shall please you you maye safely Come hoame, Heare is none now sycke neare vs, vs, [sic] yet let it not be as I wyll but at your owne best lykynge, I am glad to heare you take delight in hauckinge, & thoughe you have have [sic] worne your appayrell to Rags the best ys you knowe wheare to have better, & as wellcome to me shall you be with your rags as yf you were in Cloathe of gold or velvet, trye & see.

114. 15 March 1604. Coronation List.

After a year's postponement, King James's coronation was finally celebrated. The prerogative of patronising players, which, in Elizabeth's time had been confined to barons and above, was restricted even further by the new king, to members of the Royal Family. Worcester's Men found a new patron and became Queen Anne's Men. Their patent, drafted during the plague year, named their 'vsuall Howsen' as 'the Curtayne, and the Bores head'. The Rose was not mentioned. Allowance for red coronation livery was made to the following Queen Anne's Men listed in the Chamberlain's Accounts.

———

Christopher Beeston
Robert Lee
John Duke
Robert Palante
Richard Purkins
Thomas Haward
James Houlte
Thomas Swetherton
Thomas Greene
Robert Beeston

115. 1603. *Vertues Common-wealth* (extracts).

Stephen Gosson and Philip Stubbes, those masters of anti-playhouse diatribe, came to life again in Henry Cross. Not for twenty years had the voice of puritanical censure risen to such a howl. The tragedians of the city played out the last years of Elizabeth's reign in relative security, the pack at their heels baying only feebly. But a new king gave the hounds fresh wind. Henry Cross took up the chase with zeal. He was a man who had no time at all for cakes and ale, a man irked that 'these copper-lace gentlemen', the players, grew rich, a man incapable of appreciating why his monarch, whose speech impediment and rapidly souring relationship with his subjects exposed him to universal parody, should be made 'a May-game to all' by the players. *Vertues Common-wealth* shoots antique arrows: players are 'puft vp'; plays contribute to social decay; playwrights are 'basely imployed' using their 'noble gifts' to 'maintaine those Anticks ... that speake out of their mouthes'. Not one new accusation can be marshalled, and yet, where Gosson and Stubbes failed, Cross would ultimately succeed. It would take the cry of curs another forty years, but the playhouses would be pulled down.

―――

Must the holy Prophets and Patriarkes be set vpon a Stage, to be derided, hist, and laught at? or is it fit that the infirmities of holy men should be acted on a Stage, whereby others may be inharted to rush carelessly forward into vnbrideled libertie? ... Furthermore, there is no passion wherwith the king, the soueraigne maiestie of the Realme was possest, but is amplified, and openly sported with, and made a May-game to all the beholders. ... If a man will learne to be proud, fantasticke, humorous, to make love, sweare, swagger, and in a word closely doo any villanie, for a two-penny almes hee may be throughly taught and made a perfect good scholler. ... And as these copper-lace gentlemen growe rich, purchase lands by adulterous Playes, & not fewe of them vsurers and extortioners, which they exhaust out of the purses of their haunters, so are they puft vp in such pride and selfe-loue, as they enuie their equalles, and scorne theyr inferiours ... To conclude, it were further to be wished, that those admired wittes of this age, Tragaedians, and Comaedians, that garnish Theaters with their inuentions, would spend their wittes in more profitable studies, and leaue off to maintaine those Anticks, and Puppets, that speake out of their mouthes: for it is pittie such noble giftes, should be so basely imployed, as to prostitute their ingenious labours to inriche such buckorome gentlemen.

116. 9 April 1604. Letter.

The Privy Council wrote to the Lord Mayor and Aldermen lifting the year-long injunction against playing. Three companies – formerly the Chamberlain's Men, Nottingham's Men and Worcester's Men – were authorised to play in specific houses. The Rose was not among them,

Worcester's-Queen Anne's having abandoned her in favour of the older Curtain.

——

After our har[tie commendacions] to your [Lordship.] Wheras the kings maiesties Plaiers have given [   ] hyghnes good service in ther Quallitie of Playinge, and for as much Lickwise as they are at all times to be emploied in that Service whensoever they shalbe Comaunded we thinke it therfore fitt the time of Lent being now Passt that your *Lordship* doe Permitt and suffer the three Companies of Plaiers to the King Queene and Prince publicklie to Exercise ther Plaies in ther severall and vsuall howses for that Purpose and noe other viz The Globe scituate in maiden Lane on the Banckside in the Countie of Surrey, the fortun in Golding Lane and the Curtaine In Hollywell in the Cowntie of Midlesex without any lett or Interruption In respect of any former *Lettres* of Prohibition heertofore written by vs to your *Lordship*. Except there shall happen weeklie to die of the Plague Aboue the Number of thirtie within the Cittie of London and the Liberties therof. Att which time we thinke it fitt they shall Cease and forbeare any further Publicklie to Playe vntill the Sicknes be again decreaced to the saide Number And so we bid your *Lordship* hartilie farewell ffrom the Court at Whitehalle the ixth of Aprille, 1604.

Your very Loving ffrends
Nottingham
Suffock
Gill Shrowsberie
Ed Worster
W: Knowles
J: Stanhopp

To our verie good *Lord* the Lord Maior of the Cittie of London and to the Justices of the peace of the Counties of Midlesex and Surrey.

117. January 1604–February 1606. Sewer Records.

The Sewer Commission, whose responsibility it was to see that London's walls, ditches, gutters, banks and sewers were maintained, had authority to tax landowners or leaseholders for this purpose. Their annual inspections document in few words the last record of Philip Henslowe's Rose.

——

January 1604:	Francis, not Philip, Henslowe amerced at *6s 8d.*
4 October 1605:	Philip Henslowe amerced; return was made that the property was 'out of his hands'.
14 February 1606:	Edward Box, Bread Street, London, amerced.
25 February 1606:	Box amerced for the site of 'the late playhouse in Maid lane'.

References and Abbreviations

APC   *Acts of the Privy Council of England*, ed. J.R. Dasent, HMSO, 1890-1907. British Library catalogue no. 2073.173.

B.L. *Add. Mss.*   British Library *Additional Manuscripts* preserved in the Manuscript Room of the British Library.

CSPD   *Calendar of State Papers, Domestic;* indexed by the Historical Manuscripts Commission.

CSP Ireland   *Calendar of State Papers, Ireland;* indexed by the Historical Manuscripts Commission.

Diary   Henslowe's Diary. See *HP* below.

DNB   *Dictionary of National Biography.*

ES   E.K. Chambers, *The Elizabethan Stage*, 4 volumes (Oxford, 1925). In *Vol. IV* Chambers includes appendices on Court performances and payments (pp. 131-81) and on plague records (pp. 345-53). His section on company tours (*Vol. II*, 1) supplements J.T. Murray's *English Dramatic Companies* (London, 1910).

F & R   R.A. Foakes and R.T. Rickert, *Henslowe's Diary;* see *HP* below.

Greg, *HP*   W.W. Greg, *Henslowe Papers;* see *HP* below.

Harl. Mss.   *Harleian Manuscripts* preserved in the British Library Manuscript Room.

HP   *Henslowe Papers.* These documents, which include not only Henslowe's *Diary* but his own and Edward Alleyn's playhouse papers, are bound in several volumes and are preserved at Dulwich College, London. MS. I comprises the Henslowe–Alleyn papers while MS. VII is the *Diary.* A Facsimile edition of MSS. I and VII was prepared for the Scolar Press (London, 1977) by R.A. Foakes. *Henslowe's Diary* edited by R.A. Foakes and R.T. Rickert (Cambridge, 1961) replaced the original transcription of the complete *Diary* made by Walter Greg in 1907, but Greg's volume of criticism, *Vol. II*, has not yet been superseded. Greg also edited many of the MS. I papers in *Henslowe Papers: Being Documents Supplementary to Henslowe's Diary* (Oxford, 1931). Foakes and Rickert include the most important of these documents in an appendix to their edition of the *Diary.* In every case, the Foakes and Rickert reading is preferred to Greg's. In only one case (Muniment 16, the deed of partnership in the Rose playhouse, my document no. 1) did I find significant errors in the Foakes and Rickert transcription.

Lansd. Mss.   *Lansdowne Manuscripts*, papers of William Cecil, Lord Burghley, which, at his death, remained in the hands of his secretary, eventually passed to the first Marquis of Lansdowne, and, in 1807, were sold to the British Museum where they are preserved in the Manuscript Room. Other Cecil documents remain as State Papers; still others are at Hatfield House, where they are calendared by the

Historical Manuscripts Commission as *Salisbury Mss*. Some of these latter papers were Robert Cecil's and relate to his Secretaryship of the Privy Council.

MSC   *Malone Society Collection*. These volumes, the first published in 1907, supplement the Society's main effort of preparing definitive editions of obscure plays that might otherwise be lost. The *Collections* in many cases made transcriptions of Elizabethan playhouse documents available for the first time. They are now mostly superseded but still remain the only printed source of some documents.

Remembrancia   As instructed by the original order of the Court of Aldermen dated 5 November 1573, the *Remembrancia* were to contain verbatim copies of every letter sent by the Lord Mayor and the Court of Aldermen to the Queen and Privy Council, as well as their answers, together with every letter directed to the Mayor and Aldermen from any person 'of honor or creditt'. The post of Remembrancer was held between 1587 and 1605 by Giles Fletcher, the poet. A comparison with the Privy Council Act Books shows that many items of correspondence which deserved entry in the *Remembrancia* were not recorded there.

SR   Stationers' Register. *A Transcript of the Registers of the Company of Stationers of London 1554-1640*, ed. Edward Arber, 5 volumes (London, 1875-94).

Notes

1   Rose Playhouse Deed: *HP*, mun. 16. Printed: F & R *Diary*, 304-6; Greg, *HP*, 2-4. Simmonds Deed: *HP*, mun. 15. Printed: Greg, *HP*, 1-2 (abstract). Sewer Commission Report: *ES II*, 407 n. 2 citing C.W. Wallace, *The Times* (1914). I have settled upon the spelling Theater, in preference to Theatre, for Burbage's playhouse, since most documents refer to it by that spelling, which helps distinguish between playhouses generically and Burbage's specific venture.

2   Letter to Walsingham: *Harl. MS*. 286 no. 63 f. 102. Printed: *ES IV*, 303-4.

3   Privy Council Restraint: PC 2/14 f. 339. Printed: Dasent *APC*, *xv*, 70; *ES IV*, 303-4.

4   Privy Council Restraint: PC 2/14 f. 477. Printed: Dasent *APC*, *xv*, 271; *ES IV*, 304-5.

5   Gawdy Letter: I.H. Jeayes, *Letters of Philip Gawdy* (Roxburghe Club), 23. B.L. Catalogue no. C. 101. e. 15; *ES II*, 135.

6   Deed of Sale: *HP*, MS. I, Art. 2. Printed: F & R, *Diary*, 273-4; Greg, *HP*, 31-2. Death of John Allen: Diary, f. 3. Robert Browne: the name, being a common one, leaves the exact identity of Robert Browne open to dispute. C.J. Sisson thinks the Browne of this deed, a Worcester's Man, is the same Browne who owned and operated the Boar's Head playhouse and who 'dyed very pore, he went not into the Countrye at all' during the

plague restraint of 1603 (see document 113; C.J. Sisson, 'Mr and Mrs Browne of the Boar's Head', *Life and Letters Today*, vol. 15, no. 6, winter 1936, 99-107 and *The Boar's Head Theatre* (London, 1972)). Herbert Berry concurs: 'Our dictionaries of actors list only one Robert Browne, a man who began with the first Worcester's company in 1583, led the most conspicuous English companies in the Low Countries and Germany in the 1590s, led Derby's company 1599-1601, went back to Germany 1601-7, was a Revels patentee in 1610, and returned to Germany yet again 1618-20. Sisson, however, was obviously right to insist that there were two Robert Brownes' ('The Playhouse in the Boar's Head Inn, Whitechapel' in *The Elizabethan Theatre I*, ed. David Galloway (Hamden, Conn., 1970), 67, and 'The Boar's Head Again' in *The Elizabethan Theatre III*, ed. David Galloway (Hamden, Conn., 1973)). Willem Schrickx ('English Actors at the Courts of Wolfenbütell, Brussels and Graz during the Lifetime of Shakespeare', *Shakespeare Survey 33* (1980)) agrees that there were two Robert Brownes but argues that the Browne of this deed, who was head of the touring company in Germany, was unconnected with the Boar's Head. In this dispute Herbert Berry's opinion is to be trusted.

7 Lord Mayor to Burghley: *Lansd. Ms.* 60, Art. 19, f. 46. Printed: *MSC i*, 180; *ES IV*, 305-6.

8 Privy Council Minute: PC 2/16 f. 388. Printed: Dasent *APC*, *xviii*, 214; *ES IV*, 306-7.

9 Nashe 'Epistle': Robert Greene, *Menaphon* (1589). B.L. Catalogue no. 95.b.18 (5.). R.B. McKerrow, *The Works of Thomas Nashe, vol. III* (Oxford, 1958), 311; *ES IV*, 234-6 (reprinted from 1610 edition). For an explanation of the phrase 'latinize their necke-verse' see headnote to document 71.

10 Rose Repairs: Diary, ff. 4-5v.

11 Rose Receipts: Diary, f. 7. Warrant for Court Payment: PC2/19 f. 208. Printed: Dasent, *APC xxii*, 264. The altercation between Burbage and Alleyn was reported in depositions entered in testimony in the Burbage *v* John Brayne suit, the full text of which is printed in C.W. Wallace, *The First London Theatre, Materials for a History*, Nebraska University Studies, xiii.1, 1913. A summary is printed in *ES II*, 392.

12 Part to *Orlando Furioso*: HP MS. I, Art. 138 ff. 261-71. Printed: Greg, *HP*, 155-71. See Greg's account of the extant text of *Orlando* in *Two Elizabethan Stage Abridgements* (Malone Society: Oxford, 1923), 133-4.

13 Lord Mayor to Whitgift: *Remembrancia i*, 635. Printed: *MSC, i*, 68; *ES IV*, 307-8.

14 Guild of Merchant Tailors Minute: Guild Hall Microfilm 326 (30) f. 345. Printed: C.M. Clode, *The Early History of the Guild of Merchant Taylors i*, 236 (1888), Guildhall Library L37/M555; *ES IV*, 309.

15 Playhouse Licensing Fees: Diary, f. 6v.

16 Rose Receipts: Diary, ff. 7-8. The identity, priority, date and authorship of 'harey the vj' and Shakespeare's *Henry VI* plays are still disputed. The following should be consulted in the debate: Andrew S. Cairncross's prefaces to the Arden edition of *Henry VI, Parts I, II* and *III* (London, 1962); Clifford Leech, 'The Two-Part Play, Marlowe and the Early Shakespeare', *Shakespeare Jahrbuch* 94 (1958), 90-106; Marco Mincoff, 'The Composition of Henry VI, Part I', *Shakespeare Quarterly 16* (1965),

279-87; and Hanspeter Born, 'The Date of 2, 3 Henry VI', *Shakespeare Quarterly* 25 (1974), 323-34. The problem is this: if the 'harey the vj' play new in Henslowe's receipts on 3 March 1592 was Shakespeare's *Henry VI Part I*, why do not *Parts II* and *III* appear in Lord Strange's repertoire later this season, particularly since it is *Part III* to which Robert Greene was alluding in his famous parody, 'his tiger's heart wrapp'd in a player's hide', an attack on Shakespeare published in September 1592 (see document 21)? Cairncross, whose main concern was to dispel the late-nineteenth-century prejudice for assigning the *Henry VI* trilogy to anyone but Shakespeare on the assumption that the plays were not up to his standard, discredited attributions to Marlowe, Greene, Nashe or any collaborative combination of those playwrights. The *Henry VI* plays were definitely Shakespeare's, Cairncross asserted roundly, and were written for Pembroke's Men in 1590, but the 1592 'harey the vj' of the Diary was not, it being only another redaction of a favourite episode in English history. Cairncross's argument leaves several loose ends, the most obvious of which are Thomas Nashe's reference (*Pierce Penilesse his Supplication to the Diuell*, SR 8 August 1592) to a vastly popular Talbot play seen by 'ten thousand spectators at least (at seuerall times)', and Greene's invective, 'his tiger's heart'. Is it likely that another Talbot play besides Shakespeare's *Henry VI Part I* would have attracted 'ten thousand spectators at least' after the appearance of Shakespeare's play in 1590, or that Nashe would have referred, in what is an urgent defence of the social value of the playhouse, to a production that was staged so long ago as two years? And would Greene wait two years to publish an attack on Shakespeare, and would he rely on the two-year-old memory of a single line from the trilogy to make his point with readers? I prefer Hanspeter Born's account of the date and composition of the *Henry VI* plays. Born thinks Shakespeare was a member of Lord Strange's Men in 1592 and that Henslowe's 'harey the vj' was Shakespeare's *Part I*, premiered in March 1592; that Nashe referred to that production as the Talbot play of vast popularity in August 1592; that, based on that popularity, Shakespeare began *Parts II* and *III* for Lord Strange's Men, but that the plays were not yet ready when the playhouses were closed by plague on 23 June. They may have been well into production, or they may have opened in the provinces, but in either case Robert Greene got wind of them and used them to fuel his attack; this actually *anticipated* the London opening of *Part III* that Greene undoubtedly expected in September, the normal date for lifting of plague restraints. He seems to have planned his invective to coincide with the appearance of *Part III* when the line 'O tiger's heart' would be fresh; nor was this the first time Greene anticipated a fellow writer: he quoted Nashe's *Pierce Penilesse* before the pamphlet was in print. As things turned out, though, Greene's plan was frustrated. Lord Strange's Men did not return to the Rose in September. Instead, they disbanded (see headnotes to documents 21-3 and 27), and the *Henry VI* plays, diplomatically renamed 'the first parte of the Contention of ... York and Lancaster' and 'the true tragedy of Richard Duke of York' followed Shakespeare to his new company.

17 Lord Mayor to Burghley: *Remembrancia i*, 662. Printed: *MSC i*, 70; *ES IV* 310 (reprinted from *MSC i*, 187 and *Lansd. MS.* 71 f. 28). The *Remembrancia* letter book copy is misdated '30 May'.

18 Privy Council Restraint: PC 2/19 f. 414. Printed: Dasent *APC xxii*, 549; *ES IV*, 310-11.

19 Canterbury Chambers Accounts: Printed: *MSC vii*, 17.

20 A, Strange's Petition: *HP* MS. I, Art. 16. Printed F & R, *Diary*, 283-4; Greg, *HP*, 42; *ES IV*, 311-12. B, Watermen's Petition: *HP* MS. I, Art. 17. Printed F & R, *Diary*, 284-5; Greg, *HP*, 42-3; *ES IV*, 312. C, Warrant: *HP* MS. I, Art. 18. Printed F & R, *Diary*, 285; Greg, *HP*, 43-4; *ES IV*, 312-13.

21 Rose Receipts: *Diary*, ff. 8, 8v. Alleyn marriage: *Diary*, f. 2. *Spanish Tragedy*, *SR ii*, f. 293. *Soliman and Perseda*, *SR ii*, f. 293v. Thomas Nashe. *Pierce Penilesse* (entered *SR* 8 August 1592), B.L. Catalogue no. C.40.c.67. Robert Greene. *Groat's Worth* (entered *SR* 20 September 1592), B.L. Catalogue no. C.57.b.42. Henry Chettle. *Kind-Hart's Dream* (entered *SR* 8 December 1592), B.L. Catalogue no. C.14.a.6.

22 Privy Council Restraint: PC 2/20 f. 211. Printed: Dasent *APC xxiv*, 31; *ES IV* 313.

23 Travel Warrant: PC 2/20 f. 351. Printed: Dasent, *APC xxiv*, 212; *ES II*, 124. Sussex Warrant: PC 2/20 f. 348. Printed Dasent, *APC xxiv*, 209. Warrant for Court Payment: PC 2/20 f. 265. Printed: Dasent *APC xxiv*, 102. Loan to Francis Henslowe: *Diary*, f. 2v. Pigg's Letter: *HP* MS. I, Art. 15. Printed: F & R, *Diary*, 282-3; Greg, *HP*, 41.

24 Alleyn to Joan Alleyn: *HP*, MS. I, Art. 9. Printed: F & R, *Diary*, 274-5; Greg, *HP*, 34.

25 Alleyn to Henslowe: *HP* MS. I, Art. 11. Printed: F & R, *Diary*, 276-7; Greg, *HP*, 35-6. *Henry of Cornwall:* first reference in *Diary*, f. 7, acted 25 February 1591/2. Libels: Dasent, *APC xxiv*, 222. Marlowe: J. Leslie Hotson, *The Death of Christopher Marlowe* (London, 1925).

26 Henslowe to Alleyn: *HP* MS. I, Art. 14. Printed: F & R, *Diary*, 280-1; Greg, *HP*, 39-41. Extracts: *HP* MS. I, Art. 12, Art. 13. Printed: F & R, *Diary*, 277-280; Greg, *HP*, 36-40. A facsimile of the stage drawing is printed by F & R, *Diary*, 281.

27 Rose Receipts: *Diary*, f. 8v. *A Knack to Know a Knave*, *SR ii*, f. 304. *Titus*, *SR ii*, f. 304v. *Contention of York and Lancaster*, *SR ii*, f. 305v. For the ascription of *Titus Andronicus* to Shakespeare (and others) see John Dover Wilson, ed., *The New Shakespeare Titus Andronicus* (Cambridge, 1948); H.T. Price, *Journal of English and Germanic Philology* 42 (1943), 55-81; and J.C. Maxwell, ed., *The Arden Shakespeare Titus Andronicus* (London, 1953).

28 Privy Council Restraint: *Remembrancia ii*, 6. Printed: *MSC i*, 72; *ES IV*, 314-15.

29 Rose Receipts: *Diary*, f. 9. *King Leire*, *SR ii*, f. 307.

30 Rose Receipts: *Diary*, f. 9. *Taming of a Shrew*, *SR ii*, f. 306v. *Friar Bacon*, *SR ii*, f. 307. *Henry V*, *SR ii*, f. 307. *King Leire*, *SR ii*, f. 307. *John a Gaunt*, *SR ii*, f. 307. *Robin Hood*, *SR ii*, f. 307. *Jew of Malta*, *SR ii*, f. 307. *Henry I*, *SR ii*, f. 307v. *Wounds of Civil War*, *SR ii*, f. 307v.

31 Rose Receipts: *Diary*, f. 9.

32 Rose Receipts: *Diary*, ff. 9-11v. *Godfrey of Boulogne*, *SR ii*, f. 309v. *Richard III*, *SR ii*, f. 309v. *Tamburlaine* was first played at the Rose as part of the repertoire of the Admiral's Men on 25 August 1594 (*Diary*, f. 10) when Henslowe marked it 'j'. That symbol apparently designated not a new play but one that had been revised and consequently re-licensed. *Part II*

entered the repertoire on 19 December 1594 (Diary, f. 11). Over
the next year the two parts played seven times, usually on consecutive
days, but after 13 November 1595 (Diary f. 14) *Tamburlaine* seems
never to have been performed at the Rose again. Other Marlowe
plays were revived; *Tamburlaine* disappeared (see documents 59 and
99).

33 Lord Mayor to Burghley: *Remembrancia ii*, 73. Printed: *MSC i*, 74; *ES IV*,
316–17. The definitive work on Francis Langley and the Swan playhouse
is by William Ingram, *A London Life in the Brazen Age* (Cambridge,
Mass., 1978).

34 Rose Receipts: Diary ff. 10v, 11.

35 Bond: Diary, f. 20.

36 Company List?: Diary, f. 3.

37 Rose Repairs: Diary f. 2v.

38 Rose Receipts: Diary, ff. 11v, 12v. *George a Green*, *SR ii*, f. 130. *Old Wife's
Tale*, *SR ii*, f. 130v.

39 Rose Receipts: Diary, ff. 12v, 13. Plague Records: *ES IV*, 349. Apprentice
Disturbances: *Salisbury Mss. v*, 249, 250; *Remembrancia ii*, 97.

40 Lord Mayor to Privy Council: *Remembrancia ii*, 103. Printed: *MSC i*, 76; *ES
IV*, 318.

41 Rose Receipts: Diary, f. 14. For Burbages's acquisition of the Blackfriars
lease see *ES II*, 503 *passim*.

42 Licensing Fee: Diary, f. 40v.

43 Rose Receipts: Diary, ff. 15v, 21v.

44 Loan Account: Diary, f. 71v. *Troy*, f. 21v. *Paradox*, f. 21v.

45 Loan Repayments: Diary, f. 41v.

46 De Witt: Joseph Quincey Adams, *Shakespearean Playhouses* (Boston, 1917),
167–8. The complete Latin text is printed in *Shakespeare Survey 1*
(Cambridge, 1948), 'A Note on the Swan Theatre Drawing', and in *ES II*,
361–2.

47 Privy Council Restraint: PC 2/21 f. 317. Printed: Dasent *APC xxvi*, 38; *ES IV*,
319. Nashe Letter to William Cotton: *Cotton MS*. Julius, C.iii.f.280.
Printed: McKerrow, *Nashe V*, 194; *ES IV*, 319.

48 Loan and Repayment Account: Diary, ff. 22v, 23. *Stukeley*, f. 25v. *Vortigern*,
f. 25v. *Guido*, f. 26. Blackfriars Petition: *CSPD cc*, 116. Printed: *ES IV*,
319.

49 Rose Receipts: Diary, ff. 25, 25v.

50 Rose Receipts: Diary, f. 26. The Jones and Downton defection is surmised
from the fact that their names appear on what is possibly a Company
sharer list (document 36), undated but placed between entries dated 14
December 1594 and 14 January 1595 (Diary, f. 3), and again in players'
bonds negotiated after *The Isle of Dogs* incident (documents 55 and 57;
Diary, ff. 232–3). Jones and Downton are likewise known to have
been among Pembroke's Men at the Swan, for they are named in
litigation with Langley surrounding their departure (see note 59). For
a nearly day-by-day account of Pembroke's Men and Langley at the Swan
in these weeks see William Ingram, *A London Life in the Brazen
Age*.

51 Plot to *Frederick and Basilea*: B.L. *Add. Mss*. 10449. Printed: Greg, *HP*,
135–7.

52 Lord Mayor to Privy Council: *Remembrancia, ii*, 171. Printed: *MSC i*, 78; *ES*

IV, 321-2. The correct interpretation of these documents and events was detected by William Ingram, *A London Life in the Brazen Age*, 167-91.

53 Privy Council Minute: PC 2/22 f. 327. Printed: Dasent *APC xxvii*, 313; *ES IV*, 322. Topcliffe: *Cecil Papers* 54, 20. See William Ingram, *A London Life in the Brazen Age*, 167-91.

54 Privy Council Minute: PC 2/22 f. 346. Topcliffe: Described by Jesuit John Gerard in *DNB*. Nashe: McKerrow, *Nashe III*, 153-4. See William Ingram, *A London Life in the Brazen Age*, 167-91.

55 Players' Bonds: Diary, ff. 233, 232v. Henslowe may have derived the idea of such bonds from Francis Langley at the Swan, who seems to have been the first to hit upon the measure. Langley's forfeits were in the amount of £100. A mark was worth 13s 4d.

56 Privy Council Warrant: PC 2/23 f. 13. Printed: Dasent *APC xxviii*, 33.

57 Player's Bond: Diary, f. 232.

58 Rose Receipts: Diary, ff. 27v, 36v.

59 Loan Account: Diary, ff. 43v, 37. Alleyn's Retirement: Diary, f. 43. Pawned Cloak: Diary, ff. 33v, 50, 50v. Bird's Arrest: Diary, f. 38v. Swan Suit, Langley *v*. The Players: PRO Req 2/226/23. Printed: C. W. Wallace, *Englische Studien* 43 (1911). Adult players in women's roles: Many writers point to Cleopatra's lines, 'The quick comedians/Extemporally will stage us ... and I shall see/Some squeaking Cleopatra boy my greatness/I'the posture of a whore' (V. ii. 116-21) as indication that the role was played by a boy actor. They usually follow their comment with the observation that Shakespeare, by breaking the illusion of the play at so tense a moment in the gathering acceleration of the climax and by exposing the actor behind his character, perhaps merely for an ironic laugh, places a dangerous pressure on his play that might split it wide open. From the audience's point of view, it seems a nearly intolerable wrenching of emotions that Cleopatra, who has shown herself to be a versatile and consummate actress from her first entrance and who is now at the point of stage managing her own death, fooling others but showing herself ready to exchange illusions for realities, no longer playing her love for Antony but, in death, enacting it to the life, should sabotage such subtleties by so obvious a self-reference to the status of the actor. But what if Cleopatra were played by a man? Clearly the lovers of this play are middle-aged. Antony sees the grizzle in his beard even as he greets the 'girl' whose 'salad days' are long past and whose conquests from Pompey onwards chronicle a history of several decades: 'What, girl! though grey/ Do something mingle with our younger brown ...' (IV. viii. 18). And surely the point of Enobarbus's celebration of Cleopatra's eternal ripeness, 'Age cannot wither her', resides in the fact that Cleopatra *is* aged. Shakespeare wrote plays for a specific company of players and could capitalise upon resources he was well acquainted with. Richard Burbage would have been in his mid-forties when the role of Antony was written for him. My feeling is that Shakespeare would have partnered him with a middle-aged Cleopatra, an adult player weighty enough to balance Burbage and to carry a final wide-curving act completely unsupported by Burbage's massive stage presence. If Cleopatra were played by a man, the allusion to 'some squeaking ... boy' becomes at once more complex and more straightforward, a double bending of illusion: in the world of the play it echoes Cleopatra's appraisal of the

world's paltriness, its shrunken condition now that Antony is dead. Since 'young boys and girls/Are level now with men; the odds is gone' (IV. xv. 65-6), any re-enactment of their story in so diminutive a mortal world will be merely the squeaking of a boy. In the world of the theatre, Shakespeare is perhaps suggesting that, to this, any other Cleopatra will be a mere 'boy' whose 'squeaking', as it would have been sufficient entertainment for the 'boy' Caesar in his puppet world, will suffice for callow audiences at lesser playhouses than the Globe.

60 Player's Bond: Kendall's agreement was, at some point in the history of the Henslowe documents, cut out of the Diary from its place on f. 231. The fragment found its way into the British Library and is catalogued as *MS. Egerton* 2623, f. 19. James Bristow: Diary, f. 232.

61 Rose Receipts: Diary, f. 36v.

62 Loan Account: Diary, ff. 44, 44v. Collaborative Playwriting: See Neil Carson, 'Literary Management in the Lord Admiral's Company, 1596-1603' in *Theatre Research International*, n.s., 2 (1977); Carol A. Chillington, 'Playwrights at Work: Henslowe's, Not Shakespeare's, *Book of Sir Thomas More*' in *English Literary Renaissance*, vol. 10, number 3 (autumn, 1980); Cyrus Hoy, 'Critical and Aesthetic Problems of Collaboration in Renaissance Drama' in *Research Opportunities in Renaissance Drama* 19 (1976); C. J. Sisson, *Lost Plays of Shakespeare's Age* (Cambridge, 1936), 110-25; and S. Schoenbaum, *Internal Evidence and Elizabethan Dramatic Authorship* (London, 1966).

63 Statute on Rogues and Vagabonds: 39 Elizabeth c. 4. Printed: *Statutes, iv*, 899; *ES IV*, 324-5.

64 Privy Council Minute: PC 2/23 f. 181. Printed: Dasent, *APC xxviii*, 327; *ES IV*, 325.

65 Inventories: Malone, *The Plays and Poems of William Shakespeare, Vol. I, Part II*, 300-7. Reprinted: F & R, *Diary*, 316-25; Greg, *HP*, 113-23. Titus Andronicus Illustration: Known as the Peacham drawing and probably dated 1594 or 1595, the manuscript illustration is in the library of the Marquess of Bath at Longleat. Samuel Schoenbaum, *William Shakespeare: A Documentary Life* (Oxford, 1975), prints it together with a discussion of its problems on pages 122-3. It appears as the frontispiece to the New Cambridge edition of *Titus Andronicus*, ed. John Dover Wilson (1948).

66 Players' Bonds: Diary, f. 231.

67 Rose Receipts: Diary, f. 35. Brussels Play: *Salisbury Mss. viii*, 191, 201, 202. French Treaty: *SR iii*, f. 39.

68 Loan Account: Diary, ff. 45-48.

69 Rose Receipts: Diary, f. 48. Vestry Deputation: Printed: *ES IV*, 327, from William Rendle, *Bankside v*, in William Harrison, *Description of England ii*, Appx. i (London, 1877-81). Blind Beggar, *SR iii*, f. 40v. *Palladis Tamia, SR* 7 September 1598. Printed: *ES IV*, 246-7. Alleyn's Wager: *HP* MS. I, Art. 6.

70 Loan Account: Diary, ff. 49-50v.

71 Henslowe to Alleyn: *HP* MS. I, Art. 24. Printed: F & R, *Diary*, 285-6; Greg, *HP*, 47-8. Spencer: Diary, ff. 43, 44v. Jonson: Diary, ff. 24, 37v, 234. Drummond, *Conversations*: C.H. Herford and P. and E. Simpson eds., *Ben Jonson Vol. i* (Oxford, 1925), 139. Indictment: Herford and Simpson, i, 219. In Latin.

72 Rose Receipts: Diary ff. 48, 48v. Warrant for Court Payment: Dasent *APC* *xxiv*, 325. Burbage *v*. Giles Allen: Full text printed by C.W. Wallace, *The First London Theatre, Materials for a History*, Nebraska University Studies, xii.1, 1913. A summary is printed in *ES II*, 398–400.

73 Loan Account: Diary, ff. 50v–52. Chettle Debts: Diary, f. 51v.

74 Players' Bonds: Diary, f. 230v.

75 Loans to William Bird: Diary, ff. 38v, 41v.

76 Rose Receipts: Diary, f. 48v. Globe Lease: *ES II*, 415.

77 Loan Account: Diary, ff. 52v–54. Chettle Bond: Diary, f. 105.

78 Draft Contract: Diary, f. 20v.

79 Bird to Alleyn: *HP* MS. I, Art. 104. Printed: Greg, *HP*, 85–6.

80 Rose Receipts: Diary, f. 48v. Thomas Brand: C.W. Wallace, *The Times* (1914); quoted by Chambers, *ES II*, 415, n. 2.

81 Loan Account: Diary, ff. 54v, 63. Essex in Ireland: *CSP Ireland ccv*: 79; *ccv*: 121; *Salisbury Mss. ix*, 280–1. Bookburning: *SR iii*, ff. 316, 316v.

82 Loan Account: Diary, ff. 63–64v. Platter: Ernest Schanzer, 'Thomas Platter's Observations on the Elizabethan Stage', *Notes and Queries* 201 (1956), 466–7. Warrant for Court Payment: *ES IV*, 166. Essex in Ireland: *CSP Ireland ccv* and *ccvi* passim. Elizabeth: *Sidney Papers ii*, 127; *Penshurst Papers ii*, 396–7. Cecil on Manifesto: *CSP Ireland ccvi*:55.

83 Rose Receipts: Diary, f. 62v. Henslowe began by adding these receipts to the list he had interrupted on f. 48v where the entry of 3 June is followed by entries for 6 and 13 October. He then changed his mind, turned several pages, and began this new account. His first entry, 6 October, duplicates the entry for that date on f. 48v but is crossed out; 13 October is not recorded; 20 October begins the entries on a regular basis.

84 Shaa to Henslowe: *HP* MS. I, Art. 26. Printed: F & R, *Diary*, 287–8; Greg, *HP*, 49. Players' economics: a player's wage can be estimated from Henslowe's receipts, which represented half the gallery receipts. The other half was shared by the Company as their profit; hired men and boys were paid a fixed wage out of the sharers' pit money. In the week of 30 December 1599, for example, Henslowe's galleries were £10 8s. The ten Admiral's Men who were sharers thus took home just over £1 each that week. The week of 20 October they would have shared £4 3s, and the week of 18 November they divided £2 17s. London wages for skilled craftsmen were fixed at 5s per week, so when the sharers were each collecting £1 per week they were four times richer than their neighbours, and even in their worst weeks they were making about 3s 6d, nearly as much as their neighbour craftsmen. In 1597, one hired man who bound himself to play for the Admiral's Company negotiated a wage of 10s per week in London and 5s per week when the Company was on tour (see document 60). Two years later Thomas Downton hoped to hire a player at the rate of 8s per week and 4s during periods of restraint (see document 78). Evidently, then, sharers expected to collect more than 10s each week, for they would hardly have been willing to pay hired men more than they themselves expected to share. Calculations like these serve to make clear how inextricably the sharers' economics were bound up with their daily or weekly receipts at the playhouse door, and hence with their repertoires. They had additional expenses: first, their original investment or 'share' in the company; the only record Henslowe has of this expenditure is the £3 Humphrey Jeffes paid for his 'hallfe sheare' in

the Admiral's Men in 1597-8 (Diary, f. 36). This payment would have been more than compensated by the Company's payment to a player when he retired: Shaa and Jones had £25 each 'at ther goinge A waye' (Diary, f. 104; see document 99), the financial settlement standing in lieu of the retiring players' taking away from the Company an equivalent share in joint stock playbooks and costumes. Players seem occasionally to have bought costumes for personal use (see document 75) and to have been required to subsidise themselves on tour (see document 23). Presumably this latter payment would have been compensated by receipts on tour, that is, unless, like Pembroke's Men, the company was broken by the tour (see document 26). These were the professional expenses and rewards the sharers could anticipate. Their personal fortunes varied enormously. Edward Alleyn became phenomenally wealthy; Robert Browne of the Boar's Head 'dyed very pore'. But such discrepancies probably had more to do with individual choices and dispositions than with inevitabilities thrust upon them by the economic imponderables of their profession. It was possible as a player to make more than a tidy living. It was likewise possible to wind up destitute. The *via media* was the more typical route and men like Thomas Downton and Humphrey Jeffes more characteristic of the profession than either Alleyn or Browne. Both of these sharers in the Admiral's Men eventually left the quality for a more staid middle age. Downton married a widow and became a vintner; Jeffes, too, turned to brewing and seems to have produced a child for the baptismal font in most years. Clearly, then, their years on stage had provided them sufficient capital to set themselves up in fruitful business and domestic circumstances.

85 Loan Account: Diary, ff. 65-67. Oldcastle: Quoted by Samuel Schoenbaum, *William Shakespeare: A Documentary Life* (Oxford, 1975), 142-4. Thomas Merry Ballad: SR ii. f. 312. Fortune Lease: *HP*, mun. 20.

86 Licensing Fee: Diary, f. 81v. The fee remained £3 per month until August 1602 at least when Henslowe last recorded it in the Diary.

87 Fortune Contract: *HP*, mun. 22. Printed: F & R, *Diary*, 306-15; Greg, *HP*, 4-12. Henslowe's disbursements on the building project are recorded on the back of the contract and in the Diary, ff. 97, 97v, 98v and 99. F & R, *Diary*, print the disbursements in full, pp. 310-15.

88 Warrant: *HP* MS. I, Art. 27. Printed: F & R, *Diary*, 288-9; Greg, *HP*, 49-50; *ES IV*, 326.

89 Rose Receipts: Diary f. 62v. Warrant for Court Payment. PC 2/25 f. 41. Printed: Dasent, *APC xxx*, 89.

90 Loan Account: Diary, ff. 67-8. *Patient Grissell*, SR iii, f. 57v. *Old Fortunatus*, SR iii, f. 56v.

91 Privy Council Minute: PC 2/26 f. 78. Printed: Dasent, *APC xxx*, 146; *ES IV*, 326.

92 Vestry Minute: Printed: W. Rendle, *Bankside v*, in William Harrison, *Description of England ii*, Appx. i; *ES IV*, 327.

93 Warrant: *HP* MS. I, Art. 29. Printed: F & R, *Diary*, 290-1; Greg, *HP*, 51-2; *ES IV*, 328-9. Finsbury Petition: *HP* MS. I, Art. 28. Printed: F & R, *Diary*, 289-90; Greg, *HP*, 50-1; *ES IV*, 327-8.

94 Rose Receipts: Diary, f. 62v.

95 Loan Account: Diary, ff. 68v-70. Payments to Street: *HP*, mun. 22; Diary, ff. 97, 97v, 98v, 99; F & R, *Diary*, 310-15.

96 Shaa to Henslowe: *HP* MS. I, Art. 31. Printed: F & R, *Diary*, 294; Greg, *HP*, 55-6.

97 Payment Warrant. Printed: *MSC vii*, 18.

98 Privy Council Order: PC 2/25, f. 223. Printed: Dasent *APC xxx*, 395; *ES IV*, 329-31 reprints version from *MSC i*, 80 and thence from *Remembrancia ii*, 180. Henslowe and Tilney: *Diary*, f. 99. Curtain: Named on 10 May 1601, Dasent *APC xxxi*, 346, *ES IV*, 332; and on 9 April 1604 as one of three playhouses licensed by King James, *HP* MS. I, Art. 39. Printed: Greg, *HP*, 61; *ES IV*, 336.

99 Loan Account: *Diary*, f. 70v. The remaining Nottingham's accounts 1600-3 are recorded in the *Diary*, ff. 70v, 71, 85v-87v, 91-96, 105-109v. The 1604 accounts are found on f. 110.

100 Rose Receipts: *Diary*, f. 83. Essex: *Sidney Papers ii*, 213, 220. Proclamation of Arrest: SP 12/278/36. Printed: Hughes and Larkin, *no. 808*, 230. Eyewitness Account: *CSPD 278*: 545, *passim*. Chamberlain's Men: *CSPD 278*: 575, 578. Queen Elizabeth: Robert Cecil to Deputy of Ireland, *CSPD 278*: 547. Letter to Lord Mayor: PC 2/26 f. 119. Printed: Dasent *APC xxxi*, 218.

101 Privy Council Minute: PC 2/26 f. 193. Printed: Dasent *APC xxxi*, 346; *ES IV*, 332. *Satiromastix*, SR iii, f. 76. *Poetaster*, SR iii, f. 77v.

102 Privy Council Minute: PC 2/26 f. 514. Printed: Dasent *APC xxxii*, 466; *ES IV*, 332-3. With the entries for 31 December 1601, PC 26 ends. The next two ledgers are missing. Scanty abstracts of 1602 and 1603 are preserved as B.L. *Add. Mss.* 11402.

103 Privy Council to Lord Mayor: *Remembrancia ii*, 189. Printed: *MSC i*, 85; *ES IV*, 334-5.

104 Rose Receipts: *Diary*, ff. 115-118v. Shaa's Retirement: *Diary*, f. 104. Chettle's Bonds: *Diary*, f. 105. *Byron*, SR iii, f. 85.

105 Shaa Memorandum: *Diary*, f. 112.

106 Loan Account: *Diary*, ff. 118v-120v. Court Performance: *ES IV*, 167.

107 Personal Loans: *Diary*, ff. 113v, 114. Queen Elizabeth: *CSPD 287*: 50, 52.

108 Privy Council Minute: B.L. *Add. MS.* 11402. Printed: Dasent *APC xxxii*, 492; *ES IV*, 335.

109 Forbearance Payment: *MSC vii*, 18.

110 Proclamation: *Procl.* 944. Printed: *ES IV*, 335.

111 Loan Account: *Diary*, f. 121.

112 Lease Renewal: *Diary*, f. 114v. Original Lease: *HP*, mun. 15. Printed: Greg, *HP*, 1-2 (abstract). Tenement Sub-lets: *Diary*, f. 178v, *passim*.

113 Joan Alleyn to Edward Alleyn: *HP* MS. I, Art. 38. Printed: F & R, *Diary*, 296-8; Greg, *HP*, 59-61. Henslowe as Groom of Chamber: *HP* MS. I, Art. 11; B.L. *Add. Mss.* 5750 ff. 114, 117. Robert Browne: C.J. Sisson, 'Mr & Mrs Browne of the Boar's Head', *Life and Letters Today*, winter 1936-7.

114 Coronation List: 'The Book of the Accoumpte of the royall proceedinge of our soveraigne Lord Kinge James through his Honorable Citie of London', *Chamberlain's Accounts* 2/4 (5). Printed: *MSC ii*, 3. Patent for Queen's Men: *CSPD Jac. I*, 2: 100. Printed: *MSC i*, 265; *ES II*, 229-30.

115 *Vertues Commonwealth*: B.L. Catalogue no. C.55.d.25. Printed: *ES IV*, 247 (extracts).

116 Privy Council to Lord Mayor: *HP* MS. I, Art. 39. Printed: Greg, *HP*, 61; *ES IV*, 336.

117 Sewer Records: C.W. Wallace, *The Times* (1914).

The following three statutes lay the ground for a reading of the Rose documents. The London wage and price controls establish the official, statutory context for appreciating the players' finances and for appraising the playhouse in its most basic intent: the making of money. Henslowe's investment and returns, his daily receipts at the playhouse door, the playing companies' expenditures on individual playbooks, costumes, properties, and wages to hired men as well as the companies' daily share in the receipts must all be measured against the fixed statutory wage of a goldsmith or a plumber which in turn must be related to the cost of seven eggs in the market or a stone of best beef. Wages were reviewed 'yerely after Easter' in every shire, riding or liberty by 'discreete and grave persons ... conferring togeather respecting the plentie or scarcitie of the time' and, in London, 'having a speciall care and regard vnto the high and very chargeable prices of victuales fewell rayment and apparrell both linnen and wollen and also of housrentes and other speciall and accidental charges wherewith artificers and laborers dwelling within the saide cittie are very many and sundry times after theire power [i.e., poor] substance charged and burdened with'. In fact, wages remained practically unchanged for a decade – the statutes simply being reissued – while prices rose steadily. Between 1588 and 1599 some London prices had risen by fifty per cent. The third statute, which regulates apparel, shows how exactly it was intended that classes of Elizabethan society should be distinguished by costume. Clothing was emblematic, a constant visual indicator of a man's function in society; his status, dignity, family, and even his annual income were made obvious by colours restricted to particular privileges, by fabric and ornamentation, by liveries and badges. The original Elizabethan statute on apparel, which dated from 1565 and referred to earlier Tudor proclamations on the same issue, was never amended in one particular, the clause that stated that 'no Seruyngman in husbandrye, or Journeymen in handycraftes, takyng wages, shall weare in his doublet any other thyng than Fustyan, Canuas, Leather or Woolen cloth'. The statute has a clear relevance to the players – journeymen all – and to their expenditures on, and inventories of, costumes. By putting on 'Harey the v. satten dublet layd with gould lace' those 'fustyan kings' whose raiment should have been cut from canvas or leather, over-leapt the mandate and could be seen not only as pretentious peacocks but as subversives intensifying that 'confusion of degrees in all places' to which the statute refers. At the same time as the emblematic status of apparel in society made the players the targets of local fury, it helped them professionally. It meant that costume on stage could stand in place of setting or narrative exposition: a man's gown, his chain or spurs, declared him. A silent tableau like the Senate scene in Marlowe's *Jew of Malta*, which stands barbarian Turk exotically plumed alongside Maltese Christian, red cross blazoned on the chest, alongside Jewish gaberdine, needs no language to make its initial ironic point. Rose audiences saw such scenes frequently. Costume made it possible to dramatise the most sensitive of political issues, as for example the nature of kingship, by the migration through the play of a simple gold crown.

The statutes on prices and apparel were printed by Humphrey Dyson, *A Booke Conteining All Such Proclamations as were Published During the Reign of Q. Elizabeth*, in 1618 (British Library catalogue no. G.6463, folios 343-4, 262, and 361). A modern transcription of each appears in P.L. Hughes and J.F. Larkin, eds., *Tudor Royal Proclamations 1588-1603* (New Haven, Conn., 1969), vol. III, nos. 786 and 701. The statute regulating London wages is preserved in manuscript in the City of London Record Office *Journal of the Common Council* 22: 197-199v. Hughes and Larkin print a transcript in *Tudor Royal Proclamations*, vol. III, no. 702, but refer to the *Journal of the Common Council* confusingly as the *London Journals*.

———

STATUTE REGULATING LONDON WAGES
Westminster, 1 July 1588, 30 Elizabeth I, Reissued 1589 & 1590
[extracts]

To the best and most skilful workmen Journeymen and hired servants of any the companyes herevnder named

Clothworkers by the yeare with meate and drinke	v *li*
ffullers by the yeare with meate and drinke	v *li*
Sheremen by the yeare with meate and drinke	v *li*
Diers by the yeare with meate and drinke	vj *li* xiij *s* iiij *d*
Taylours hosiers by the yeare with meate and drinke	iiij *li*
Drapers being hosiers by the yeare with meate and drinke	iiij *li*
Shoemakers by the yeare with meate and drinke	iiij *li*
Pewterers by the yeare with meate and drinke	iij *li* vj *s* viij *d*

Whitebakers by the yeare with meate and drinke	iiij *li* xiij *s* iiij *d*
Brewers by the yeare with meate and drinke	x *li*
Blacksmithes by the year with meate and drinke	vj *li*
ffletchers by the yeare with meate and drinke	iiij *li*
Glouers by the yeare with meate and drinke	iij *li* vj *s* viij *d*
Cookes by the yeare with meate and drinke	vj *li*

To the workmen Journeymen or hired *servantes* of any the companyes herevnder named

Gouldsmythes by the yeare with meate and drinke viij *li*   by the weeke iij *s* iiij *d*   by the day vij *d*   without meate and drinke by the weeke vj *s*   by the day xij *d*

Skinners by the yeare with meate and drinke iiij *li*   by the weeke iij *s* iiij *d*   by the day viij *d*   without meate and drinke by the weeke v *s*   by the day xiij *d*

Plumbers by the yeare with meate and drinke iij *li* vj *s* viij *d*   by the weeke iij *s* iiij *d*   by the day viij *d*   without meate and drinke by the weeke vj *s*   by the day xiiij *d*

Joyners by the yeare with meate and drinke v *li*   by the week iiij *s* vj *d*   by the day ix *d*   without meate and drinke by the weeke vij *s*   by the day xiiij *d*   His *servant* by the yeare with meate and drinke iiij *li*   by the weeke ij *s*   by the day iiij *d*   without meate and drinke by the weeke iiij *s*   by the day x *d*

Carmen by the weeke with meate and drinke ij *s* vj *d*

Watermen by the yeare with meate and drinke xl *s*   by the weeke xij *d*   by the day iiij *d*   without meate and drinke by the weeke iij *s*   by the day vij *d*

Common *laborores* with meate and drinke by the day v *d*   without meate and drinke by the day ix *d*

STATUTE REGULATING LONDON VICTUALS PRICES
St James, 7 August 1588, 30 Elizabeth I
[extracts]

First a quarter best wheat cleane and sweet in the Market	xx.*s.*
And a quarter second wheat in the Market	xvi.*s.*
Item a quarter third wheat or best rie in the Market	xii.*s.*
And a quarter second rie in the Market	x.*s.* viii.*d.*

Item a quarter best mault cleane and sweet in the Market	xi.*s*.iiii.*d*.
And a quarter second mault in the Market	x.*s*.
Item a kilderkin of the best Ale or Beere at the brewers with cariage	iiii.*s*.
And a kilderkin single Ale or Beer at the brewers with cariage	xx.*d*.
Item a thirdindell of the best Ale or Beer within and without euery house	i.*d*.
And a full quart of good single Ale or Beer within and without euery house	*ob*.
Item a pound of butter sweete and new the best in the Market	iii.*d*.
Item a pound of good Essex cheese in the shop or in Market	i.*ob*.*q*.
Item seuen egges the best in the Market	ii.*d*.
Item a stone best bief at the butchers weighing viii pound	xii.*d*.
Item a pound of Tallowe Candles made of wicke	iii. *ob*.
Item a fetherbed for one man one night and so depart	i.*d*.
Item a fetherbed with necessary apparrell there-vnto for one man alone by the weeke	vi.*d*.
And the like fetherbed and furniture by the weeke for two lying together	viii.*d*.
Item a mattrice or flockbed for one or two together by the weeke	iiii.*d*.
Item hay and litter day and night for one horse within euery Inn	iii.*ob*.
And the like hay and litter day and night for one horse within euery other house being no Inne	iii.*d*.
Item a hundred good faggots keeping the assise with cariage	iiii.*s*. iiii.*d*.
And three of the same faggots within euery house	ii.*d*.
Item a quarter of Charcoals conteyning viii bushels with cariage	viiii.*d*.
Item a vacant or emptie roome, either chamber roome or stable by the whole weeke	iiii.*d*.

In August 1599 when troops were being mustered for the Irish wars these prices were revised, presumably to discourage black-marketeering. Best wheat cost 30*s* a quarter; second wheat, 26*s* 8*d* a quarter; best malt, 20*s* a quarter; second malt, 18s a quarter; best ale was 4s a kilderkin; single ale 2s; a quart of single ale or beer cost a penny. Butter was 4d a pound; Essex cheese 1½d; 8 lb of beef cost 1s; a pound of tallow candles was 4d. Hay and litter for a horse, day and night, cost 3½d, while one hundred faggots were 4s 8d. The price of eggs remained unchanged: seven for 2d.

ENFORCING STATUTES AND PROCLAMATIONS OF APPAREL
Greenwich, 6 July 1597, 39 Elizabeth I
[extracts]

Whereas the Queen's Maiestie for auoyding of the great inconuenience that hath growen and dayly doeth increase within this her Realme, by the inordinate excess in Apparel, hath in her Princely Wisedom and care for reformation thereof, by sundry former Proclamations straightly charged and commanded those in Authoritie under her to see her Lawes prouided in that behalfe duely executed; Whereof notwithstanding, partly through their negligence, and partly by the manifest contempt and disobedience of the parties offending, no reformation at all hath followed; Her Maiestie finding by experience that by Clemencie, whereunto shee is most inclinable, so long as there is any hope of redresse, this increasing euil hath not bene cured hath thought fit to seek to remedie the same, by correction and seueritie to be vsed against both these kindes of offenders, in regard of the present difficulties of this time, wherein the decay and lacke of Hospitalitie appeares in the better sort in all Countreys, principally occasioned by the immeasurable charges and expences which they are put to in superfluous apparelling their wives, children, and families, the confusion also of degrees in all places being great, where the meanest are as richly apparelled as their betters, and the pride that such inferiour persons take in their garments, driuing many for their maintenance to robbing and stealing by the hie way ... For Men's Apparell Her Maiestie doeth straightly charge and commaund, that None shall weare in his Apparell

Cloth of gold or siluer tissued, Silke of colour Purple, vnder the degree of an Earle, except Knights of the Garter in their purple Mantels onley.

Cloth of gold or siluer, tincelled Sattin, Silke or cloth mixed or imbrodered with Pearle, Gold, or Siluer, woollen Cloth made out of the Realme, vnder the degree of a Baron, except Knights of the Garter, Privy Counsellors to The Queenes Maiestie.

Passemaine lace or any other lace of gold or siluer or mixed with gold & siluer, with gold and silke, with siluer and silke, Spurres, Swordes, Rapiers, Daggers, Skaines, Woodkniues, Hangers, Buckles, or studs or girdles, Gilt or Damasked with gold or siluer, Siluered, Under the degree of a Barons sonne, except Gentlemen in ordinarie Office, attending vpon her Maiestie in her house or chamber: Such as haue bin imploied in Ambassage to forren Princes: Such as may dispend v. C. [500] marks by the yeere, for terme of life in possession aboue all charges. And Knights for wearing onely of Spurres, Swordes, Rapiers, and Daggers, and those other things therewith ensuing. And likewise Captaines being in her Maiesties pay.

Veluet in Gownes, Cloakes, Coates, or other vppermost Garments, Embroderies with silke, Netherstocks of silke, Under the degree of a Knight, except Gentlemen in ordinarie Office, attending vpon her Maiestie in her house or chamber; Such as haue bin imploied in Ambassage to foreine Princes. The sonne and heire apparant of a Knight. Captaines in her maiesties pay: and such as may dispend CC. *li.* [£200] by the yeere for terme of life in possession aboue all charges.

Veluet in Jerkins, Hose, Doublets: Sattin, Damaske, Taffata, Grogeran in Gownes, Cloakes, Coates or other vppermost Garments. Under the degree of a Knights eldest sonne, except Gentlemen in ordinarie Office, attending vpon her maiestie in her house or chamber: Such as haue bene imploied in Ambassage to forein Princes: And such as may dispend C. *li* [£100] by the yeere for terme of life in possession aboue all charges.

Sattin, Damaske, Grogeran, Taffata in Hose, Doublet, Under the degree of a Gentleman bearing Armes, except Gentlemen in ordinarie Office, attending vpon her maiestie in her house or chamber: Such as have bene imploied in Ambassage to forein Princes: And such as may dispend xx. *li* [£20] by *the* yeere for terme of life in possession aboue all charges.

INDEX OF PLAYS

The repertoire of the Rose playhouse 1592–1603 is recorded *inter alia* in Philip Henslowe's Diary. Henslowe's receipts accounts, being calendars of performances, provide a record of several companies' actual Rose repertoires. His scattered loan accounts give evidence of a *potential* repertoire. The loans record transactions on plays commissioned by companies at the Rose, some of which plays were obviously completed and produced, paid for 'in fulle', licensed and costumed across successive entries in the accounts. Other plays, however, may never have reached completion. Partial payments on them lapse or first instalments are not followed by work 'in fulle'. Yet in other cases where payments to playwrights do not indicate a play to have been completed, a subsequent loan for a licence or a costume shows that the play was being produced. Upon the fullness of Henslowe's individual entries in these loan accounts, therefore, depends the possibility of deciding which works-in-progress may finally have been performed and of establishing from the potential repertoire what may have been the companies' active repertoire. The following index is a near-complete index of Rose plays. Some sixteen additional plays, edited from the Diary extracts that make up the present volume, are listed here:

An index of Rose plays is not of course a complete list of play titles recorded in Henslowe's Diary since Henslowe continued to use his book to enter the loan accounts of Nottingham's Men once that company had left the Rose for the new Fortune playhouse in 1600. Some seventy plays therefore belong to the Diary but not to the Rose. Like the plays documented in the earlier loan accounts the Fortune plays that eventually reached the stage can usually be determined by the details of Henslowe's entries. Among Nottingham's repertoire are several revivals of plays staged years earlier at the Rose; these are documented by new production expenses disbursed on them. Another handful of plays was sold back to the Company by players who would have come to possess them privately over the years as their personal share in joint company stock. In the absence of entries recording new production expenses, however, these plays cannot be indentified as revivals or even assigned to the Company's active repertoire. Nottingham's plays include:

A third category of plays – ones mentioned in the present volume but not in Henslowe's Diary – are indicated with an asterisk in the following index. Only those plays mentioned in the Introduction are indexed by page number, i.e., 'p. 3'. All other index references are to document numbers, not to page numbers. Italicised references indicate play titles that appear in the headnotes. Roman type references are to the documents themselves. For a more extensive index to the play titles of the Diary see Foakes and Rickert, Henslowe's Diary. Fuller cross-referencing, alternative spellings and titles, and forged entries are cited there.

GENERAL INDEX

(See note on p. 236 for conventions)